# The Art of Facilitation

## The Essentials for Leading Great Meetings and Creating Group Synergy

Dale Hunter
with Stephen Thorpe
Hamish Brown
Anne Bailey

**16**

EasyRead Large

# Copyright Page from the Original Book

National Library of New Zealand Cataloguing-in-Publication Data

Hunter, Dale, 1943-
The art of facilitation / Dale Hunter.
Includes bibliographical references and index.
ISBN 978-1-86941-817-5
1. Group facilitation. 2. Communication in small groups.
3. Group decision-making. 4. Teams in the workplace. I. Title.
302.34—dc 22

A RANDOM HOUSE BOOK
published by
Random House New Zealand
18 Poland Road, Glenfield, Auckland, New Zealand
www.randomhouse.co.nz

Random House International
Random House, 20 Vauxhall Bridge Road,
London, SW1V 2SA, United Kingdom

Random House Australia (Pty) Ltd
20 Alfred Street, Milsons Point, Sydney,
New South Wales 2061, Australia

Random House South Africa Pty Ltd
Isle of Houghton
Corner Boundary Road and Carse O'Gowrie
Houghton 2198, South Africa

Random House Publishers India Private Ltd
301 World Trade Tower, Hotel Intercontinental Grand Complex,
Barakhamba Lane, New Delhi 110 001, India

First published 1994 by Tandem Press
This edition published 2007

© 1994, © 2007 Dale Hunter

The moral rights of the author have been asserted

ISBN 978 1 86941 817 5

Design: IslandBridge
Cover design: Katy Yiakmis
Printed in Australia by Griffin Press

# TABLE OF CONTENTS

Having used the original version of this book for a number of years, I found this latest version to be a practical and relevant resource for both new and 'veteran' facilitators alike. Packed full of useful information, research and thinking, an invaluable resource to add to any facilitator's toolbox. It certainly made me pause, breathe and rethink about some of my own facilitation practice; I would recommend this book to anyone in the field of professional facilitation.

*Gary Austin*
*Senior Consultant Facilitator, circleindigo, UK*

Reading and using this completely updated edition of *The Art of Facilitation* is, for me, an experience of pure joy, meaning and hope. Dale Hunter and colleagues are magicians in the art of enabling groups to connect with their potential and act on it so that wellbeing and sustainability can be emergent at every level, not only within organisations, but also within individuals and ecosystems. It is grounded in clear values and ethics, and a philosophy of co-operacy and caring; and its practical wisdom and tips for effectiveness are profoundly informed by lifetimes of working at the cutting edge of facilitation and change. All who work in the challenging and exciting borderlands of transformation and progressive change will certainly benefit from reading and using this 'best book on the topic by far'.

With her enviable balance between wisdom and knowledge, she also balances scientific rigour with understandable pragmatism in this new edition. I whole-heartedly and unconditionally recommend this book, as I have to hundreds of my facilitation students throughout Latin America, for any person who wants to better understand and practice the art, science and technology of facilitation.

*Dr. Gilbert Brenson-Lazán*
*Presidente Ejecutivo, Amauta International, LLC,*
*Colombia*

# Acknowledgements

A big thank you to Zenergy team members Stephen Thorpe and Hamish Brown for contributing chapters to this book and to Marilyn Hunt, Sabine Druekler and Flora Wolfgram for contributing in other ways. I especially acknowledge the untiring technical assistance and good company of Stephen Thorpe on many writing retreats and days of polishing and refining. I also acknowledge Anne Bailey and Bill Taylor for their contributions.

The thinking that makes up this book is necessarily a collective effort. Many hundreds of participants in Zenergy training programmes and groups that I have facilitated or participated in have contributed to building the body of knowledge expressed in these pages. In recognition of this collective effort, scattered throughout this book are some insights from Zenergy graduates.

There are many people around the world who have inspired me and shared their wisdom with me. Many of these good folk of courage and integrity are members of the International Association of Facilitators, the Australasian Facilitators Network and the Global Facilitators Service Corps.

A special thanks to mentor Professor Stuart Hill, founding chair of Social Ecology at Hawkesbury now part of the University of Western Sydney; my lifetime peer group coaches, Bevin Fitzsimons, Marijke van Battenburg, Gill Ellis (The Group), Shirley Hardwick,

Diana Elliot, Ngaire Lynch, Rachel Friedlander (now in France), the Commandos and all co-creators of the Heart Politics Network of New Zealand.

Thank you to publisher Nicola Legat and the Random House team.

I also thank and acknowledge Remedios Ruis for allowing us to reproduce her adapted description of purpose; the Department of Conservation Bay of Plenty Conservancy for allowing us to reproduce their Community Relations and Technical Support Team Charter; Lester Milbrath for allowing us to reproduce his Proposed Value Structure for a Sustainable Society; Glyn Thomas for allowing us to reproduce his Dimensions of Facilitator Education Model; the Earthsong Eco Neighbourhood for allowing us to reproduce their Group Decision Making Process from their Body Corporate Rules; and The Zhaba Facilitators Collective for allowing us to reproduce their hand signs.

Arohanui to all my family and friends, and thank you for your continuing love and support.

# About the contributing authors

**Dr. Dale Hunter** is a group facilitator, mediator, coach and author. She is a founding director of Zenergy Ltd, a company that provides facilitation, mediation and coaching services to government, business and community sectors. More than 1400 people in New Zealand and Australia have participated in modules of the Zenergy Diploma of Facilitation, codesigned by Hunter. In addition, she has led workshops in the UK, USA, Canada, China, Malaysia and Taiwan.

Dale is the principal co-author (with Anne Bailey and Bill Taylor) of *The Art of Facilitation* (original edition), *Handling Groups in Action: The Use of Distinctions in Facilitation, The Zen of Groups* and *Co-operacy—A New Way of Being at Work.* She has also contributed chapters to the International Association of Facilitators (IAF) Handbook of Group Facilitation and Creating a Culture of Collaboration.

Her doctoral thesis is entitled 'Facilitation of sustainable co-operative processes in organisations' from the Social Ecology Research Group (SERG) at the University of Western Sydney, Hawkesbury, Australia. She is a former trustee of Heart Politics New Zealand, and Vice Chair International of the IAF.

**Stephen Thorpe** is a Zenergy facilitator specialising in online facilitation. He is undertaking a PhD in online facilitation and storytelling. He also lectures at tertiary level in computing, and is an associate editor of the IAF Group Facilitation Journal.

**Hamish Brown** is a group psychotherapist trained in the psychodrama method. He is also an organisational facilitator and has worked with a range of organisations throughout New Zealand and internationally. Hamish is a director of Zenergy Ltd.

**Anne Bailey** is a facilitator and was a founding director of Zenergy. She was a co-author of the first *Art of Facilitation* and also *The Zen of Groups, The Essence of Facilitation* and *Co-operacy—A New Way of Being at Work* together with Dale Hunter and Bill Taylor.

# Welcome

Tena koe. Haere tahi tatou me enei roopu.

Welcome to everyone working in groups.

Welcome to the art of facilitation.

We invoke the spirit of cooperation through the ages—past, present and future—and welcome into existence the word 'co-operacy', a new distinction which brings forth government through cooperation.

We acknowledge Aotearoa for nurturing us, Maungawhau for watching over us, and the waters of Manukau and Waitemata for connecting us to the world.

We acknowledge our families, communities, networks and all the groups that have 'grown' us.

We acknowledge our company, Zenergy, which is dedicated to creating synergy on the planet.

> He aha te mea nui o te ao
> Maku e ki atu
> He tangata, he tangata, he tangata.
>
> Ask me what is the most important thing in the world
> And I will tell you
> It is people, it is people, it is people.

# The taste of Banzo's sword

Matajuro Yagyu was the son of a famous swordsman. His father, believing that his son's work was too mediocre to anticipate mastership, disowned him. So Matajuro went to Mt Futara to find Banzo, the famous swordsman. But Banzo confirmed the father's judgement. 'You wish to learn swordsmanship under my guidance?' asked Banzo. 'You cannot fulfil the requirements.'

'But if I work hard, how many years will it take me to become a master?' persisted the youth.

'The rest of your life,' replied Banzo.

'I cannot wait that long,' explained Matajuro. 'I am willing to pass through any hardship if only you will teach me. If I become your devoted servant, how long might it be?'

'Oh, maybe 10 years,' Banzo relented.

'My father is getting old and soon I must take care of him,' continued Matajuro. 'If I work far more intensively, how long will it take me?'

'Oh, maybe 30 years,' said Banzo.

'Why is that?' asked Matajuro. 'First you say 10 and now 30 years. I will undergo any hardship to master this art in the shortest time!'

'Well,' said Banzo, 'in that case you will have to remain with me for 70 years. A man in such a hurry as you are to get results seldom learns quickly.'

'Very well,' declared the youth, understanding at last that he was being rebuked for impatience. 'I agree.'

Matajuro was told never to speak of fencing and never to touch a sword. He cooked for his master, washed the dishes, made his bed, cleaned the yard, cared for the garden; all without a word of swordsmanship.

Three years passed. Still Matajuro laboured on. Thinking of his future, he was sad. He had not even begun to learn the art to which he had devoted his life.

But one day Banzo crept up behind him and gave him a terrific blow with a wooden sword. The following day, when Matajuro was cooking rice, Banzo again sprang upon him unexpectedly. After that, day and night, Matajuro had to defend himself from unexpected thrusts. Not a moment passed in any day that he did not have to think of the taste of Banzo's sword. Matajuro learnt so rapidly that he brought smiles to the face of his master. He became the greatest swordsman in the land.

# Introduction

*The Art of Facilitation* has influenced many aspiring group facilitators and helped to define the profession we call facilitation. Well-thumbed copies inform many facilitators' work. It is now time to bring the new knowledge gained in the last 13 years into the familiar pages, to re-energise the book and, hopefully, all who browse in it.

The first edition of *The Art of Facilitation* was written by Dale Hunter, Anne Bailey and Bill Taylor, and published in 1994. It is a leader in the field of facilitation writing, a consistently favoured facilitation text, and a long term Top-10 bestseller on Amazon in the categories of facilitation and facilitation of groups.

This fully revised and updated edition of *The Art of Facilitation* has been written by Dale Hunter, with contributions from Stephen Thorpe, Hamish Brown and Anne Bailey. While retaining the freshness and simplicity that have made the book so popular, it incorporates new thinking and research from the last 13 years and brings the book into the thick of facilitation debate.

The first three chapters of Part 1 are mostly new material, and describe the development of group facilitation as a profession, the role of the facilitator and a conceptual framework for facilitation. The remaining chapters in Part 1, addressing key elements of facilitation, have all been revised.

Only the first chapter of Part 2 was in the earlier book, and this has been revised. The new chapters explore facilitation in organisations, facilitation and ethics, sustainability, therapeutic group work, and online facilitation using the medium of the Internet and computing technology. Chapter 7, 'Mapping the field of facilitation', covers some of the wide variety of approaches and methods that have now emerged in the field of facilitation.

Part 3 offers a training programme that can be used by a group of aspiring facilitators as a peer learning framework. A variety of processes and some useful design frameworks are included in this section.

The chapter notes and bibliography provide a thorough list of references that many readers will find useful. The interviews that formed part of the original book have not been included in this new edition.

This is a user-friendly book for aspiring and experienced facilitators, team leaders, managers, coaches and others who are called on to facilitate groups and want a thorough understanding of the field of facilitation. Enjoy.

# Abridged introduction to the first edition

The Earth is running out of energy resources, but there is a source of special energy that has scarcely been tapped. It is the power available in groups—the power of group synergy. Tapping into group synergy is made possible through powerful group facilitation.

Effective group facilitation is an artful dance requiring rigorous discipline. The role of the facilitator offers an opportunity to dance with life on the edge of a sword—to be present and aware—to be with and for people in a way that cuts through to what enhances and fulfils life. A facilitator is a peaceful warrior.

Group facilitation is moment-by-moment awareness; being and awake in action—awake in the way a hunter stalks a tiger or a mother watches over her newborn infant. The facilitator protects the group culture at the same time as cutting through unproductive or sabotaging patterns to get to what enhances and fulfils the group purpose.

This book reveals the secrets of the art of facilitation. It provides access to the source of group empowerment and how to create this with ease. *The Art of Facilitation* is the second book by the authors of *The Zen of Groups—A Handbook for People Meeting with a Purpose.* That book focused on the role of the group member and explored how effectiveness can be vastly increased through accessing synergy. *The Art of Facil-*

*itation* provides a deeper cut into developing group effectiveness by focusing on the role and skills of the facilitator.

The purpose of the book is also to provide a training resource for facilitators, and to enable group members to understand and take on this role.

When working with groups, the authors use the first person 'we' to include themselves in any statements. In this book, on the advice of our publisher, we have mainly used the second person 'you' to address the reader directly. This does not imply that we know better or that we are separating ourselves from the reader. On the contrary, we find it empowering to know that we don't know everything and that we are always learning and in training. As part of the development of cooperative technology, we ask for and welcome suggestions and feedback on our books, which we see as a developing 'conversation' rather than final texts.

# part 1

## Chapter 1

# preparing the ground

## What is facilitation?

Facilitation is about process—how you do something—rather than content—what you do. It involves movement—from A to B—towards an agreed destination. A facilitator is a process guide, someone who makes a process easier or more convenient. Facilitation enables a group of people to achieve their own purpose in their own agreed way.

The word 'facilitate' comes from the Latin 'facile', and means to make easy or more convenient. In some languages there is no direct translation for the word 'facilitator'. This is the case in German, for example, and a facilitator is often known as a moderator.

Facilitation (or group facilitation) is designed for groups, organisations, networks and communities. It is the body of expertise associated with cooperation and collaboration among equals, and is concerned with ways of ensuring that everyone in a group can, if they wish, fully participate in all decisions that affect them.

The people who have the knowledge or intuitive ability to lead groups towards self-generated knowledge, participative decisionmaking and consensus have become known as facilitators.

# Where did facilitation come from?

Group facilitation has a rich history and many influences. Many indigenous peoples used forms of consensus in their tribal councils and other deliberations. In more recent times, the Society of Friends (known as the Quakers) has been associated with consensus as a way of being and meeting. Cooperative organisations and movements, peace movements, women's groups and feminist movements, group psychotherapy, community and organisational development, conflict resolution, participative and radical education, and many kinds of action research all require or benefit from facilitation and facilitative leadership.

The work of many individuals and groups, including Paulo Freire, Carl Rogers, M. Scott Peck, Chris Argyris, John Heron, Laura Spencer and Brian Stanfield of the Institute of Cultural Affairs (ICA), Fran Peavey, Gil Brenson-Lazan, Roger Schwarz and many more, have contributed to the development of facilitation and the various approaches within this field. In Australia and New Zealand, a group of writers, many based in academic settings, have contributed to the literature on facilitation. These include Bob Dick, Christine Hogan, Glyn Thomas, Stuart Hill, Stephen Thorpe and myself.

Works by all these people are listed in the bibliography.

In the late eighties and throughout the nineties, facilitation became associated with the business sector through the total quality movement (TQM) of continuous step-by-step improvement; the promotion of teamwork as a way of coping with rapid change, complexity and advances in technology; and the introduction of organisational processes such as strategic planning, performance management and public consultation. A rush of facilitator activity sought to exploit these opportunities and facilitation was introduced at all levels of government and business.

All this activity led to the emergence of facilitation as a new profession, and the International Association of Facilitators (IAF) was established in the USA in 1994. The IAF went on to develop a set of professional facilitator competencies, a code of ethics, a certification procedure for facilitators, various e-groups (listservs), as well as publishing several journal issues and co-publishing handbooks on facilitation and collaboration.[1] In 2006 the IAF had 1400 members and was actively associated with facilitator conferences and forums in Europe, North America, Asia, Latin America, the Caribbean, Africa and Australia/New Zealand.

The introduction of facilitation into government and business attracted both praise and criticism. It was praised for creating the opportunity for more equal and respectful relationships and knowledge sharing. Facilitators enabled better information-sharing within and across teams, more effective group decisionmaking, and more conscious organisational development. However, facilitation was also decried as a form of management 'fascipulation'[2] in which the facilitator manipulated the participants to 'buy into' the management agenda.

This criticism had some validity, as many facilitators were initially confused about how to work effectively in hierarchical organisations. The criticism and resulting collegial reflection within the profession contributed to the collective development of the Facilitator's Code of Ethics, which was adopted by the IAF in 2004.

# Why focus on facilitation?

Why focus on facilitation rather than other ways of working with groups, such as management, leadership or being a 'boss'?

The facilitator does not get involved in the content of group deliberations, but facilitation is not and cannot be value-neutral. Facilitation starts from the premise that every person has an equal right to speak and participate in dialogue and decisionmaking. The inherent value of the individual, the collective wisdom of the group, cooperation, choice and consensus are all values that underlie facilitation.

Facilitation does not support oppression, coercion, bullying or any other behaviour that involves having 'power over' others. Instead, the right use of power is understood to be 'power with'. Effective facilitation encourages each person to value, develop and express their full sense of self, and be in authentic relationship with others individually and as part of a group working towards collective goals.

The relationship between group facilitation and organisational hierarchy tends to be difficult. The facilitation values of equal worth, full participation and consensus are undermined when a manager has the positional power to recommend people for promotion, instigate disciplinary procedures and the right to 'hire and fire'. These 'power over' roles contrast with that of the impartial facilitator, who does not take sides or get involved in content or decisionmaking.

# Why is consensus decisionmaking important in facilitation?

One of the key differentiators of facilitation is its preference for consensus decisionmaking (also called collective decisionmaking). Consensus is based on the belief that every person has a right to be involved in decisions that affect them.

Most people know something of committee procedure and rules, and how to take a majority vote—these skills are very much part of many societies. However, the processes and skills involved when people want to reach a consensus or collective decision are not so well known, and often it can seem too hard to get everyone to agree.

Yet consensus decisionmaking is used widely. Consensus is used within intentional communities and cooperatives of all kinds. In business, some boards, executives and teams require consensus before taking major actions. Most juries in criminal justice procedures require consensus. On the world stage, within the World Trade Organization and the United Nations Security Council consensus is required for major decisions. At a national and regional level, the electoral systems of many countries ensure minorities are represented and legislation requires more than a majority vote to pass legislation.

In the book *Co-operacy: A New Way of Being at Work* (by Dale Hunter, Anne Bailey and Bill Taylor) we describe the cooperative paradigm (which rests on collective decisionmaking) as distinct from democracy (which rests on majority decisionmaking) and autocracy (which rests on one person deciding on behalf of others). We write about the cooperative ways of working that need to be developed, invented or rediscovered so that they can become a readily available choice. These ways of working are what we name the 'technology of co-operacy'.

At present, most countries practise a version of democracy, or at least have the democratic model as the ideal. Democracy requires cooperation between people and participation in decisionmaking, but has as its bottom line the belief that the majority is right and majority decisionmaking the best way to make decisions. Democracy means that the minority can be overruled and marginalised.

If you draw a continuum of decisionmaking, with autocracy (one person deciding on behalf of all the rest) at one end, you will see that co-operacy is at the other end, with democracy in between.

All points on the continuum have a place in decisionmaking, and are the best choice in some situations. However, we have a bias towards co-operacy and believe the reason it is not used more often is that its skills, attitudes and values are not yet an everyday part of our culture. People want full cooperation and participation, but when it comes to the crunch they believe the only thing to do is to take a vote, with the majority deciding, or even to ask someone (the boss?) to make the decision for them.

Figure 1.1.1 Continuum of decisionmaking

# How can we get to co-operacy?

The shift from democracy towards co-operacy involves an enormous culture shift. It could be likened to the historical shift from feudalism (autocracy) to democracy. It could also be described in personal development terms as the shift from dependence (autocracy) through independence (democracy) to interdependence (co-operacy).

Collective decisionmaking and facilitation are part of the technology of co-operacy. Underpinning collective decisionmaking are some beliefs and values. These include the beliefs that:

- all people are intrinsically of equal worth;
- difference is to be valued, honoured and celebrated;
- it is possible for people to live and work together cooperatively;
- the best decisions are made by those people who are affected by them.

For collective decisionmaking to work well there needs to be an underpinning commitment to reach agreement by all those involved. This is sometimes spoken of as 'an agreement to reach agreement'. This does not mean that everyone needs to agree on everything. Everyone may agree to disagree, delegate the decisionmaking to one or more individuals, agree in smaller groups to do different things, or even agree to use a simple majority or other percentage for decisionmaking as an interim measure.

It does mean, however, that everyone is committed to working issues through without resorting to coercion or violence. There is an imperative for the people disagreeing to propose another course of action, and actively take part in the effort to find a solution that will work for everyone. There is no power of unmoving veto, such as, 'This is my position, I'm

9

sticking to it and I won't discuss it.' This would be autocracy in reverse (and is a problem in the operation of the United Nations Security Council).

Over time, I and my colleagues have learnt some of the skills and ways of being that are needed to make cooperative decisionmaking a practical and workable alternative to democratic or autocratic models. We want cooperative processes and consensus decisionmaking to be as well-known and accessible as committee procedures and majority voting in groups, organisations, communities and nations.

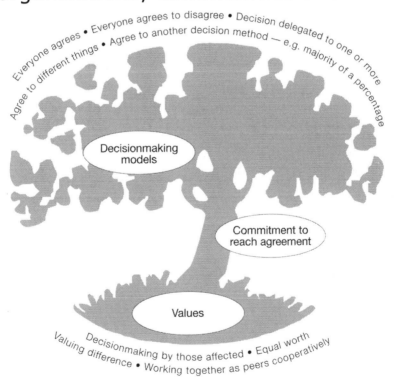

Figure 1.1.2 The co-operacy tree (from Co-operacy: A New Way of Being at Work)

What is more, we believe using cooperative methods makes it possible to more easily access a very important and critical resource for the world. This is group synergy—the alternative fuel for the twenty-first century. We may be running out of some key energy resources, but group synergy, in which collective intelligence can be added together with a multiplying effect, has great untapped potential. The planet needs group synergy because it is group intelligence and effort, on small through to large scale, that will heal our planet and ensure that it is able to support human life. This cooperation and collaboration for the common good is needed to ensure the sustainability of human and ecological systems.

The potential of facilitation has not yet been fully realised. There is more discovery, learning, development and education to be done. The challenge of creating a sustainable world gives this journey urgency.

## Summary

Facilitation is the body of expertise associated with leading cooperative groups and cooperative processes. It is based on values of equal worth, full participation, consensus and celebration of difference. The development and growth of facilitation in the last 20 years is reflected in its usage in government and business as well as in its traditional home in the community sector. In addition, published writing, facilitator training, networking among facilitators and more recently academic research have led to the development of the profession of facilitation.

# Chapter 2

# the role of the facilitator

In an earlier book, *The Zen of Groups,* we describe the role of the facilitator as a leadership role in which the facilitator's job is to guide the group process towards the achievement of the group's agreed purpose. In a fully effective group, each participant may have the skills and experience to facilitate the group and the role may be rotated. In practice, the skills associated with group facilitation are not always  well known, and the facilitator may be the person (or persons) in the group who has facilitation skills. An external facilitator may also be brought in by the group to play this role.

The facilitator is an aware and conscious listener, and a clear communicator, who understands group dynamics and provides process expertise, usually in the form of questions and suggestions. She/he grows meaningful relationships, participation and collaboration, focuses a group on its purpose and guides its development through organic cycles, using cooperative processes and collective decisionmaking. The facilitator is also impartial and does not get involved in the content of the group deliberations.

The facilitator is chosen by and accountable to the group—he/she is not imposed without agreement. Sometimes, for example in a public consultation process, this can be challenging, and involves conferring with representatives of the groups involved rather than all the individuals.

These descriptions of the role of the facilitator are somewhat similar to the role of a chairperson in a democratic majority voting committee, since a chairperson is also in charge of process and responsible for following group rules. However, unlike a chairperson, who has a vote (and sometimes an extra casting vote if numbers are tied), a facilitator does not have a vote at all, or any direct or indirect say in the content of decisions that are made.

The psychologist Carl Rogers, who was a pioneer of facilitation, describes the role of facilitator as follows:

> The facilitator is genuinely free of a desire to impose ready-made truths or to control the outcome.

> The facilitator has skills in helping people engage in genuine dialogue.

> The facilitator respects the capacity of the group to discover the nature of their own problems and has the skills to help people to express that capacity.

> A respectful hearing is given to all attitudes and feelings, no matter how 'extreme' or 'unrealistic'.

The members of a group are permitted to choose, collectively and individually, their own processes and work towards their own goals.

If these conditions apply, then a process is set in motion that has certain characteristics.

# The Process

Long-suppressed feelings will surface, many of them angry and bitter. Because these feelings are accepted and not judged, more people will express themselves, and the range of feelings will widen.

As people become vocal, visible and known, trust and mutual respect will be strengthened.

Irrational feelings lose their power, both by being fully expressed, and by feedback from others.

Feelings based in common experience are clarified and strengthened, leading to a greater self, and group, confidence.

Collective understandings become more realistic and less irrational.

Power struggles between members are resolved, and collaboration increases.

Actions emerge that are aimed at changing the existing situation. In a good group, these actions will be innovative and transformational, as well as realistic.

Group solidarity is strong enough to support individuals to take even radical action.[1]

Carl Rogers' description recognises the place of the emotional and instinctive in human behaviour. This fits well with recent advances in neuroscience that recognise the functions of the instinctive reptilian brain, the limbic brain (the seat of emotions) and the neocortex (where language, logic and ability to manipulate numbers reside). Recent neuroscience research by Candace Pert also shows an inevitable connection between thoughts and emotions through the chemical charges released in the brain.[2]

In the books on facilitation that are now available, the role of the facilitator is described in a variety of ways. Here are some of these descriptions, dating from 1967 to the present day.

...a leader is needed who plays a role quite different from that of the members ... This type of approach to group processes places the leader in a particular role in which he must cease to contribute, avoid evaluation, and refrain from thinking about solutions or group products. Instead he must concentrate on the group process, listen in order to understand rather than to appraise or refute, assume responsibility for accurate communication between members, be sensitive to unexpressed feelings, protect minority points of view, keep the discussion moving, and develop skills in summarising.

—Norman R.F. Maier[3]

To facilitate means 'to make easy'. The group facilitator's job is to make it easier for the group to do its work. By providing non-directive leadership, the facilitator helps the group arrive at the understandings and decisions that are its task. In a consensus group the facilitator's focus is on the group and its work. The role is one of assistance and guidance, not of control.

—Michel Avery et al.[4]

The primary role of a facilitator is to assist parties to have a constructive dialogue. Facilitators usually help groups set an agenda and manage the process of discussion ... For example, facilitators help the parties to recognise how their own styles of interacting or the institutional prejudices that they embody may interfere with constructive problem solving. Here the objective is to promote understanding among the parties. Additionally, facilitators may propose a series of process steps to keep the discussion on target. Facilitators may also explicitly help parties find a mutually agreeable solution to a dispute.

16

—Barbara Gray[5]

...a facilitator is a person who helps a group free itself from internal obstacles or difficulties so that it may more efficiently and effectively pursue the achievement of its desired outcomes for a given meeting ... In the purest sense, when wearing the 'facilitator's hat' an individual acts as a neutral servant of the people. By that I mean the person focuses on guiding without directing; bringing about action without disruption; helping people self-discover new approaches and solutions to problems; knocking down walls which have been built between people while preserving structures of value; and, above all, appreciating people as people. All of this must be done without leaving any fingerprints.

—Thomas Kayser[6]

The facilitator's job is to support everyone to do their best thinking. To do this, the facilitator encourages full participation, promotes mutual understanding and cultivates shared responsibility. By supporting everyone to do their best thinking, a facilitator enables group members to search for inclusive solutions and build sustainable agreements.

—Sam Kaner et al.[7]

Facilitation is the design and management of structures and processes that help a group do its work and minimise the common problems people have working together. Facilitation is therefore a neutral process (with respect to the content and participants) that focuses on: what needs to be done; who needs to be involved; design, flow, and sequence of tasks; communication patterns, effectiveness, and completeness; appropriate levels of participation and the use of resources; group energy, momentum, and capability; the physical and psychological environment.

—Tom Justice and David Jamieson[8]

A facilitator ... is a process guide; he or she does not evaluate or contribute substantive ideas to a discussion. The facilitator is the servant of the group, not its leader, and works to ensure that the group accomplishes its goals. He or she does this by offering process suggestions, enforcing ground rules agreed to by the group. Keeping discussions on track, protecting group members from attack, and ensuring that all members participate.

—David Straus[9]

Roger Schwarz, a leading contemporary writer on facilitation, takes a group-centred approach:

Group facilitation is a process in which a person who is acceptable to all members of a group, substantively neutral, and has no decisionmaking authority, intervenes to help a group improve the way it identifies and solves problems, and makes decisions, in order to increase the group's effectiveness.[10]

Schwarz divides facilitation into basic and developmental facilitation. The two approaches imply different roles for the facilitator. In basic facilitation, although the group may influence the process at any time, in general it expects the facilitator to guide it using what he or she considers effective process. In development facilitation, members expect to monitor and guide the group's process, and expect the facilitator to teach them how to accomplish this goal.

Schwarz also stresses that facilitation is value-based, and that these values guide effective group behaviour and effective facilitator behaviour. He lists the key values as valid information (sharing and understanding information), free and informed choice, and internal commitment to these choices (people being personally responsible for the choices they make as part of the group). In 2002, in a new edition of his book *The Skilled Facilitator,* Schwarz added a fourth core value, that of compassion.

Facilitators enable groups to improve their process by helping them to act in ways that are consistent with these core values. In development facilitation, Schwarz finds that over time the group members develop the ability to identify when they have acted in ways that are inconsistent with their core values, and to correct their behaviour—without a facilitator's help. In basic facilitation, the group uses a facilitator to help it act consistently with the core values, temporarily, while working with the facilitator.

On a different tack, Harrison Owen, the inventor of the facilitation method known as Open Space, describes the facilitator's role as facilitating the journey of spirit using mythos (story) as a key.[11] Form follows spirit.[12] 'Spirit cannot be bought, ordered, directed. It responds positively to a very different treatment called *inspiration.*'[12]

# Co-facilitators

The role of the facilitator is not always taken by one person alone. There are times when the role is shared. Three common ways are:

- Two or more facilitators work together as equals.
- One facilitator takes the primary role and has one or more assistant facilitators, who are often in training with the primary facilitator.
- One primary facilitator and a number of secondary facilitators who facilitate smaller break-out groups as needed.

In all these scenarios the facilitators need to clearly and transparently negotiate and monitor their various roles, and make these transparent to the participants. Any unclear or manipulative power relationships will undermine the 'power with' value base of facilitation and lead to problems and confusion in the whole group. Particularly in longer workshops and organisational interventions over time, lack of role clarity can undermine the effectiveness of the facilitation.

On the other hand, when it is done well, co-facilitation can model an effortless weaving of energies and interactions that appear seamless. Effective co-facilitation by people of different genders, cultures and abilities can be inspirational. The benefits of co-facilitation include sharing of work tasks, increased collective intelligence, and better monitoring of the group dynamic.

Another important benefit of co-facilitation is the deflection of negative projections onto a facilitator from group participants. Participants can unconsciously project onto the facilitator(s) perceptions related to past relationship distress (often involving the family of origin or early authority figures). Strong projections can sometimes weaken the effectiveness of a facilitator's work, and understanding this dynamic is an important part of facilitator training (see 'Identity check, Process 43',).

Co-facilitation can interrupt this negative dynamic by providing alternative personalities with whom participants can relate. In some highly charged situations co-facilitation is undertaken specifically for this reason. For example, groups or organisations in which there are ethnic or religious tensions may need a mix of facilitators that mirror the group or organisational diversity.

# Facilitator and facilitative

I have described the role of the facilitator in some depth, but some further clarification is needed. It is important to distinguish between a facilitator as a practitioner and someone who is facilitative, i.e. acting in a facilitative way.

Almost anyone can be facilitative if they seek to provide space for others to build relationships, think and reflect, exercise choice and express their creative potential. For example, teachers, leaders and parents can all be, and hopefully often are, facilitative. They listen, encourage and support others to become their full selves. The limits to being facilitative would be in situations where choices have already been denied or severely curtailed. An extreme example would be that of facilitating with people in prison.

There are some disciplines where facilitative skills are regularly used and highly regarded. These include mediation, teaching or training, coaching, group psychotherapy and some kinds of leadership. Facilitators are often asked what the difference is between their discipline and these other disciplines, so I will address this here.

## *Mediator*

Professional mediation has been in use longer than facilitation and is well established internationally. Mediation is used at all levels of society, from neighbourhood disputes over boundary fencing through to disputing and warring nations. The mediator guides the process of two or more opposing parties (individuals or groups) towards an agreement which the parties design themselves. The mediator does not make a decision on behalf of, or for, the parties. The skills of mediation are allied to those of facilitation in that both are process guides.

The main differences are that a mediator works *between* the opposing parties or groups when they are unwilling to talk or engage with one another directly. A mediator 'mediates' a dispute. In addition, the mediator works specifically in the area of conflict. A conflict can be assumed, otherwise a mediator will not be required.

Although a facilitator also works with conflict, this is only part of their role. The facilitator works within the context of a group or organisation and is involved in processes of all kinds, including many that do not relate to conflict.

## Teacher or trainer

A teacher or trainer has as their primary role the transferring of information or knowledge to individual participants. The trainer or teacher also needs to manage the group process while this individual learning is taking place. A teacher can be very facilitative, and this is naturally to be encouraged. However, the primary role is individual learning within a particular sphere of knowledge.

The difference between a facilitator and a trainer is that a trainer or teacher's job is to transfer knowledge to individuals. The individual's learning is likely to be assessed in some way by the teacher. The teacher needs to focus on individual learning more than the group dynamic. A facilitator works primarily with the group dynamic and is not involved in assessing individual performance. This is done by the group itself, or possibly by some other party outside the group.

It is unfortunate that trainers are often called facilitators, as this muddies the waters for facilitators who work with group process only.

A further confusion arises when people are being trained as facilitators, i.e. being taught how to facilitate. A facilitator who trains other facilitators is necessarily placed in the role of teacher, and needs to make the differences between facilitation and training clear to those she/he is teaching.

## *Coach*

A coach is very similar in skills and approach to a facilitator. Coaching is indeed part of the facilitator's role, particularly when it relates to encouraging an individual to plan and implement goals.

A 'business of life' coach usually works with an individual. However, a coach can also be involved with a work, sporting or other team.

I tend to put facilitation and coaching close together on a continuum of skill sets, particularly when referring to team coaching. However, coaching in its traditional role, as in sports coaching, can include choosing the team and firing individuals, which is never part of the facilitator's role.

# Manager

A manager in a traditional organisation is often the role name for someone with positional power over a group of people, including the right to assess performance and 'hire and fire'. However, the term 'manager' can also refer to someone with little or no positional power, and a particular role which involves managing the workflow of others. For example, successful creative people and sportspeople are likely to hire personal managers.

Whatever the definition of the manager, there is certainly a place for them to be facilitative, particularly if the power relationship is loaded unequally.

# Group therapist

A group therapist or psychotherapist has the primary role of creating personal healing with individuals and is likely to be very facilitative when working in a group. For example, a group psychotherapist will need to build the group so that it is safe enough for the participants to reveal themselves to each other.

A group psychotherapist will work with participants who are not expected to have the same knowledge about human development, and may work with the group for a long period of time. In some groups, such as violence prevention groups, the participants will have been ordered to attend by a court; in this case the psychotherapist also has the power associated with required attendance and lack of choice.

Psychotherapists have their own codes of ethics, and generally these codes make the relationship boundaries very explicit in order to protect the rights of participants.

## *Leader*

Leadership is a term that has a very wide range of interpretations; it is a generic term and is not often well defined. If someone takes initiative and others follow then we can see that there is a leader. If someone takes initiative and others don't follow, there is no leader.

A leader may be charismatic, inspirational, ruthless, coercive or brutal. We often describe leaders as good or bad. Certainly leadership requires followers, and is not always needed or desirable if everyone is thinking and acting proactively in an aligned way.

A facilitator is in a situational leadership role. This is the kind of leader who will take initiative at times but is always looking to empower the group and encourage initiative and alignment within it. An effective leader may also be facilitative and exercise many of the skills of a facilitator. A leadership role similar to that of a facilitator is that of the 'servant leader', as described by Robert Greenleaf in his book *Servant Leadership.*

However, a leader who has a designated position of some kind is likely to be using other skills in addition to those of a facilitator. This may include exercising power over others, deciding for them, and influencing them to go in a certain direction which is favoured by the leader or some outside agency.

## What's next?

These descriptions and comparisons of the role of the facilitator are interesting because they help to illustrate the development of the role, and the efforts of practitioners to explain what they do.

While explaining or describing the role of facilitator is helpful, a framework or 'architecture' for facilitation is also essential. In the next chapter I describe a framework that has been developed by Zenergy and is used in our facilitator training programmes.

# Chapter 3

# A framework for facilitation

As our work in facilitation developed, my colleagues and I began to train facilitators through our cooperative company Zenergy. At this point we found the need to create a conceptual framework for facilitation that describes what a facilitator does, where a facilitator focuses her or his attention, and how he/she creates a safe and productive environment. Such a framework is helpful both for the understanding of the facilitator and for those being facilitated.

Here is the framework for facilitation that I developed for Zenergy training programmes. As the framework is a model, it does not contain everything a facilitator is or does. It is an effort to state or create the architecture or pattern that underpins the work of a facilitator.

Figure 1.3.1 Zenergy model of facilitation

# Zenergy model of facilitation

The key elements of the framework are the topics covered in this chapter and the three following chapters: 'Facilitating yourself', 'Facilitating another' and 'Facilitating a group'.

The triangle illustrates the relationship between self-facilitation (working with and monitoring our own thoughts, feelings and actions, and making appropriate choices); facilitating another (coaching one other person to empower themselves and make choices), and facilitating a group towards meeting its stated purpose (working with the whole group dynamic). Stating the group purpose—having it displayed prominently and referring to it often—focuses the group and answers the following question.

# Why are we here, or what do we want to achieve?

The circle represents the container, which holds the group agreement on **how we will be together** —the agreed internal environment, culture and group contract (including possibly a code of conduct or ground rules). Outside the circle is the external culture or environment—all the influences, formal and informal, that affect us as citizens and members of organisations and cultures. These influences will come into the group unconsciously and may lead to misunderstandings and conflict. Although misunderstandings cannot be avoided entirely, the best way to minimise them is to create an explicit agreed and written group culture which itemises the key aspects of how you will work together.

This framework can also usefully be expressed as a three-dimensional pyramid with the group purpose as the top point and the third lower point representing the whole group. The graphic is useful in illustrating the need for alignment between individual and group purpose.

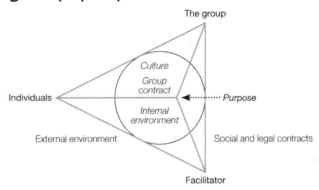

Figure 1.3.2 Pyramid model of facilitation

In this diagram the purpose becomes the apex of the pyramid and the group becomes the third angle of the lower triangle. The relationships (facilitator, individuals and the group) are represented by the lower triangle. The separation of group and purpose provides more clarity and allows the model to be extended to include several groups that share the same purpose within an organisation, or a dispersed network of groups dedicated to a specific purpose. For example, an NGO such as Oxfam or

Greenpeace, or a decentralised business such as Visa, could be illustrated in this way.

The primary role of the group facilitator is to focus the group on its purpose and act as guardian of the group culture. This may involve drawing attention to the purpose and culture through speaking, or it may be more subtle and energetic. This key work for the facilitator can be described as 'holding the group'. Holding is an embodied function—it involves the head, heart, belly (brain, emotions, intuition)—powers of listening, being with and mindfulness—all the presence that the facilitator can access. This primary work of the facilitator is done in silence, and to the untrained eye it may look as if the facilitator is not doing anything at all.

The processes used are, however, the useful steps (or means) towards achieving a purpose. Processes can be very different and still help the group meet its purpose. It is common for people to think that facilitation is only about using processes (even 'applying' them, like sticking plaster) because this is what participants see the facilitator doing that is tangible.

One of the advantages of the Zenergy model is that it provides a strong container (or structure) for the group (the purpose and culture), and allows for maximum flexibility within this structure. Processes can be planned in advance and then adapted, new processes can be created as needed or desired, or the group can work in a spontaneous and anarchic way. The facilitator is not dependent on any set processes once the group purpose and culture have been agreed.

The advantages of setting the purpose or intention and the key 'bottom line' rules, while allowing for maximum flexibility within this, are discussed in the book *Blink* by Malcolm Gladwell. He calls this the Red Team approach, and he contrasts it with the Blue Team (logical, structured and hierarchical) approach in exercises that saw the Red Team performing consistently better.

The framework of facilitation gives importance to the group purpose and the group culture. These together determine the parameters for everything that happens in the group. Purpose and culture define the boundaries and focus of the facilitation role. Having an explicit group purpose or intention provides clarity, certainty, transparency, safety and trust.

# Purpose

## *Where are we going? What is our direction?*

A group or team needs a purpose. A group purpose focuses the intention of the group. Without a purpose a group is likely to be unintentional. In his book *Servant Leadership,* Robert Greenleaf describes purpose (here adapted by Remedios Ruiz):

Purpose is our deepest dimension. Purpose is not a thing. Purpose has a way of ordering time and energies around itself; that is the real power behind the purpose. It often involves refocusing our work in order to bring out our talents and full potential.

If there is no clear purpose everyone is obliged to assume the purpose—and assumptions are most likely to be different. Even mild differences about the purpose of a group can and will lead to misunderstandings. Facilitators or group members who say there is not time for setting a purpose do not understand the power of setting intention. Wayne Dyer's book *The Power of Intention* includes some interesting comments about the close relationship between purpose and the universal field of intention.

A purpose may take time to establish, and sometimes it may be elusive at first. Rather than rush the setting of the purpose it can be allowed to emerge as relationships in the group deepen and energies come into alignment. In this case the purpose can be something to look out for and recognise when it comes to the group attention, probably in the form of an 'aha' moment.

The facilitator guides the process of a group towards setting and then meeting its purpose. Naming the group purpose allows the group to align. This alignment can happen on many levels, including mentally, emotionally and energy-wise.

The facilitator can then 'stand in' or 'come from' the group purpose with the authority of the group and provide the processes to move the group in that direction. If the purpose is unnamed or unclear, where does the facilitator take the group and on what authority?

The setting of the group purpose is so basic that it can seem self-evident. Yet it is often missing in groups, and many group problems arise because the group purpose is unclear.

## EXAMPLE

A telecommunication company team adopted a practice of checking for meeting purpose after attending one of our training programmes. They introduced the practice to others, and soon observed a 30% reduction in meetings generally and a much larger percentage of people choosing not to attend meetings that were unrelated to their particular focus. Consider the savings in time and money for this company.

### When purpose is missing

When purpose is missing in a group:

- Group members may say they feel confused or frustrated.
- The group may be unfocused.
- Group members may complain of wasting time.
- Group members may tend to misunderstand or speak 'past' each other.
- The group may get bogged down and stuck.

### Generating purpose

- The time to establish the general purpose of a meeting is in advance, so people know why they are there.
- It is important to confirm the purpose at the beginning of the meeting. Write it up so it can be seen and referred to. Clarifying the purpose at the beginning saves confusion and time-wasting later.
- Bring people back to the purpose when they become unfocused.
- In the moment, ask: *Where are we? Where do we go from here? Where is this taking us?* This will lead us to a conversation about purpose: *Why are we here? What results are we here to achieve?*

## Ownership

To get full ownership of a group purpose it is necessary to involve all the group participants in the process. This can be done at the first group meeting of an ongoing group. An imposed purpose will not have the same degree of ownership as one designed by the group itself because language is very personal. The group needs to put its purpose in its own words.

## Purpose for each discussion

On the micro level, every agenda item and discussion also needs a purpose. Establish this at the beginning. What is it the initiator wants from the discussion? *The purpose of this agenda item is to ... The purpose of this discussion is to ...* Clarify this first, before getting into the detail. Come back to this purpose if the group gets distracted. Keep focusing the group.

# Process ideas

## *Developing an aligned purpose*

1. Contact participants before the meeting and ask them what they understand the purpose of the meeting(s) to be. Collate the responses and form a draft purpose. Feed this back to the participants and ask for their comments. Rework the purpose to incorporate these suggestions until the group is satisfied.

2. At the first facilitated meeting of an ongoing group, have a round on the purpose. What do people understand it to be? Is it clear? One description may stand out. If there is alignment, write the purpose up. If the purpose is still unclear work in subgroups to make a succinct, one-sentence statement of purpose. Write these up. Find the commonality and create a purpose that everyone aligns on. Look for what lights people up.

3. Invite participants to draw or paint images that represent their individual purpose for being involved in the group process. Encourage people to look at one another's work and notice the images and colours used. What are the commonalities and differences? A similar image may show

up in several drawings. This may provide a clue to the group purpose. Ask individuals to speak the purpose they see emerging. Encourage people to be succinct and express only one potent idea. Listen for the purpose that has resonance for the whole group. Watch people's faces, watch for nods and listen to their 'mms' and other sounds. Write the purpose up only when alignment has been reached. (This process helps to circumvent unnecessary wordsmithing by people used to bureaucratic ways of working.)

Purpose addresses the issue of direction, where we are going; culture addresses the issue of how. This is the relationship between ends and means. Both matter.

# Culture

## *What is group culture?*

Culture is about how we will be together, or 'the way we do things around here'. On a group level we could also call this the group agreement, group contract, charter, ground rules, mores, understandings or desired behaviours. On a structural level you could see culture as the container within which the group operates.

As with the group purpose, it cannot be taken for granted that there is agreement about how things are done. On the contrary, there will be many different perceptions, which can range from deeply held cultural beliefs through to minor preferences. Differences of behaviour and expectations will lead to misunderstandings and conflict if they are unrecognised and unattended. Social norms such as competitiveness, blaming and bullying will prevail.

The development of an explicit culture allows for the group to become conscious about different beliefs and perceptions and to actively choose the qualities that are important to them. These can then be encouraged and 'lived into' by group members. This kind of culture is empowering rather than prescriptive. Specific rules about behaviour can also be made. A culture is a dynamic work in progress and should be added to or subtracted from as needed.

### Groups without culture

When culture is missing from a group:

- Behavioural differences will come to the surface and be interpreted in negative ways, leading to ongoing tension and misunderstandings.
- People may become tetchy and short with one another, and start avoiding some group members.
- People may begin to complain about one another to others *(She is so ... I wish he wouldn't ... I find her very...)*.
- Factions may form within the group.

### Generating culture

- Culture can be developed through **culture setting.** The questions to ask are: *How are we going to work together to achieve our group purpose? How do we want to be together?*

- A culture can include words and symbols. It is best if it is concise and memorable. It is helpful to write the culture up, perhaps as a mind map or drawing, and also to memorise it. See Figure 1.33 below.

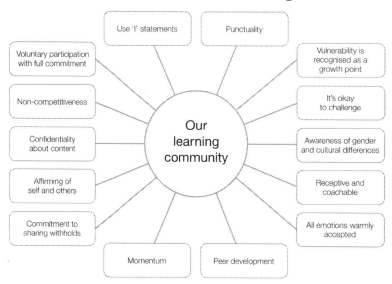

Figure 1.3.3 An example of a group culture, developed for a learning community

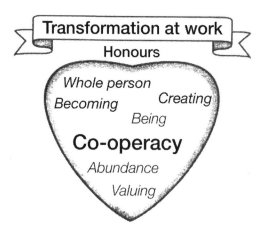

Figure 1.3.4 Zenergy culture—this example of a culture is more symbolic, and the words are triggers for an already understood way of working

- A culture is alive and needs to be reviewed regularly. Additions and subtractions can be made as needed by general agreement.

# Process ideas

## *Developing a culture*

1. Brainstorm how you want to work together. Clarify. Identify key elements and side issues. Discuss disagreements and link similar ideas. Choose between three and six of the most important aspects of the culture. Write, draw or mindmap the culture and pin it up where it can be seen each time you meet. Claim it as a dynamic document that is referred to and added to each time you meet and that can be added or changed as needed.

2. Ask each participant to identify one or two elements of culture that are particularly important to them. Group these. Ask people to meet in the groups and refine their understandings. Have them pick one idea from each group. Set a limit of five or six. Invite someone to create a drawing of the culture including the key words.

3. Now practise being the culture. How does this feel? Is anything missing?

   Processes 6–8, are for developing group purpose and group culture.

40

Figure 1.3.5 A team culture can also be developed into a charter.
This example is from the Department of Conservation's Bay of
Plenty Conservancy

# Chapter 4

# facilitating yourself

Knowing others is wisdom.
Knowing the self is enlightenment.

—Lao Tsu, *Tao Te Ching*

The most important work for any facilitator is developing one's own capacity to be and become an embodied, grounded, self-aware and self-reflecting person—to facilitate yourself.

Facilitating yourself is about going on a life journey—a scary and exciting journey that will take you to places within yourself that will surprise, delight, inspire, as well as disturb, horrify and disgust you. This happens in all aspects of our lives, including the physical, emotional, mental and spiritual. It is about the whole of us and it requires an holistic approach. There is so much to learn and accept about ourselves that most of us will (or could) be at work until we take our last breath.

Your body shape, tone and stamina are affected by food and exercise. You can modify your body for strength and flexibility and to build up certain muscle groups for the performance of special functions, for example as sportspeople, musicians, dancers and singers. There is a universal acceptance of the importance of healthy food in the development and maintenance of the body, although there is incessant debate about what is the 'right' food. Clean air and the absence of toxic substances from the body are also recognised as important to healthy living and the length of our lives.

Many people in the healing professions now believe that sickness, including life-threatening illnesses such as cancer and AIDS, and healing of the body are or can be influenced by our thoughts. You could debate the extent to which physical, emotional, mental and spiritual development is natural (just happens), or is facilitated by yourself or others. This is the 'nature or nurture' debate, which is still held among scientists. But the debate is not so important. Why not consider that most of your development is self-facilitated and that you can increase this through your own actions? That way you take responsibility for your own development.

# Being with yourself

The first step in facilitating yourself is to 'be with yourself'. To get access to being with yourself, it will help to consider the following questions:
- Are you comfortable with yourself the way you are right now?
- Are you comfortable with your body?
- Are you comfortable with your feelings?
- Are you comfortable with your thoughts?

- Are you comfortable with your gender and sexual orientation?
- Are you comfortable with your cultural and national affinities?
- Are you okay about being you?

It has been said that many people live lives of quiet desperation:

- 'I'm not okay, and I hope you don't find out how awful I am.'
- 'I'm not good enough, and I never will be.'
- 'I'm unloveable, and this can't change.'

Life then becomes dominated by covering up and compensating for 'not okayness'.

Before you get involved in facilitating other people you need, in the main, to accept yourself and be at work on this. Facilitating yourself is about growing, developing and training yourself—but not about 'fixing up' yourself. Can you get a sense of the difference? 'Fixing up' is always about compensating for something being 'wrong'—it actually holds 'wrong' in place.

Accepting ourselves is the biggest hurdle for most people:

- 'I accept myself completely.'
- 'I am a magnificent human being.'
- 'I am fully alive now.'

# Empowering yourself

Through self-facilitation you can empower yourself. Empowerment is coming into your own unique place of power where you are most truly your own self. It is about recognising when you are 'in your power' and how you experience this, and bringing it into all aspects of your life. It is about being at home in your body and in your personal space. It does not always mean being strong and confident. You may be most 'in your power' when you are feeling very vulnerable—it is more to do with being truly authentic and present.

Being strong and confident over the top of nervousness and vulnerability will be experienced by others as just that—a cover-up, or a sense of incongruence they can't put their finger on. When you are in your power, your words and actions have a different ring to them—things happen more spontaneously and you have access to synchronicity and miracles. You can train yourself to keep coming back 'into your power' and get others to coach you when they notice you are out of your 'place of power'.

Passive and proactive self-facilitation is about empowering yourself. Passive self-facilitation happens when you put yourself into a situation where things will happen to you which you believe will be empowering. You may choose a particular house to live in with ready-made flatmates, or work at a particular workplace with other people. You may put yourself into a training programme of some kind. You may choose to watch a movie or go to certain cafés or bars, or to holiday in a particular place.

Passive       Proactive

Figure 1.4.1 Passive and proactive

Through placing yourself in certain situations, you are provided with experiences that affect you more or less profoundly. An extreme example would be if you sat in the middle of a busy road at night—you would be passively facilitating getting yourself killed or injured. (This is hardly likely to be empowering, however.)

Proactive self-facilitation is when you consciously choose to alter your behaviour—to interrupt how you normally do things, believing this can benefit you. You may choose to speak or listen or behave in a new way, expressing feelings you usually hide, sharing thoughts that had been self-censored, wearing different clothes, exercising regularly and so on. You take the initiative—it is your idea, your choice, your action.

You can allow and move through the thoughts, feelings and body sensations which resist the change in behaviour and use your will as the impetus or touchstone to keep you on course. Exercise your free will. As you become more and more proactive, your will also becomes stronger. Just as taking on a fitness programme will develop and strengthen your body, exercising your will to change your behaviour develops and strengthens the will—and your capacity to be proactive.

# Self-facilitation as a training tool

For a facilitator in training, self-facilitation is essential. You need to take on training yourself to be as fully conscious and awake as possible. How can you usefully facilitate others if you don't facilitate yourself? This would be hypocritical. As a facilitator, you need to be constantly in training and at work on yourself. You need to be an in-training Olympic athlete in self-awareness. Questions to ask yourself are:

To what extent am I responsible for my own actions?

...my own thoughts?
...my own emotions?
...my own physical sensations?
...my own environment?
...my own relationships with others?

Can I right now choose my own thoughts?

...my own feelings?
...my own physical sensations?
...my own actions?
...my physical environment?

What about now?

And now?

Perhaps now then?

Or now?

Start to observe yourself, and keep observing yourself as often as you can remember. Write the following question on a card and place it on your desk or mirror.

What am I choosing now?

Am I choosing to be well?

...to be loved?
...to be comfortable?
...to be stimulated?
...to be bored?
...to be sad?
...to suffer?

Doing this exercise is very useful as it will assist you to become more selfaware. And there is no right answer. The value is in the looking.

What fascinating choices you have every moment!

Perhaps each moment you have a choice to:

expand—give—contribute—appreciate—live
or to:

contract—take—pull back—criticise—die

The usefulness of this process of inquiry is in looking at yourself and developing some awareness that is other than your thoughts, feelings and body sensations. Consider the possibility that you are totally responsible for all your thoughts, feelings, body sensations, physical environment, the people you are with, and all your circumstances (food, money, clothing, housing, belongings). You don't have to believe it is completely true, although it may well be, but just consider the possibility to see what alters when you take on this way of being in the world.

Try it as an exercise. As you experiment with this for a while (days, weeks) ask yourself the following questions:

What do I choose to learn from this (choice, situation)?

If I am choosing to be sad, angry, upset, ill, what can I learn from this?

How is this fulfilling my present needs?

How is this situation fulfilling my beliefs about myself, about others, about the world?

This process of inquiry is only for use on yourself. Don't apply it to others. It is about developing your awareness, not assessing others—that would entirely miss the point.

One way to be with others is to notice that:
They are choosing to do ... to say ... to be...
How interesting! This is where they are choosing to be. It may be life-enhancing or not for them. Only they will know.

To be a facilitator requires you to extend and develop the part of yourself that can give free attention—that part of your awareness not caught up with thoughts, feelings (emotions) and body sensations. To do this you need to explore and find personal development methods that will enable you to heal old upsets (hangovers from the past). Upsets are 'set-ups for you to grow'. They often date from your early childhood when you were very impressionable.

There is a wide range of personal development methods to choose from, including action methods such as psychodrama, co-counselling, voice dialogue, NLP(Neuro-LinguisticProgramming),psychosynthesis, the Landmark Education programmes and many more. Other methods to increase your available free attention are also useful. These include meditation, prayer, creative visualisation and ritual.

# Upsets

You also need to develop ongoing practices to help avoid picking up more baggage (upsets) than you already have. To do this you need clearing techniques (see Processes 36–38,).

If you are upset for more than, say, a few minutes, something has been activated from the past—the upset is no longer solely in the present. It helps to look at what has been triggered from the past—what specific incidents spring to mind and how can you heal or complete these?

This is how I have described how I deal with old upsets:

There are several ways I handle my own old upsets when they get triggered. One way is to acknowledge the upset (I may be feeling angry or scared or sad and am not sure what it's about) and keep doing what I have to do to keep my commitments. I put the upset on hold. If the up-set is related to a particular person I know well, I may request a clearing session with them. [See Process 37.] This requires some in-depth reflection on my part, however, before I decide this, as, mostly, for me anyway, upset is more about me than the other person.

I may also work with another facilitator to ac-cess the cause of the upset and begin the healing process. Another process I use to release and transform the energy of an upset is through vig-orous dancing or going to the gym.

What I often do is take time out and fully ex-plore the feelings that have come up. I call this my healing process. I like to do this by myself: I lie down on the sofa under my favourite blanket, relax and begin to breathe into the feelings, allow-ing them to totally reveal themselves, in their fullness, so that nothing is left unfelt. I relax into them, no matter how awful they seem at the time. I give up any resistance to them—any judgement of them. This is a very healing process for me. I stay with and allow the feelings for as long as it takes—it could be half an hour to several hours.

Usually I will slip into a meditative space and become very sensitive to my body energy, and sounds and movement around me. I keep watching my breathing and relaxing my body. After a time (and this varies enormously) there will be a shift in my consciousness. The feelings will begin to move and dissipate as though they have had their say and been listened to. Often during this process, I have insights and visual or word images which clarify the nature and source of the upset and suggest ways I might do some things differently. After this process I am freed up, clearer and less at the effect of those particular feelings. They have loosened their grip.

Upsets are a bit like children, demanding to be heard and given full attention. When they are fully heard, they become satisfied and contented. This is my favourite way of facilitating my own emotional healing.

I suggest that you experiment and explore a range of techniques and processes until you find the ones that work best for you. There is no right answer here. It is a personal matter. Be gentle and tender with yourself—a loving parent. (Usually we are far more critical of ourselves than anyone else is ever likely to be.) As you try things out and get to know yourself, your confidence in your own choices and your own truth will grow. Trust yourself and your wisdom. Self-facilitation is the key to the effective facilitation of others.

Although it is easier to see other people's blocks, seeing and healing your own is a vital, ongoing and lifetime journey with many joys and challenges along the way. It is a process. There are times when the way is clear. At other times nothing is clear. The process may be like going down a tunnel, seeing a dim light at the end, moving through the tunnel and coming out into the light—then going into another tunnel and repeating the process over and over.

For information on centring while facilitating and debriefing, and after a facilitation, see Processes 50 and 51.

# Chapter 5

# facilitating another

Facilitation calls forth people's best intentions.

—Zenergy programme participant

## One-to-one facilitation

A group is made up of individuals, and much of the time a group facilitator will be interacting with the individuals in the group. In addition, the facilitator may sometimes work on a one-to-one basis as a coach. Like facilitating yourself, facilitating another person (one-to-one facilitation) is an important part of facilitating groups.

It is important to distinguish between different types of one-to-one facilitation, including coaching and therapeutic counselling. Facilitation takes place in a group setting and involves one-to-one interaction. Coaching is one-to-one facilitation (usually in private) where the person being coached (the coachee) is focused on exploring and clarifying an issue or achieving an objective or goal. Therapeutic counselling is a relationship that addresses such deep-seated conditions as trauma or depression. Sometimes there will be a crossover or grey area between coaching and therapy, so it is important to be on the alert for this and to know the level of your own knowledge and expertise.

If you are facilitating or coaching someone and you feel out of your depth, or they are very fearful, confused, withdrawn or acting strangely, don't persevere. Contact a more experienced facilitator or therapist for your own coaching or recommend that the person see a therapist or doctor.

# Facilitation is not giving advice

Facilitating another person tends to come more easily than facilitating yourself. It is easier to see other people's patterns and blocks than to see your own. Often you want to tell others what to do—this is called giving advice.

Advice is telling someone what you think they ought to or should do. It comes from 'I know better'. Advice is not facilitative, especially if it is not requested. Even if it is requested, it is often not helpful because it fails to take into account that everyone is different and unique and will choose different experiences and ways of learning.

Facilitation recognises that each person is perfect just the way they are—they are already whole and complete (which includes having problems and difficulties like all other human beings).

The values of respect and honouring underlie facilitation. I respect and honour you. It is a privilege for me to be with you and you with me. We matter: our time together matters.

This attitude of respect and honour is necessary before you can facilitate someone. 'Attitude' means where you as facilitator are coming from, or where you are 'standing'. You will come from not assessing or judging people or taking account of society's view of them. You will accept them as whole people with their own values, behaviours and world-view.

If your attitude is that there is something wrong with the person you are to facilitate, then you are going to want to fix them up, or will expect the person to fix him-or herself up (with your help). This is more of 'I know better', and it implies that you know what that person 'being fixed up' looks like. This is not a powerful place for a facilitator to come from.

Another way of saying this is that you need first to accept people the way they are if you are going to work with them as their facilitator. This does not mean that you need to like them or agree with them. But if you are unable to honour, respect and be with them, you cannot facilitate them.

If you are asked to give advice ('What do you think I should do?') to another person or within a group, you may like to use one of the following responses. All redirect the question to the advice-seeker.

'What alternatives can you generate for yourself?'

'I suggest you answer that question for yourself?'

'I notice a "should" in there. Have you got some judgements or assessments about what is the right thing to do?'

'Would you like the group to generate some
   suggestions?'
'Are you asking for my opinion?'
'Is it illegal, immoral or unhealthy?'
If illegal: 'What is the law?
If immoral: 'What is the principle or belief?'
If unhealthy: 'What is the risk?'

# Being with another

The first step in facilitating another person is to
be able to be with them. This involves, firstly, being
with yourself, in your own body, your own space, with
your own thoughts and feelings, and being comfortable and at home with who you are. Secondly, it involves being with another, being comfortable and at
home with them. Ask yourself the following questions:

Am I comfortable being with (name)?
Am I comfortable with their body?
Am I comfortable with their appearance?
Am I comfortable with their voice?
Am I comfortable with their expression of
   feelings?
Am I comfortable with them expressing their
   thoughts?
Am I comfortable with their gender or sexual
   orientation?
Am I comfortable with their ethnic group or
   culture?

Are they okay?

If you can be with another person with respect and honour—not wanting to make them different or better, or to fix them up—you are ready to learn about facilitating others. (See Being with another, Process 20.)

# Living in different worlds

Everyone has a view of the world. Every view of the world is different.

Everyone lives in different worlds.

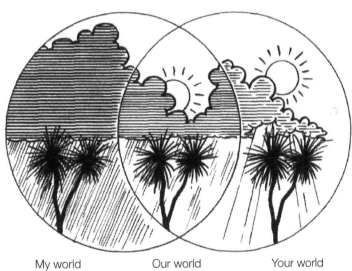

My world          Our world          Your world

Fig 1.5.1 My world, your world

I have a view of the world.
My world-view is unique.
This world-view is all-encompassing.
This is the way the world is.
You have a world-view.

Your world-view is unique.
Your world-view is all-encompassing.
This is the way the world is.

It is easy to assume that someone else's world is the same or similar to your own. Your way of experiencing the world is the way the world is. You assume others perceive (see/feel/think) things in the same way that you do. Otherwise how can you understand them?

Consider the possibility that you can never fully understand another person. Their mix of life experience (including culture, gender, sexual orientation, communities of interest and place, family, schooling, friends, age, work, recreation, values and beliefs) will always differ from your own. They are and will always be something of a mystery. This is both the joy and frustration of being with other people. You can have moments of being 'at one', but this will not be ongoing.

What often happens is that people make a mental jump from seeing that another's perceptions are different to assuming that their own perceptions are better.

'The way I see things is "right". The way you see them is "wrong".'

Or:

'My experience with (childhood, school, marriage, work) was..., therefore you must have had similar experiences.'

Or:

'I believe ... about (sex, religion, marriage, politics, and so on). Surely you must have similar beliefs.'

Or:

'I feel strongly about (abortion, the environment, child abuse, the role of women, and so on). Surely you must feel strongly about these things too.'

If another person's behaviour, beliefs and values are unacceptable to you (and some people's will be), don't work with them as a coach. It is important to recognise your own limits and not try to be more accepting than you really are. You may be able to refer the person to someone else who has more experience or a world-view that is more like theirs. (See My world, your world, Process 22). As a group facilitator, however, you will come across people in groups with whom you have little empathy. Here you will need to practise the discipline of compassion. Try imagining the person as the innocent child they once were.

# Projection

Another thing to become more conscious about is how you 'project' your world (your past experiences) on to other people and situations. We all do this all the time. This is the way we make sense of and quickly interpret the world. It can be a safety mechanism to help us recognise danger quickly, but it also acts as a filter to experiencing the present directly.

Consider that you are 'blinded' by your projections. You mostly see things through a 'projection fog', playing your old movie over the top of what is happening now and connecting the moment-by-moment present with your past. You may often become disappointed or surprised by other people because they do not fit your preconceived picture of how they might behave—based on other people you have known in the past who resemble them in some way. So you are often relating to a projected person rather than the real one who is with you.

We also live out our unresolved past experiences through new scenarios:

'All tall dark men remind me of my father and my unresolved feelings about him. I never date anyone who looks like that as all my unresolved feelings are stirred up immediately. I avoid those guys like the plague.'

'When anyone who looks like or behaves like my mother is my boss, the relationship is always difficult. I always end up feeling misunderstood and not appreciated. It is so stupid. Even though I now have some consciousness about this, it still seems as if I go onto automatic pilot.'

Such is the power of projections.

The identity check exercises (Processes 43 and 44) are very useful for identifying your own projections about people and situations. This was my experience the first time I did this exercise:

We did the identity check in pairs and then shared in the whole group. There were 30 people there and we were sitting in a large circle. I have never forgotten the shock of looking around the room and 'seeing' my mother, sisters, childhood friends, and adults I had known as a child, all present in the circle. I had been projecting my early 'world' on to the present and was relating to all these people as though they were my family, early friends and associates. The people I warmed to reminded me of people I liked from the past and the people I was not attracted to reminded me of people who were associated with unpleasant memories.

Often you will be unconscious of the power of projections and the fact that most of your experience of the world is perceived second-hand through your version of reality.

## Listening

Communication has been described as 80 percent listening and 20 percent speaking. Listening is a very important part of facilitation. Listening powerfully is a skill and a way of being with people. Listening can be full of assessments and judgements about the person being listened to, or it can be a period of time-out from speaking yourself. During this time you may mentally rehearse your own lines or fantasise about other things triggered by the conversation.

Alternatively, listening can be a powerful energy, which draws forth the authenticity of the other person. The listener can listen actively for the 'gold' in the speaking, and create such a positive listening energy that the speaker will begin to speak and share themselves in a totally new way. Perhaps you can recall someone listening to you like this—you would have felt powerful and honoured.

As a facilitator you need to be training your listening constantly. Listen to each person with whom you come into contact as though they are the most important person in the world. The irony is that the conversation you are having is indeed the most important one at that moment. Listen as though your life depends on it. Listen for the commitments, the dreams, the love, the vulnerability of the speaker. Listen for what lights the speaker up and makes them enjoy life. Listen for what expands, energises and enlivens them.

As your listening develops, you will be amazed at how magnificent every person is and how love is present in your conversations.

Listen also for the conversation itself—what is being said and what is not being said; what is spoken from the heart and what is spoken from the head—'I feel' as opposed to 'I think'. Is the speaking a series of complaints, blaming others, self-criticism and descriptions of events, or is it creating a vision or dream, and opportunities to have this happen through action? What happens at the beginning, middle and end of the conversation (the structure)? Is the conversation left hanging in the air or is it complete and with opportunities for action?

# Speaking—interventions

Out of powerful listening comes facilitative speaking. This is speaking that empowers the listener. Facilitation involves the use of questions and suggestions (interventions) that encourage the other person to clarify and explore their own thoughts and feelings, and move themselves forward in line with the insights and connections they make.

Facilitating a person is about empowering them to:

- Fulfil their dreams.
- Create something new.
- Have something happen that wasn't going to which will make a difference in their own lives and in their world.
- Catch their own patterns and blocks.
- Identify what they want to happen next.

Facilitation is not about interpreting someone else's world. Interpretations are only valid or useful if there is agreement by the client. And it is not about giving advice or your opinion.

## *Facilitative speaking can be reflective*

You can reflect back the content of what has been said:

'What you have said is...'
'What I heard you say is...'

Or you can reflect back the spirit of what has been said in an empowering way:
'I can hear that you are concerned about...'

...are committed to...'
...are making a contribution towards ... project through...'
...have a vision about...'
...want to do something about...'
...are accomplished at...'

For more about this see Mining the gold, Process 26.

# Interrupting disempowering conversations

Our first response to upset is usually to blame or discount ourselves or others. Facilitative speaking will interrupt the conversations that disempower the speaker.

'I notice you said you are "hopeless" at that. Can you say that some other way that is more empowering?' (For example, 'This is an area I am in training with.')

'I notice you said you "should" do that—it sounds like you don't have a choice. Is that so?'

'I notice you said you can never remember names. Could you say that in a way that doesn't reinforce your forgetfulness?' (For example, 'In the past I have found it difficult to remember names, but I am now remembering names more and more easily.')

See also Empowering Interpretations, Process 27.

Facilitative speaking will also interrupt conversations where the speaker disempowers others—blaming. The facilitator is not there as a 'blame policeperson', but rather as someone who notices the blaming and encourages the client to move through and see it as a preliminary to understanding the underlying issue. Blaming is often the way we find out how we feel about something, so the facilitator will encourage the client to explore this—maybe by exaggerating the blaming until it becomes ridiculous.

'Blame ... blame ... blame ... blame ... oops!
'What is my role or responsibility in this?'

Remember, blaming is always disempowering, at least for the speaker, and is always about avoiding responsibility. Caution: people are so attached to blaming that this may not be popular news.

# Encouraging lightness

Humour is another way to interrupt disempowering conversations—if you can see the lighter side to a 'problem', your perception of it often shifts. Gently encourage the person to see the humour in the situation. If handled sensitively, the person will be able to laugh gently at themselves.

'I suppose my shouting at the boss, stomping out and tripping over as I went was quite reminiscent of Charlie Chaplin. I missed the opportunity to throw a pie at him though.'

# Coaching

Sometimes it is appropriate for the facilitator to offer coaching in the group. A request or an offer can be accepted or declined freely, and this needs to be made very clear. To decline coaching does not mean anything about you or the other person; it is merely an ongoing choice.

One-to-one coaching (in private) can be more directive than interactions with one person in a group. To train yourself to coach others one to one, it is important to have lots of experience in being coached yourself. There is plenty of written material and training available for one-to-one work. Useful books include Landsberg's *The Tao of Coaching* and *The CCL Handbook of Coaching* edited by Ting and Scisco.

Coaching is a contractual arrangement—without agreement it is potentially abusive. So let's say that someone has requested coaching or a facilitated session with you, that you understand they are well, and you have agreed to facilitate them. You now have a contract.

# Coaching for action

If your friend or client has decided to take some action, they may like support by way of ongoing coaching. This will take the form of encouraging the person to invent and carry out the actions necessary to accomplish their plans and projects. Coaching is particularly helpful when the going gets tough and lots of reasons come up (disempowering conversations) as to why in retrospect a project may not be such a great idea.

Some coaching interventions are:

'What is something you can do to have ... happen?'

'What resources do you have or need to do that?'

'Is there anything stopping you from having that happen?'

'Is there a small step you can take now towards that larger project?'

'Can you draw up a plan which will get you from A to B?'

'What support will you need to implement your plan?'

For example, the friend who yelled at the boss may have decided to make another appointment to clear up the issue, but he or she may need encouragement to actually make the appointment.

'When are you going to make the appointment by?'

'I request that you phone me at 5 pm and confirm that you have made the appointment.'

'What is it that you want to say to him? Will that be complete for you then?'

'How can you ensure that you do say that? Do you need to write it down?'

'Phone me after the meeting, say by 3 pm.'

(In this example, the person may have a pattern of stewing over incidents like this for days or weeks rather than going back and clearing them up quickly, something they want to do but don't because it seems scary.)

This kind of ongoing coaching (sometimes called life coaching) is popular in business and some facilitators also offer this service. You can develop your coaching skills through coaching training, and through participation in programmes of experiential communication skills training in your region. These skills are very useful to a group facilitator.

# Chapter 6

# facilitating a group

Facilitation is like dancing. If you go unconscious, you miss the rhythm and trip.

—Zenergy programme participant

A purposeful group is not just a collection of individuals. A group is an entity in itself. It is a living system with its own physical form, its own personality, its own potential and its own limitations. You are part of a group a bit like an arm or a leg is part of a human body. While you are not joined physically, you are (or can become) joined emotionally, intuitively, intellectually, energetically and spiritually. And you are part of and bonded to a number of groups—family, household, work, recreation and community.

Being in a group can cause anxiety for most of us as it brings up our fear of losing our own identity and autonomy. You might be afraid of losing your free will or being dominated by others. Perhaps you don't know what you have to contribute or where your limits are. You might be swayed by the views of others against your better judgement. These fears are real.

As children and teenagers, we are often subjected to powerful peer pressure to conform to a particular group's values and behaviour. Our own families can exert a very controlling form of group pressure: 'You must do what we [Mummy and Daddy] say or be punished.'

A cooperative group can be particularly threatening in this way because everyone is supposed to reach agreement on major decisions.

Will I feel pressured to agree?

Will I be compromised and give in to peer pressure so people will like me or so I don't stick out?

A facilitator needs to be aware of the individual's need for autonomy, of the collective need for cooperation, and of the group as a whole system/organism with a particular culture and personality. Individuals will have different requirements for privacy and disclosure depending on their personalities and cultural conditioning. Individuals will be at different places on their life journeys towards full autonomy and self-expression.

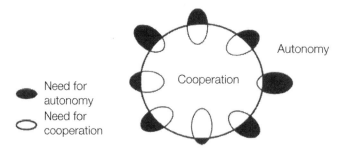

Figure 1.6.1 Autonomy/cooperation in a group

The relationships between group members are also complex and form a web of interaction, with each strand having its own unique character.

Figure 1.6.2 A web of interaction

# Being with a group

Being with a group is a development of being with yourself and being with another. Being with a group is being with yourself and with a number of others. It is being part of a larger self, part of an organism or entity with its own purpose and personality.

As a facilitator, ask yourself the following questions:

Am I comfortable being with myself and others in this group?

Am I comfortable being part of this group entity?

Am I comfortable with the way this group works?

Do I know the values of this group?

Am I comfortable with them?

Am I comfortable with the 'culture and personality' of this group?

Is there someone in this group who I find particularly triggering?

Have I done an identity check with them directly or indirectly (that is, not in their presence)? (See Identity Check, Process 43.)

Also ask yourself these questions:

Do I want to dominate this group?

Do I feel dominated by this group?

Am I afraid of this group?

Do I 'know what is best' for this group?

Do I have the 'right process' for this group?

Am I an 'expert' on the subject this group is addressing?

Do I like/agree with some of the members of this group but not others?

Am I the only person who will work well with this group?

(Check each of these out with yourself or with your coach. 'Yes' answers to these questions are all good reasons for not working with a particular group.)

And ask yourself these questions too:

Coming from an attitude of 'I don't know', am I committed to empowering this group to achieve its purpose?

Am I committed to taking care of every person in the group and creating a safe environment for them to be fully self-expressed and authentic?

('Yes' answers to these questions are good reasons for working with a group).

# Facilitating a group is putting yourself on the edge of the sword

Facilitating a group takes a certain fearlessness (and this includes feeling scared). It takes sufficient awareness of yourself to realise that you don't know how to do it (even though you have a toolkit of skills), and a willingness to go with the flow of the group—to tap into the group mind and creativity (which includes challenging the group and halting the flow if it is sabotaging the group purpose).

Group facilitation is moment-by-moment awareness, being awake and in action—awake in the way a hunter stalks a tiger or a mother watches over her newborn infant.

A group facilitator needs:
- Self-awareness (being with yourself).
- Awareness of others (being with others).
- Commitment to the group fulfilling its purpose.

# The facilitator's relationship to the group

The role of facilitator is granted by the group. It is a different relationship to that of a teacher and a class, a parent and children, a manager and staff, or a conductor and an orchestra. In these situations most of the responsibility and accountability rests with the teacher, parent, manager and conductor, and is to an outside source. The facilitator, however, is responsible and accountable only to the group (and her-or himself).

The role of facilitator is a role of honour and trust given by the group. The group has recognised the importance of the group process and contracts with the facilitator to guide this process towards the fulfilment of the group purpose.

We trust you to guide the process of our group so that the group can wholeheartedly achieve its purpose.

# Starting work with a group

When working with a new group, the facilitator will want to check out the group's expectations of the facilitation role. What the group expects from the facilitator will depend on their previous experience. Ask the group:

What are your expectations of a facilitator?

You, as facilitator, will also want to share your own values and ways of working with a group, and your expectations of the group. Sharing these things means you can be quickly known by the group, and it encourages an open atmosphere of sharing in the group.

I will tell you something about myself and my way of working with a group.

This initial checking-out process will establish if there are marked differences between the expectations of the group and the facilitator. If there are, they will need to be addressed straight away and clarified to check if it is appropriate for the group to work with that particular facilitator. This process is usually best carried out in advance by representatives of the group 'interviewing' the facilitator before he or she is hired. For more on this see Part 2 Chapter 1, 'Facilitation and the client'.

# Guidelines for a facilitator

Group facilitation is the art of guiding the group process towards the agreed objectives. A facilitator guides the process and does not get involved in content. A facilitator intervenes to protect the group process and keep the group on track to fulfil its task.

There is no recipe for a facilitator to follow, and there is no one right way to facilitate a group. But here are some guidelines, techniques and tips that you may find useful (these guidelines include material from *The Zen of Groups: A Handbook for People Meeting with a Purpose*).

# *A group is capable of more than any one member thinks*

One+one+one+one=5 or more. This is the equation of synergy. A group is capable of much more than each individual member thinks is possible. You have no idea what you can achieve in a group. Maybe you can achieve almost anything in the world as a group, although it may take some ingenuity to discover how you can achieve it. Effective facilitators know that group members are stopped mainly by baggage from the past, and they can achieve amazing results. A facilitator is out to tap the energy of the group and tap into the group synergy.

# Trust the resources of the group

The facilitator trusts that the group will have the resources to achieve its task and work through any process issues. Trust in this sense is an attitude of confidence that the resources are present and will be discovered. The facilitator enables the group to explore and find these resources. This is the way a group becomes empowered. This does not mean that the task will always be fulfilled. It means you don't give up when the going gets tough and all group members may be wilting.

# Honour each group member

Facilitation is about honouring each group member and encouraging full participation while having the group task achieved effectively and efficiently. Always approach group members as capable, aware and fully functioning people who are committed to the group purpose. Even if they are behaving in disruptive ways, always treat them as if they were acting honourably and for the good of the group.

# Keep the group space safe

It is important to keep the room or space safe from interruptions and distractions. The facilitator ensures the physical space is safe and guarded from interruptions and intrusion. A group also has an 'energetic' space, and the facilitator is aware of this and watches out for it in the same way a mother looks out for a child who may wander unconsciously into danger. On a spiritual level, group space is sacred space.

# Stand in the group purpose

Always keep in mind the group purpose. It can be useful to have this on a large sheet at each meeting. 'Presencing' the group purpose will keep the group on track and grounded, and provide you with a place to stand when the group gets distracted or bogged down.

# Be adaptable

There is no one technique that will always work at a particular time for the group. It is a matter of choosing, in a particular moment, what to do—whether or not to intervene, and how to intervene. You can plan ahead but you always need to be ready to adapt to what is happening in the moment.

# Remember that beginnings are crucial

Group meetings and workshops have a beginning, a middle and an end. Getting started is like setting out on a journey or laying the foundation of a house. The first part of a group meeting or workshop is crucial to the whole process and time needs to be allowed for the process of starting.

# Take everything that occurs as relevant

A facilitator takes everything said or done in the group as group interaction, including individual exchanges, side comments, and accidental occurrences. For example, if someone falls off their chair, that becomes part of the group process rather than an interruption. Some facilitators use outside interruptions as well, like someone coming into the room accidentally.

# Work with conflict

A facilitator is comfortable with conflict and always encourages it to be expressed openly. Disagreement is the natural result of different personalities, different views and opinions. If a group is to develop to maturity, it will need to work with conflict, rather than avoid it. Creative conflict resolution can be synergistic, leading to major breakthroughs and forward movement in a group. Remember: don't get tripped up by conflict or get involved in the content.

# Be awake

Your most important asset as a facilitator is your awareness. Be 'awake' and 'present' to each moment,

moment by moment—listening, looking, sensing—100 percent present. Personal development work, meditation, consciousness-raising, discussion, training and development in experiential learning techniques are all useful ways to develop awareness. Experiment to find ways that work for you.

## Be yourself

As a facilitator, you will be most effective when you are being your natural self and allowing your own personality to be expressed. People get permission to be themselves from the way a facilitator behaves—through modelling. If you are stiff and formal, the group tends to be like that. If you are relaxed and self-expressed, the group tends to be like that too. Keep checking to see in what way the group is reflecting you.

## Develop discernment

Make sure your eyes and ears are open all the time. Listen and see without judgement, but with discernment. When is someone tripped up? When is someone 'asleep', upset, caught in a pattern or triggered? When are people tripping one another up or sabotaging the group? Are they aware of it? Do they want to stop? Who has given up and why? Who is raring to go and frustrated by the non-action of others? Discern when these behaviours are present and if an intervention is necessary.

## Stay clear

This is similar to being awake and present moment by moment. As a facilitator, notice when you get tripped up by your own or others' baggage. When you do get tripped up, note the 'trigger' word or phrase (for you to work through later), recover yourself quickly and carry on. Don't take personally, or get drawn into any comment on, ideas or beliefs expressed in the group, nor any criticism, no matter how personal. If you get triggered and are unable to recover quickly, use the process 'Clearing yourself when facilitating', Process 50.

## Get the job done

Always remember you are there to get the job done. Make sure you know the purpose of the group and the desired outcome for the particular meeting you are facilitating. Check how much time the group is prepared to spend on group process issues.

## Don't be attached to your own interventions

You may come up with what you think is a brilliant intervention, but if it doesn't work, drop it. The only reason to use an intervention is to keep the group focused, not because you think it is brilliant. Your job is not to show how clever you are.

## Use questions and suggestions

Questions and suggestions are the usual way a facilitator intervenes. Avoid giving advice. Use 'I suggest...' rather than 'What you should do is...' Also avoid giving the answer to an issue. Your job as facilitator is to guide the process, not be involved in the content, even if you've got the answer.

## Negotiate and contract

A facilitator is an effective negotiator within groups. The structure and framework of meetings and processes are developed through negotiation. Proposals and counter-proposals are encouraged until agreement is reached. Agreement=the contract. Most group decisions—including ground rules, time limits, personal responsibilities, roles, commitment, membership, values, purpose, aims, objectives and evaluation methods—are negotiated.

## Be sensitive to cultural differences

Sensitivity to cultural differences is essential for a facilitator. When you are working with people from cultures other than your own, some knowledge of the customs, rituals and sensitivities of those cultures is most important. If you do not have this knowledge, you need to say so and seek advice from people in the group to ensure cultural difference is respected. Community sensitivities also need to be addressed in a similar way. Don't assume—ask.

## Create space

An important part of facilitation is creating space for everyone in the group and for all that is happening in the group. Be inclusive. Keep enlarging the psychic or energetic space for the group to be together. This holding role is just as important as saying anything. If you have the opportunity practise holding the space of the group as a participant as well. When participants and the facilitator hold the space together there is room for emergence—unexpected new possibilities will begin to arise.

## Improvise

Facilitation is an improvisatory art within an agreed and negotiated structure. In this way, it is like jazz rather than classical music. Don't get stuck doing things a certain way. Remember, there is no one way or technique. Be flexible and stay awake.

## Acknowledge and affirm

A facilitator gives frequent acknowledgement and affirmation to a group. Encourage your group to keep going during long or difficult processes by affirming progress and acknowledging completion of tasks. Model the giving of acknowledgement and affirmation, and encourage group members to affirm and acknowledge one another.

## Use humour

A sense of humour is a great asset to a facilitator. The use of humour can usefully defuse some tense moments. There is nothing better than a light touch at the appropriate time.

## Keep intervention to a minimum

Intervene in group discussion only when it is necessary to interrupt behaviour that is:
- impeding progress towards fulfilling the task without the agreement of the group;
- off track in the discussion and the result of someone having tripped over baggage from the past;
- undermining the possibility of group synergy occurring;
- physically dangerous.

## Monitor the energy level

Monitor the energy level of the group at all times. This is your barometer. Energy is indicated by tone of voice, body posture, eye contact, level of participation and level of activity directed towards the task. Are people awake or asleep? Engaged or disengaged?

The energy of a group will alter all the time. At the beginning of a day people often have lots of energy. After lunch they are very often low in energy. Short breaks or active exercises can help keep energy up for longer sessions. For most people, concentration is hard to maintain for longer than 30 to 40 minutes. Keep some active exercises in your repertoire to use when energy is low and the meeting is long (see Games and energisers, Processes 32–34).

## Seek agreement and alignment

A facilitator seeks agreement from everyone and uses collective decisionmaking processes (consensus) unless there is agreement by everyone to do otherwise. Voting, majority or otherwise, is not a recommended way of reaching a decision in a facilitated group. A more potent version of agreement is alignment. This involves identifying a clear direction/purpose and alignment on both this and how to proceed towards it.

## When in doubt, check it out

'When in doubt, check it out' is a useful guideline for a facilitator. If you are not clear that everyone is in agreement with a decision or task, ask if everyone agrees. If necessary request a response from everyone—a yes or a no. Silence does not necessarily mean assent.

## *If you don't know, say so*

If you don't know what to suggest or do when an intervention seems to be needed in a group, say so and ask for suggestions. Someone else may have a good idea, or their suggestion may spark off an idea in you. Don't pretend you know everything—nobody does. Trust the group.

## *Invite feedback*

A facilitator invites feedback during and at the end of group meetings. All feedback is useful. Specific comments are more useful than general ones. One feedback technique is the use of rounds of negative and positive comments.

## Synergy

Synergy is about tapping into group energy so that the group members are able to accomplish more than they thought possible. Tapping into group energy dramatically increases the speed at which a group takes action. Synergy is about flowing and working together harmoniously. It is about coordinated action and being inspired by one another.

How can you tap into this group energy in a conscious way rather than by accident? In everyday life, people usually feel separate from one another. We are all individuals and different from everyone else. We like it this way. It is a function of the different 'baggage' we carry, and it keeps us separate from others.

The ability to let go of your 'baggage', even momentarily, will allow you to identify with and feel for others in a more direct way. In a group, this can be experienced as trust, closeness, peacefulness, understanding, happiness, joy and exhilaration (all aspects of love in its broadest sense). This is what people crave when in groups—unity, acceptance and trust (love).

Increasing group and facilitation skills will open up the pathway to experiencing synergy in your group. Group skills increase the level of cooperation in a group—members begin to listen to one another in a new way, and start to recognise when they are in tune with others. Differences are quickly voiced and worked through. Group members take responsibility for their own baggage and strive to stay 'clear' with one another.

But synergy is not the result of following rules. It is more subtle than that. It is something to value and generate. Force will produce the opposite to synergy—separateness, and the rigid taking and defending of positions.

A facilitator trains to listen for the subtleties of group energy—what will enhance it and what will detract from it. This is the art of facilitation. Developing and using the techniques in a skilful way is the craft.

# Some signposts to synergy

At Zenergy we have identified a number of signposts or milestones which may assist your group in finding a pathway to synergy. These are:

- **Purpose**—the group has a clear purpose and group members are committed to it.
- **Vision**—a powerful vision is developed by the group. Building the vision, and recording it in some way—in words, art or music—serves as an ongoing inspiration to group members, particularly when the going gets tough.
- **Values**—implied in the group purpose and vision will be a number of values. These are teased out by the group and referred to particularly when making tough decisions.
- **Clarity**—the group clarifies roles and commitments such as membership, ground rules, expectations and limits.
- **Projects**—the group invents projects to achieve its purpose with clear accountabilities and action plans.
- **Identity**—group members develop a strong group identity. Trust is developed through group members sharing themselves honestly with one another. Members honour one another and make allowances for each other's baggage.
- **Communication**—the group finds agreed ways to work through conflict rather than avoid it. Conflict

is seen as normal. Feelings are seen as normal. People agree to communicate even when it's hard.

- **Learning**—group members increase effectiveness by identifying what they have learned as they go along through group process and project monitoring and evaluation.
- **Acknowledgement**—group members acknowledge their contributions and the contributions of others to the group.
- **Celebration**—group members celebrate together the accomplishments of the group.

See also Part 2 Chapter 2, 'Cooperative processes in organisations', especially the figure showing the FACTS model for maintaining sustainable cooperative processes in organisations.

Chapter 7

# making interventions

Peace is an active force, not just an agreement not to harm one another.

—Zenergy programme participant

The technical term for what a facilitator does or says is an 'intervention'. The idea behind this is that everything a facilitator does affects the group in some way. Even being present and listening is an intervention, although the term is usually applied to the more obvious actions of the facilitator such as speaking or using gestures.

The facilitator's job is to make it easy for the group to achieve its purpose, and to empower the group to tap into its full synergistic potential. The facilitator begins by accessing the power of listening and speaking.

## Listening

Listening is the primary skill of facilitation. The quality of your hearing will profoundly affect the group. Listening is active, focused and affirming. You listen for the whole group, and for each person in it. You hear where the group has been, where they are going and how they might best get there. You listen for the group purpose, projects and commitments, and the magnificence of each person. You listen to the spoken and unspoken conversation. You listen for what is present and for what is missing. The group is focused and energised through the power of your listening.

Your facilitation also trains the listening of the group through modelling and reminding. As noted earlier, listening is usually full of assessments and judgements—this is distressed listening. What you are developing as a facilitator is distress-free listening.

# Speaking

Powerful speaking is whole-body speaking—the body is centred, the breathing is deep and relaxed, the voice comes from deep in the chest. The voice resonates and projects. It has a ring to it. As a facilitator, you use your voice like a musical instrument. You can use it to direct, encourage, support, calm, inspire and play. Your voice is the authentic expression of your intent as a facilitator. It makes available the whole range of your human expression—from your gentle and vulnerable inner child through to your stress-free authority and power.

Speaking is the obvious way a facilitator intervenes. The interventions of the facilitator can be described as a kind of dance with the speaking and listening of the group members, drawing forth cooperation and creativity, probing the group, blocks, and disarming the barriers to synergy. As facilitator, you guide the group process and guard against the tendency of participants to trip up on their baggage.

## How does a facilitator know what to say?

A facilitator doesn't know what to say in advance. You listen for what needs to be spoken to facilitate the group. This is what you speak 'in the moment'. You become an instrument of the group purpose. You are there for the group. You tap into the 'higher purpose' of the group, whether it is spoken or unsaid. You speak to have the group win and synergy occur.

Facilitation is an improvisatory art. Like tennis, swordsmanship and jazz, you can practise the strokes or riffs, watch or listen to other practitioners, and seek to understand the philosophy and values. The facilitation itself can occur only in the practice of it—by being in action.

## Intervention training

To assist facilitators in training themselves, this chapter provides a range of interventions in a number of areas that will give you a feel for the way a facilitator works. The interventions will provide you with an indication of the way to work with a group. Notice how the interventions usually take the form of questions and suggestions.

Use these interventions if you want to, but preferably read them, and consider both the attitude of the facilitator using them (where they are coming from; who they are being) and the possible response from the group when each is used.

## Climate and culture setting

How would you like the seating arranged?

How do we want to work in the group?

What roles do you want to cover (facilitator, recorder, timekeeper)?

Who would like to take the role of (recorder, timekeeper)?

What ground rules would you like? Any suggestions?

What values are important?

What processes for joining and leaving do you want?

What are the characteristics of your ideal group? Let's have a brainstorm.

What do you not want to see happen in this group?

If you were to be in this group for the next five years, what would you like to be set in place now (processes, rules, guidelines)?

Is this group discussion to be confidential to the group? Any exceptions?

Is trust important in the group? (Suggest techniques to develop it.)

What are your hopes and fears regarding the group? Let's have a round to share these.

## Managing time

This session will end at (time). Is everyone in agreement with this? Anyone not?

The breaks will be at ... and ... Any problems with these?

Let's put times beside the agenda items.

How long will we spend on this issue?

Our time is up. We will stop this discussion now.

How much more time do you propose?

Does everyone agree?

Not all of the group wants to extend the discussion so we will stay with the original time agreed.

It is now time to start again.

Bill, can you please ask people to come back in from the break. We need to get started.

I want us to start in two minutes. Please be ready.

## Getting participation

Let's have a round and see what everyone is thinking (or feeling).

What about people who haven't spoken so far? What do you think (or feel)?

What do you think, (person's name)?

What are your feelings about this, (person's name)?

Let's have a brainstorm. Call out your ideas. Don't censor them.

(Name), could you please write up the ideas on the whiteboard?

Who'd like to speak first?

Share with your neighbour (the person next to you).

Who would like to share with the whole group?

Now let's go round the whole group. We'll start here.

Remember it's okay to pass or decline.

Who can sum up the (issue/main ideas/areas of difference/where we have got to)?

## Being present and awake

Does anyone have anything they would like to say to be here (fully present)?

You look worried/upset. Is there anything you would like to say?

Share with the person next to you any concerns you have about this issue.

Is there anything you would now like to share with the group?

Are there any concerns about the group or the process?

The energy is low. Often this indicates there are things that people are holding back. Does anyone have anything they would like to say?

Find someone you feel comfortable with and share something you have been afraid to say in the whole group.

Let's stand up and stretch (swap seats or do an energising exercise) to get the energy moving.

Let's have a round of things we've been withholding.

What would it take to wake everyone up? Any suggestions?

Here's a joke that might wake everyone up.

## Creating a future

What are your hopes and dreams about this?

What can you see developing out of this in the future?

What will this lead to in three years' time?

If you stand in the future (say 10 years from now), what do you see?

Let's do a group visualisation exercise and see what's in the future.

Let's pretend we have been travelling in space and arrive back to find that three years have passed. What do you see?

What are we building?

How will your children see this?

What might your children say about this in 10 years' time?

What do you want to end up with (or put in place)?

What are the steps that will lead us into the future?

If we look through the fog, what do we see?

What's the best way this can turn out?

What's the worst thing that can happen?

## *Drawing out issues*

What are the issues here? I'll write them up.

There are several issues within this discussion. Let's tease them out and address them one at a time.

Would someone like to play the role of devil's advocate?

There seems to be an underlying issue here, which we are missing. Can anyone identify it?

How do these issues fit together? Can someone put up a model on the board? What is the key issue here?

## *Keeping on task*

We are getting distracted. Let's get back on task.

Can anyone summarise where we are up to?

How can we move this issue forward?

What is the main task?

What steps can we take?

Let's put this new issue on the agenda for later and get back to the first issue. Who will take responsibility for carrying out this task?

When will it be done by?

There are a lot of distractions happening—let's get back to the issue/task. What do we need to consider or take into account to have this resolved?

## Shifting levels

How are people feeling about this issue now?

How is the energy level?

Who has a sense of what is going on in the group?

Is everyone comfortable or do we need a stretch (or a break)?

What do you think about this issue? Let's set up a continuum to get a picture of the range of views.

Who can speak for the higher purpose (or wisdom) of the group?

Could you, (name), be the Goddess of Wisdom, and speak to the group?

How would you like to start this session? Can someone suggest a ritual we can adapt for the group?

Let's raise the energy of the group by using this technique.

There seems to be some yucky baggage spilling into the group. Can anyone say what it is?

Some people have gone very quiet. Can you tell us what is going on for you?

This sounds very rational. What do people feel about it?

This sounds very emotional. What do people think about it?

# Interrupting unhelpful behaviour

You have said what you don't want to happen, (name). Can you tell us what you would like to happen?

Can you propose an alternative, (name)?

This conversation is going around in circles. Let's have a proposal we can work on.

You have made a number of criticisms, (name). What is your bottom-line concern?

(Name), you have now had the opportunity to put your view. Let's hear from someone else.

Please don't interrupt when (name) is speaking.

Can we have one conversation at a time?

Let's have a role-play or fishbowl to work on this issue.

Let's separate the person from the issue.

## *What's not being said*

I sense that there is something present here that is not being said. What is it? There is something going on under the surface. Can someone articulate it/say what it is?

There is a gremlin in the works. Can someone see it and tell us what it is? What do you really want to say, (name), and are holding back?

102

The unsaid is louder here than the spoken.

There seems to be a lot people are not saying.

There is constipation present in the group. It's time for the shit to hit the fan.

Who can say what's missing here?

Let's have a round on what's missing in this discussion.

How do you account for the (low energy/anger/lack of participation/etc.) in the group?

What does it suggest to you?

What do you think is happening here?

# Identifying agreement and disagreement

Can someone sum up the agreement already reached?

Now we'll check that out with the whole group.

The agreement we seem to have reached is ... Does everyone agree?

The areas of agreement are: (a)..., (b)..., (c).... The areas of disagreement are: (a)..., (b)..., (c).... Is this how everyone sees it?

Does this wording (on the board) capture the agreement reached?

We do not have agreement. Let's capture the different perspectives on the whiteboard.

Can you or someone else summarise your perspective?

Who is not happy with this solution?

What would you like changed?

What words would you like added or deleted?

Please say 'yes' if you agree, 'no' if you don't.

I take it that everyone agrees? (Silence means assent?)

Can you live with this decision?

104

Thank you for allowing this decision to be reached without using a veto.

Would you like your contrary view written down in the records?

# Learning

What did you notice?

Were there any surprises?

How does this link in with what you already understand?

How will you use these ideas?

If you did this again, what would you like to be different?

What have you learnt from this (project/workshop/seminar)? What is the essence of your learnings, in one sentence?

# Feedback and acknowledgement

Let's have a round of constructive criticism. Let's have some feedback on that idea.

Is there any further constructive criticism?

Now let's have positive feedback and acknowledgement.

I acknowledge you, (name), for....

Let's have a round of acknowledgement.

Find someone in the group whose work you appreciate, and go and acknowledge them now.

Write down the names of three people in the group you admire and what it is you appreciate about them.

We will write the feedback on the whiteboard in two columns: Constructive Criticism/Acknowledgement. Let's have two rounds—the first on constructive criticism and the next on acknowledgement.

I request your feedback on my facilitation. First, constructive criticism, please? Thank you, I have some useful learning from that. Now for acknowledgement please? Thank you. Yippee!

# *Completion*

What do you need to say to be complete on this?

What do you need to say so that you can move on?

What would you say now if you were never able to be with this group again?

If a bomb were going to explode in two minutes, what would you want to say now?

What would complete this for you?

What is stopping you being satisfied with the outcome?

Is there anything more you need to say or do?

Is anyone still incomplete?

Is there anything you would like to say after you leave this group? Please say it now.

# Chapter 8

# shifting levels

Now I see that, instead of trying to not be 'overbearing', I can be a dance.

—Zenergy programme participant

A group, like each individual in it, is multidimensional and operating on many different levels. Group facilitation works within and between these different levels. This is part of the magic or alchemy of being a facilitator. A facilitator working on different levels may appear to people in groups as a magician:

How did you pick that up?

What did you see that had you make that suggestion?

When you said that, the group came together.

What did you do that had us all get into action?

Awareness of the different levels develops gradually for the facilitator. It is useful training to practise distinguishing the different levels operating in the group. Here are some notes on different levels. Explore them. You may come up with some more of your own. Note that in calling them levels the intention is not to suggest they are in some kind of a hierarchy. They could also be called aspects of a continuum.

# The physical level

The physical level is about people being comfortable and having their physical needs attended to. Care needs to be taken with:
- Seating arrangements.
- External noise.
- Room temperature.
- Clean air.
- Adequate food and drinks.
- Bathroom facilities.
- Breaks for food, toilet and other physical needs.
- Effective lighting.
- Resources—whiteboards, videos, PowerPoint as needed.
- Special needs—language interpreters, child minding, access for wheelchairs, etc.

The environment needs to suit the function and style of the meeting and the culture of the organisation.

Encourage:
- Planning for physical needs in advance.
- People saying what they need to be comfortable at the beginning of a meeting.

- People being on time to start and restart after breaks.
  Avoid:
- Ignoring participants' physical needs.
- Insufficient preparation.

# The thinking level

The thinking, or intellectual, level is the predominant mode used by work and project groups. This level invokes:
- The sharing of ideas.
- The exploration of issues.
- Brainstorming.
- Creative thinking.
- Inspiration.
- Analysis.
- Critical thinking.
  At this level you will notice the words used are:

I think...
I've noticed...
I understand...
My vision is...
Can you imagine...?
We need to consider...

By sharing our thoughts, we inspire one another, share visions and create the future. We discover common values and build commitment, recognising each person's individual contribution. By thinking through and analysing how, we determine how we can *do things together.*

Encourage:

- Speaking about future possibilities.
- Speaking that moves the conversation forward.
- Intentional speaking—*'This will be.'*
- Sharing ideas—not holding back.
- Full participation.
- Mining the gold (listening for people's magnificence).
- Diversity of ideas.
- Dialogue.

Avoid:

- Withholding.
- Thinking small.
- Domination by a few.
- Complaining and negative speaking.
- Discussion that doesn't go anywhere.
- Criticising personalities.

# The emotional level

Research by neuroscientists suggests that every thought has a corresponding emotional charge that is set off by chemical reactions throughout the body. This means that emotions are always present in some form as we think, although we may not always be conscious of them.

The emotional level is more conscious when we are:

- Sharing experiences.

- Sharing feelings.
- Expressing feelings (grief, anger, fear, love, enthusiasm).
  At this level the words used will be:

  I feel...
  I care...
  I'm concerned...

We can access heartful speaking, authentically speaking in a way which moves others, finds empathy with them and arouses their feelings.
  Encourage:
- Sharing from the heart.
- Participants owning their own distress.
- Listening for one another's magnificence.
- The presence of love.
- Trust.
- Empathy and compassion.
- Caring for the planet.
  Avoid:
- People shutting down their feelings.
- Shutting down the expression of feelings by others.
- Filling up the silence.
- Distress projected onto others (blaming and fault-finding).
- Pretending the distress will go away.

# The intuitive level

This is speaking that encapsulates the essence and finds the common chord, intuiting what is going on for people. Words used will be:

I sense that...
There is something not quite right here.
There is something off here.
We are onto something—I've almost got it.

Intuitive speaking is in tune with the group—speaking that expresses what is present yet unsaid.

Encourage:
- Listening for the whole group.
- Listening for what needs to be said.
- Speaking the unsayable.
- Recognition of the group wisdom.

Avoid:
- Ignoring the unspoken upset.
- Ignoring the group wisdom.
- Ignoring your own intuitions.

# The energy level

This is a non-verbal level where you pick up or sense the energy by observing behaviour/posture/tone and animation of voices/attentiveness/'vibes'. At this level, you appreciate where people are at: how 'awake' the group is, how 'attuned' and focused it is. You can develop an awareness of the way the energy works in a group. It occurs rather like the tide coming in and out.

Neuroscientists now suggest that we perceive objects by resonating with them. In her book *The Field,* Lynne McTaggart says: 'At our most elemental, we are not a chemical reaction, but an energetic charge. Human beings and all living things are a coalescence of energy in a field of energy connected to every other thing in the world.'

At times you will need to be able to move the energy.

Encourage:
• Awareness of energy by participants.
• Recognition of natural energy flows and ebbs.
• Allowing the natural flows to occur.
• Recognition of key energy points and shifts.
• Recognising times to shift the energy level.

Avoid:
• Ignoring the group energy.
• Always maintaining the same level—e.g. high level.
• Mistaking a natural energy ebb for boredom or stuck energy.

# The spiritual level

The spiritual dimension is where you tap into the higher purpose of the group—the fine energy of the higher consciousness, the 'God' energy. This is done by the use of music, dance, art, meditation and ritual to invoke the higher/spiritual energies, compassion and love/at 'oneness'/beyond worlds/planetary consciousness/universal love and joy/essence/spirit of peace.

Encourage:
- Development of group rituals by the group.
- Fun, joy and self-expression.
- Practices that deepen the group experience.
- Simple, powerful practices.
- Embracing cultural diversity.
- Inclusion of all.

Discourage:
- Superimposing rituals designed by others.
- Rituals that don't inspire everyone.
- Rituals that have become meaningless or boring.

# The synergistic level

This is the level of transformation, of heightened awareness that occurs when the group is at one—aligned, attuned and integrated. This is the level at which the group recognises itself as an organism with one mind. Each group member has direct access to this mind and is able to speak it. The energy of the group is palpable and there is clarity, spaciousness and timelessness. These are the magic experiences you will always remember and treasure—and everyone in the group will feel them.

At this level, group members:
- Have 'aha' experiences as others say what they were about to say or think.

- Speak with voices that have changed in quality and seem to resonate.
- Feel in tune and at one with the group.
- Drop their judgements of others.
- Feel that suddenly there is plenty of time even though an issue is urgent.
- Notice others in a new way.
- Feel guided or supported by a higher self.
  Encourage:
- Alignment with the group purpose.
- Clearing.
- Attunement.
- Spontaneity.
- Lightness.
- Humour.
- Creativity.
- Stretching beyond usual limitations.
- Not stopping.
- Sharing at a deep level.
- Appreciation.
  Discourage:
- Discounting of self and others.
- Cynicism.
- Negativity.
- Small-mindedness.
- Members hanging on to positions or behaviours.

# Noticing the levels

A facilitator observes the group at a number of levels and notices when a change will advance the group purpose. Noticing the levels can be accessed through:

- Listening to the sound, tone, pitch and speed of participants' speaking.
- Watching body movements, facial expressions and body language.
- Listening to the length and quality of silences.
- Sensing energy changes.
- Sensing the presence of love and the higher energies.

After noticing the levels, it is helpful to share these experiences with another facilitator so that you develop a fuller and more developed sense of the subtleties involved. Ask one another, 'What did you see or notice?' and share your experiences. You may have similar or different experiences. Just notice, don't try to make one another right or wrong. Keep sharing experiences and see if there is some agreement.

# Working with the levels

Working with or drawing attention to a number of levels is a skill a facilitator needs to develop. The simplest way to develop this skill is through:

- Noticing the different levels.
- Sharing your observation with the group.
- Inviting the group to share their observations.
- Modelling moving to the various levels (for example, speaking from the heart will encourage participants to do the same).

- Encouraging group members to shift levels as they feel appropriate.

## *EXAMPLE*

The group has been meeting for an hour. A discussion has become bogged down and is going nowhere. People are looking tired and are slumped in their chairs. The facilitator notices that the group is stuck 'in their heads' (thinking level) and that the energy is low (energy level).

She shares her observation with the group, and invites them to stand up and stretch for two minutes to increase the energy (physical level). The group agrees to do this. After the break, she invites them to have a round, each sharing their feelings about the issue (emotional level) for two minutes.

The comfort level of the facilitator will determine the degree to which the levels can be explored by the group. The facilitator's ease will give participants permission to explore the levels, and build the trust and safety necessary for exploration to occur. As the group opens up to different levels, participants find new ways of relating to one another.

If you want group effectiveness and synergy, you need to know you can't get there without taking care of the multi-dimensional nature of the group. It's like an iceberg—probably 90 percent of what is really going on is submerged and will go unnoticed unless the facilitator or a participant draws attention to it, bringing it to the consciousness of the group as a whole.

The facilitator is always looking for the balance and pathways which will allow each group to become synergistic. There will be a workable balance of levels for each group for full effectiveness. See Part 2 Chapter 2, 'Cooperative processes in organisations', for an in-depth look at achieving sustainable synergy.

Most work groups tend to operate well at the thinking level, but may not be fully aware of other levels. A group that operates only on the thinking level will not bond unless they also access the emotional level. Sports teams are often more aware of the importance of emotional bonding, which they often do while socialising after the game.

A group whose purpose requires creativity (design, innovation, development, envisioning) will need to raise its awareness of and tap into the intuitive level to fully access this creativity.

Chapter 9

# dialogue and storytelling

Humans have a deep need to understand and find meaning. Many group activities are action orientated. Many are not. This chapter explores some reflective group activities.

## Dialogue

Dialogue in groups has been happening since the time humans learned to string sentences together. It is part of all indigenous cultures and is often associated with sitting in a circle, perhaps around a fire. It would be difficult to find a culture that had no words for this practice of sharing experiences and engaging in learning through deeply and consciously being together in a communal setting.

Through dialogue individuals and groups can share knowledge and uncover meaning. Dialoguing can bring out all the perspectives in the group, revealing what is important for each person—their dreams, concerns, expectations, hopes and fears.

Dialogue also enables the quest for deeper meaning in life, death, existence and all the big questions we have about 'all of it'. Facilitators can hold the space and encourage processes that enable potent stories to be shared and deep meaning to be uncovered. Such spaces can be deeply nurturing, restoring and feeding the soul. They can also provide the insights that lead to thoughtful action and social change initiatives.

In addition, group dialogue builds the collective intelligence of the group—the capacity of the group brain. It is this group intelligence or group synergy that is needed to solve the complex problems of the present day (whether they are organisational, community-based, national, regional or global) for peacemaking, resource allocation and system redesign.

Taking this to a deeper level again, dialogue in a space of deep listening opens up access to the whole field of consciousness, sometimes called the fourth dimension, and the unlimited knowledge available beyond the constraints of time and space. We can learn to access this expanded consciousness as a normal part of human interaction. This depth and width can be available to most of us if we take the time and suspend disbelief, and allow ourselves to be in communion with ourselves, others, the whole group and beyond. Some call this 'sacred space'.

# Methods of dialogue

The method of dialogue Zenergy favours is dependent on a respectful, accepting culture, deep embodied listening, the ability to be in silence together, the willingness to speak from one's own experience or knowing, and the willingness to suspend judgements.

The dialogue also needs each participant to 'be with' him-or herself and others without becoming too triggered or encumbered by recurrent baggage, or at least to be able to put her/his baggage aside for a while. Most people can do this, with some support, and it is not helpful for individuals in the group to begin judging one another's abilities. If this occurs, build a more respectful culture. (Preferably have this written up and placed on a wall to remind people, along with the purpose or focus of the dialogue.)

Participants listen deeply to themselves, to one another and to the whole environment, and speak when they feel moved. Participants listen for meaning and resonance, with all contributions being considered important, including the bird and animal life within earshot. The facilitator's main job is to hold the space through light awareness and ground the energy through being grounded in her-or himself. In addition, the facilitator ensures that the group culture is respected and there are no external interruptions.

If this process is unhurried and listening is profound, a sense of expansion and resonance will emerge. It is as if the embodied consciousness of each person in the group is expanded and the group is resonating to a larger, more global consciousness. People will begin to speak from a more expanded awareness and speaking may be peppered with recognition, such as 'I was thinking [or about to say] the same thing.' After some time, poems, song and dance may be shared. Laughter takes on a lighter and more sparkling quality. Tears may flow. It is as if the group brain is working as a single, wonderfully complex unit, and each individual is part of it and also fully autonomous.

If you wish to explore this kind of dialogue it can be helpful to practise 'Being With' and 'Powerful Listening' exercises first (see Processes 20, 21 and 26).

# Checking in

An entry into dialogue for new groups can be through the practice of 'checking in' (see Rounds, Processes 1 and 2). Checking in is usually practised at the beginning of a meeting or gathering. Each person has the opportunity to presence and share something of themselves within the context of the group purpose.

Often there is a rule that this sharing will be uninterrupted. Sometimes, however, some interaction is part of the round. The order of participants is usually as people wish to speak, or in turn around the circle. There may be a time limit at first, but it is better if the time can be flexible.

Experience with checking in is a good way to begin a group's journey toward in-depth dialogue. When ready, the group can take off their trainer-wheels, allow several hours or days and move into in-depth dialogue.

# Strategic questioning

Fran Peavey, a social-change activist from the USA, wanted to talk to people around the world and develop in herself a 'global heart'. The people she knew and loved were mainly in California and Idaho, and she had not travelled much outside the USA. She came up with the idea of sitting in public places with a sign saying 'American willing to listen'. She travelled to Japan, India and other countries, listening to people's concerns. She sat for days at the railway station in Varanasi, India and out of many conversations she saw a project grow in the community to begin the process of cleaning up the sacred Ganges River. This project brought together many people under community leadership. It caught the attention of Indira Gandhi and later her son Rajiv, who as prime minister created the Ganga Action Plan. The project is continuing.

Fran's method of working in such sensitive areas of social change involved listening and asking questions, often obvious ones that no one wanted to ask for fear of appearing stupid. Fran called her way of working 'strategic questioning', and developed the skills of asking questions that will make a difference. Strategic questioning is a powerful tool for personal and social change as it helps people to discover their own strategies and ideas

124

for change. It is a process that changes the listener as well as the person being questioned.

In her book *Heart Politics Revisited,* Fran writes:

> In the early '80s, one of the unaskable questions for me was, 'What shall we do if a nuclear bomb is dropped?' You couldn't answer that without facing our overwhelming capacity for destruction, and the senselessness of it. That question allowed many of us to move beyond terror and denial, and work politically to keep it from happening.

Fran likes to use the analogy of water and flow, and talks about 'water' questions that work to find a way through, a reality that moves, a focus on 'to' rather than 'is'. She describes a water question as taking the form of the container into which it is poured, rather than being a form unto itself.

# Focused conversation

The Institute of Cultural Affairs (ICA), which is based in Chicago, has developed a technology of participation (ToP) after extensive work in facilitating community and organisational development in many countries. Their ORID method codifies their dialogue process by the kind of questions to ask at each stage of a conversation. ORID takes a group through four stages of questioning to reach deeper levels of understanding and more effective decisions.

The focused conversation uses the following levels, which form a template or pattern from which innumerable conversations can be drawn.

1.  The *objective* level—questions about facts and external reality.
2.  The *reflective* level—questions to call forth immediate personal reaction to the data, an internal response, sometimes emotions and feelings, hidden images and associations with the facts. Whenever we encounter an external reality (data/objective) we experience an internal response.
3.  The *interpretive* level—questions to draw out meaning, values, significance and implications.
4.  The *decisional* level—questions to elicit resolution, bring the conversation to a close, and enable the group to make decisions and resolves about the future.[1]

# Strategic dialogue

Peter Senge named a process he devised to uncover meaning in groups as 'strategic dialogue'. He writes about strategic dialogue in his book *The Fifth Discipline,* which also describes the five key disciplines that underpin the learning organisation. These five disciplines are systems thinking, personal mastery, mental models, building shared vision and team learning. Senge notes:

All these five disciplines must be employed by the learning organisation in the never ending quest to expand the capacity of the organisation to create its future.

In the book *Presence,* Senge describes the development of a group he was part of, who met for several days at a time over two years. He describes their ability to dialogue deeply, and sums up the centrality of 'presence'.

> We've come to believe that the core capacity needed for accessing the field of the future is presence. We first thought of presence as being fully conscious and aware to the present moment. Then we began to appreciate presence as deep listening, being open beyond one's preconceptions and historical ways of making sense ... Ultimately, we came to see all these aspects of presence as leading to a state of 'letting come,' of consciously participating in a larger field for change.

> In the end, we concluded that understanding presence and the possibilities of larger fields for change can come only from many perspectives from the emerging science of living systems, from the creative arts, from profound organisational change experiences—and from directly understanding the generative capacities of nature.

# Storytelling

Storytelling has been around as long as there have been people to tell stories. Throughout the world, storytellers use stories in intentional ways to bring about transformation and change within individuals, organisations, communities and in public spaces.

Cultural memory resides in stories from before the written word. Stories of ancestors and key events were told and retold until they became the myths and legends that reside in the recesses of our unconscious memories and define our various present-day cultural traditions.

There are a variety of books on storytelling. One wonderful book, which took 37 years to write, is by the British author Christopher Booker. Called *The Seven Basic Plots: Why We Tell Stories,* the book describes the patterns underlining storytelling as 'the seven gateways to the underworld'. Booker identifies these universal themes as overcoming the monster, rags to riches, the quest, voyage and return, comedy, tragedy and rebirth. He suggests that 'all kinds of story, however profound or however trivial, ultimately spring from the same source, are shaped around the same basic patterns and are governed by the same hidden, universal rules'.

Having a group explore its own story (narrative), or the narrative of its context, can be the key to its transformation. In his book *The Leader's Guide to Storytelling,* Stephen Denning refers to the discipline of storytelling as the sixth discipline of learning organisations, in addition to the five suggested by Peter Senge in *The Fifth Discipline.*

Denning introduces several story forms that can be used in the leadership of organisational change.

These story forms include sparking action, communicating values, fostering collaboration, taming the grapevine, sharing knowledge and leading into the future.

Storytelling can play an important part in the group development, and facilitators are learning to create safe and potent environments for stories to be shared. Through stories we can access deep aspects of humanity, and share the otherwise unsayable things that we may be experiencing as deep impulses and yearnings. Personal and mythic stories paint verbal pictures that inspire and terrify us as we add in the colours, imagine the context and 'connect the dots'.

Stories are also a means through which groups articulate and perpetuate their cultural knowledge.[2] When personal stories are shared in a group context, an individual experience may come to represent the group's shared experience. This occurs in social space where members are exploring the narrative of their context and situation. As personal stories begin to shape the group narrative, each individual story builds on previous stories. The forming narrative becomes a new framework for thought and a blueprint for action.[3]

It is by telling our stories that we come to know ourselves, and whenever we hear another's story we understand them. We come to appreciate their strengths and vulnerabilities, their joys and sorrows. Storytelling teaches us to listen and enables us to find our voice. It entertains us and challenges our thinking. Story continues to enhance our lives and bring us closer together.[4]

Storytelling is useful for promoting meaningful relationships. It provides a forum for mutual recognition and awareness. It can allow people to express events, issues or perceived problems in a non-threatening way. Story provides for the presentation of experience without opinion and judgement, and this leads to expanding possibility.

When I tell a story, an introduction of myself, I get in touch with my personal culture. In a sense I lay down a carpet so that others can come and sit on it. When I hear someone else's story, I pick up something of their values, their beliefs, and the many wonderful things about them.[5]

The check-in process is one way of introducing ourselves as stories. Other storytelling processes are included in Processes 28–30.

You are also encouraged to develop your own ways of storytelling. Gathering in a circle, around a fire, a candle, a table or under a tree are all associated with storytelling. The starting point for storytelling is deep listening, a sense of mystery and wonder, imagination, and a willingness to share from the heart and soul.

# Rituals

There is a history of groups meeting for ritual purposes from the earliest human history, especially to celebrate and assuage nature at the change of the seasons, harvest and spring planting. Ritual groups have taken many forms and continue to this day in all religions and in the contemporary New Age movements. Women's consciousness-raising and spirituality groups; men's groups, including drumming, sweat lodges and other ritual activities; informal and formal spiritual groups—all are happening in their hundreds of thousands in all countries in the world wherever people gather. One spiritual tradition that has deeply influenced the development of modern groups dedicated to peace and finding alternatives to violence is that of the Society of Friends (Quakers), who sit in silence until moved to speak and practise finding consensus in all their activities.

You are encouraged to research these and other groups' activities, which are so numerous they cannot be covered adequately here. See also Part 2, Chapter 7, 'Mapping the field of facilitation'. Do also consider devising your own unique processes or adapt existing processes for your own circumstances. The field of facilitation is always changing and open to innovation.

# Chapter 10

# getting to consensus

Facilitation is creating a space within which people can empower themselves.

—Zenergy programme participant

The decisionmaking mode associated with facilitation is that of consensus. For cooperative groups involved in action, decisionmaking is very important, and the process skills for consensus decisionmaking are a key aspect of the facilitator's role.

Consensus decisionmaking (also called collective decisionmaking) draws out the collective wisdom of the group and encourages each group member to own all decisions made. Consensus decisionmaking may take time at first, but with practice it can be quick. And this form of decisionmaking allows for synergy to occur.

To be effective, consensus decisionmaking requires an underlying agreement by the whole group to reach decisions in this way. Individuals take on a commitment to reach agreement by concensus and give up the right of veto. This agreement can take the form of a contract that is written into the group charter or constitution. It can be useful to have a written agreement so that when new people join the group or organisation there is no need to revisit this basic premise.

# How to make decisions

Having a consensus-based group or organisation does not mean that everyone necessarily takes part in all decisions. There are various possibilities, including the following:

- Everyone is actively involved in all decisions.
- Those who want to be are involved in all or any decisions.
- Those directly affected by a decision are involved in the decision. (All group members agree in advance what 'directly affected' means.)
- The whole group agrees to give authority and responsibility to make decisions, within agreed criteria or other limits, to individuals or subgroups (that is, to delegate).
- The group agrees that in particular specific circumstances majority or even autocratic decisions can be made (for example, in an emergency).
- Group members agree to disagree. Disagreements can be noted and not hold up individual action in some specific circumstances.

One group, organisation or community is likely to include most or all or these decisionmaking modes in their repertoire. How to make various kinds of decisions is best considered near the beginning of the group life, and it also needs to be revisited on a regular basis. Be careful, however, that this review does not become a rehashing of particular decisions.

Note: In some groups and organisations there is a fall-back position to be used only when all consensus decisionmaking processes have been tried without success. This is usually agreement by 75 percent of the group. It is much less likely to be majority or autocratic decisionmaking.

# *Recording and revisiting decisions*

How and where decisions are recorded is important, particularly for those who have not been able to attend a particular meeting. Groups will need to decide if and when decisions can be revisited. Usually, for example, groups limit the right to revisit decisions to the next meeting only. Proxies are not usually allowed.

# Raising awareness

Taking part in consensus processes allows participants the opportunity to raise awareness and develop a new relationship with agreement and disagreement. We can of course have opinions and agree and disagree on just about anything, and some of us are prone to this. We can debate how, when, where, why, by whom and on what basis (values and information) decisions are made. There is a lot of scope for conflict and also for creativity when people come together and share diverse perspectives. There are also personal development opportunities for freeing ourselves up, from always having to be involved, having to be right, or having to get our own way.

It helps when group members develop a working trust in their own and others' decisions. A willingness to follow the flow of energy and listen for emergent action is also useful to the group. There is an opportunity to develop discrimination and wisdom as an ongoing practice. As the facilitator you can help this consciousness-raising by maintaining a lightness in your energy—like a feather on water. Ask questions such as:

What is trying to emerge here?

Who is articulating this?

Can you align with this urge and support it actively?

Is there some thread or perspective missing that is needed?

Do you want/need to shift the flow of the group into a new pathway?

Is that urge coming from a clear place or from a distressed place?

What would happen if we expanded our field of awareness to feel into the group as a collective consciousness?

How does your view fit now?

# Consensus decisionmaking processes

There are a variety of processes that can be used for reaching consensus decisions. Some stress the importance of participants remaining proactive and actively involved in seeking solutions rather than being stuck in a particular position (see Process 13). Other processes require the development of criteria for the decision before proposals are discussed (see Process 15).

These decisionmaking processes are task-oriented and may not always acknowledge the emotional impact of decisionmaking.

## *Emotional honesty*

When deep personal relationships are involved it is necessary to acknowledge and honour emotional honesty. This can be more important than getting the decision made. Here is a way to do this:

First, align on the real purpose and need to make a decision.

Next, encourage everyone (perhaps in a round) to express their views and proposals whether in agreement or disagreement. Encourage participants to share their true motivations without fear of judgement or alienation from anyone in the group.

After all views and motivations have been shared, check to see if alignment is already present or can been reached.

If emotional alignment is not reached, acknowledge that more time may be needed to think about and integrate the discussion, and that the group may not yet be ready for the proposed idea.

Identify one or more practical steps forward towards making a decision. (More information may be needed or other people may need to be involved).

## Listening for agreement

A very effective way for a facilitator to work with consensus is to listen for it during a free-ranging discussion. Often participants reach consensus without consciously noticing it (they are caught up in the excitement of the discussion) and the group moves on without noting the agreement that has been reached. A skilful facilitator listens out for such moments and notes them, and then intervenes in the group to check out the agreement reached—almost in passing (see Process 14).

# Barriers to reaching agreement

Many people drawn to cooperative groups have fears about consensus decisionmaking.

How can you get everyone to agree?

Won't it take too long?

It will waste too much time.

Collective decisionmaking can take longer than majority decisionmaking, but the decisions 'stick' and are often put into action more quickly and effectively because they have been agreed to by the whole group. Often a lot of time is spent before a majority decisionmaking meeting by factions canvassing for votes, and the real decisionmaking is taken out of the meeting itself and done on the sidelines.

With collective decisionmaking, discussion time is spent in the meeting and everyone is involved. Majority decisionmaking may mean shorter meetings, but decisions often leave people unhappy or unwilling to implement them wholeheartedly. Then time is often wasted because these decisions have to be revisited. Thus, collective decisionmaking is often shorter in the long run. As your collective decisionmaking skills improve, the time taken to make decisions will decrease.

There are a number of barriers to reaching agreement, however, and the facilitator must become aware of these and skilled at dismantling them.

## Making one another wrong

This comes from a failure to recognise that your world is different from another's world—the 'I'm okay, you're not okay' approach we all fall into at times. 'Your opinion is different from mine, therefore it must be wrong.' Getting stuck in 'I'm right and you're wrong' impedes reaching agreement.

Dismantle this barrier by reminding participants that both or all points of view are valid. Remind them of their common purpose and values, and ask them and others in the group to suggest a number of alternative solutions that can then be explored. Brainstorming is a useful technique here.

## Not being proactive

This is when participants get stuck and can't or won't think of any alternative solutions. They will usually also be stuck in 'making one another wrong' mode.

Dismantle this barrier by reminding participants that 'every problem holds its own solution', and affirm that they can come up with an agreement everyone can align with. A short break or a physical exercise, such as changing seating positions, can be useful here.

# I have nothing to contribute

This may be the thought pattern of some group members who then stop themselves from taking part in decisionmaking processes.

Dismantle this barrier by reminding the group that everyone has something to contribute and the people who are contributing the least to the discussion are likely to be the ones who can contribute the most to the decisionmaking process. Affirm and write up on sheets of paper or a whiteboard all contributions, even if they initially seem unhelpful or off track.

Also check your own listening. Are you listening more generously to some members of the group than to others? Why do some members feel they have nothing to contribute?

# Getting stuck on one particular outcome

This is called 'getting positional', and it is similar to making one another wrong. Some participants may be so attached to their 'solution' that they can't or won't let go of it. They become like a dog with a bone and are unwilling, or 'unable', to let go.

Dismantle this barrier by allowing the 'attached' participant(s) to have uninterrupted time to explain their proposal, and encourage everyone to give it their full attention and to listen generously. Allow them to take as much time as they like without any interruptions. This can be followed by questions for clarification, not argument (be rigorous about this). Allow equal space for other points of view and then have a round in which people indicate agreement, disagreement or part agreement (without discussion or argument).

If there is disagreement or part agreement, request that the 'attached' participants put their solution 'on hold' while everyone brainstorms alternative solutions. Look to see how any part agreement reached can be noted and incorporated into other proposals.

## Negative and stuck energy

People may become negative, resigned, have stopped or have given up.

Dismantle this barrier by calling a short break, a stretch, physical exercise or an energiser such as someone telling a joke. Don't resume the decisionmaking process until the energy has shifted. Check there is sufficient fresh air in the room and that people are not hungry. There could be physical reasons for low energy. If there is no physical reason, the group may need a clearing session or an opportunity to recreate the group vision.

# Cheap closure

Everyone seems to agree, then the decision is challenged or people start reacting to one another or the facilitator.

Dismantle this barrier by checking the decision again and requesting that each person say 'yes' or 'no' to it as a round. Note: Do not fall into the trap of assuming silence means assent and rush through decisions without checking them out in an active way.

# Not taking responsibility

The group has agreed on a particular course of action, but no one is willing to commit to the individual actions required to carry out the decision.

Dismantle this barrier by challenging the decision. People may be coming from we 'should' do this rather than from a genuine commitment. Or it may be personally risky or threatening to carry out the decision (as in a protest group deciding on direct action). If people are still unwilling to commit to action after consideration, request that the group revoke the decision.

# Group think

Within a group, 'us' and 'them' behaviour is expressed through the phenomenon of 'group think'. When a group has been going a while and has established its identity, what is likely to emerge is a tendency to think of itself as special, and 'better' than other groups. Our group is 'the best' and 'right'; your group is 'lacking' and 'wrong'.

Being in the group feels good and more powerful than being alone and feeling scared and powerless. Being in a group fulfils our need for belonging and identity. On a large scale, this bonding and identity becomes community, culture, race and nationalism.

The danger arises not from being different and special (unique), but from believing that different is also better. We all indulge in this in sport, particularly on a national level. We believe our sports teams should win, and we need someone (or something) to blame if they don't—the wrong players or coach were selected, the opponents cheated, or it was the fault of the referee or the weather. Our pride is at stake and (we imagine) our own personal sense of worth.

The 'isms'—sexism, heterosexism, racism, ageism, adultism, and so on—are all about this kind of right/wrong, insider/outsider, good/bad interpretation of the world through the eyes of group identity.

Group exclusivity is a result of the 'unconscious' leap from different to better. It fails to recognise our own and others' full humanity. It is a cruel joke which can only backfire as it must mean in the end that our group is disconnected and alone.

'Group think' is this kind of unconscious behaviour in the group. Group members start to talk about 'we' or say that 'the group is this or that and thinks this or that' without taking the time or energy to think individual issues through freshly. Group think is automatic and unconscious behaviour. And it tends to permeate the whole world. Most of us indulge in this behaviour, as it is very convenient. 'I' statements are important here, as is not making assumptions about what the group is or wants.

The facilitator will alert the group to any tendency to become automatic and unconscious, and encourage participants to stay awake and aware. *Different in some ways, yes. Better—never.* The way to bridge the gap between groups is to establish commonality of values, purpose, vision and shared experiences. Full humanity covers the whole range of human emotions including love, joy, sadness and loss. Consciousness leads us towards one another, unconsciousness leads us away.

# Non-verbal aids to consensus

There are some useful non-verbal aids to consensus.

## *Coloured card systems*

Some groups and organisations use coloured cards to assist with decisionmaking. For example, participants hold up yellow cards if they have questions; green for answers; blue for opinions, ideas or statements; orange for something that is more emotional or personal, and red for 'stop process, we are off track'.[1]

In Appendix A, you can find the method used by the Earthsong Eco-Neighbourhood for consensus decisionmaking using coloured cards.[2]

## Hand signals

They are a number of ways to use hand signals to assist in consensus decisionmaking. These include taking a straw poll using the hand or arm (e.g. 'Hold your hand up high if you enthusiastically support this proposal, lower (or horizontal) if less enthusiastic, down low (point towards the ground) if you don't support it at all.')

The Zhaba Facilitators Collective has published a booklet describing a series of hand signals that are very helpful for people with language differences or in a very large group. These include a raised open hand for a question (as many of us used in school); rolling both hands forward to indicate that the point has already been made; both hands fanning down meaning 'Slow down, you're talking too fast', and both hands up waving, meaning 'This sounds like a good idea' or 'I agree'. A raised fist means 'No! Stop! I block this idea.'[3] (See Appendix B.)

Chapter 11

# addressing conflict

This chapter covers conflict and a number of related issues, including sabotage, scapegoating, factions and challenges of various kinds.

## Conflict

Conflict in groups is normal and inevitable. Conflict reflects the rattle of individual egos as a group moves towards alignment on its purpose and then into congruent action. It is part of the normal dissonance of a mature group as it balances task and process with individual and collective needs.

Conflict can range from mild disagreement to angry outbursts. It can also be experienced very differently by participants in the same group. Some may have clearly articulated views and understandings, some may lack clarity and be confused, while others may be aware only of uncomfortable feelings or physical symptoms which indicate to them that something is amiss.

A highly creative group is likely to have a quite a lot of conflict. Lack of any conflict in a group may indicate apathy, lack of interest, boredom, people feeling unsafe to share, and low self-esteem among group members.

Groups often give more credence to those who are articulate, however the more intuitive and less articulate members of the group have as much to offer in handling conflict productively. Some participants may consider themselves unaffected by conflicts in their group and impartial about the outcomes. These participants can often offer the best suggestions for moving forward.

# Prevention and early intervention

Much conflict can be prevented by attending to group set-up issues early on in the life of a group. These issues include having a clear purpose, a stated group culture or ground rules, clear decisionmaking processes, record-keeping and an agreed conflict resolution process. Once a group has become conflicted it is more difficult to work on these matters. When you are hired to facilitate a conflict, check that these are in place; if they are not, endeavour to establish them after you have attended to the conflict. Don't try and do this in the midst of a conflict. Unfortunately, groups often consider hiring an external facilitator for the first time when they are in conflict and have tried and failed to resolve it themselves.

When conflict does occur, and it will, it is best handled by attending to it at once. If conflict is left, it will tend to escalate and blow up—leading to hurt and resentment—or simmer, with occasional repetitive bickering. Sometimes it will go underground and be reflected in lack of energy, people avoiding one another, indirect attacks, low levels of cooperation and even subversion of other group members' efforts.

Working through and resolving conflict calls for sensitive and creative facilitation.

Trust that the group members can work any conflict through and that each person has an important role to play in this. If you as facilitator practise deep listening, treat each group member with respect and compassion, and encourage others to do the same, this will reduce the likelihood of group members feeling hurt or damaged by the conflict or your intervention.

The facilitator's work is to hold the container (the group purpose and culture) and encourage participants to listen deeply for one another's best intentions, while compassionately and intentionally searching for truth, honesty, connection and alignment. The art of the facilitator is in knowing when to intervene and when to suggest a process to assist the group. And, of course, there is no right answer—each facilitator will intervene differently.

People in conflicts need to be held, heard and healed (the 3 H's). The holding refers to energetic holding by a group of people who create a safe space in which to address the conflict and stay until the process is complete. Hearing refers to deep listening. Healing most often comes from the first two and happens from within each person as they are held and heard.

148

Acknowledged conflict is usually best handled by appointing a facilitator, usually one of the group members who has skills in facilitation and is not involved directly in the conflict. If the conflict is serious an outside facilitator must also be considered, particularly if the group has tried unsuccessfully several times to resolve the conflict from its own resources. Conflicts that are not attended to well can become nasty, hurtful and damaging, and affect the group for a long time.

Process 16 is highly recommended as a simple conflict-resolution tool. This is a highly effective method that requires a minimum of facilitation.

# Sabotage

Sabotage is behaviour that undermines the group's ability to fulfil its purpose. Sabotage happens often in a group, usually at an unconscious level, but sometimes at a conscious level. It is usually connected with one or more group members not taking full responsibility for their actions, and then acting out their individual distress in the group (reverting to childlike behaviour). Often other group members get hooked into rescuing or punishing the persons concerned.

## *EXAMPLE 1*

Stephen sometimes falls into a 'victim' behaviour pattern which developed from experiences in his early childhood. He took on a number of tasks in the group but has not fulfilled them by the time agreed. Other members of the group comment on the fact that he has not kept his commitment. Stephen reacts as a victim, saying that people don't understand the pressures he is under. He blows his nose and looks dejected (like a little boy). Group members feel sorry for him, apologise and offer to take on some of his work. In reality, Stephen is able to handle the workload and has given other tasks priority.

What is the sabotage here? The group is in victim/rescuer mode—patterned behaviour that will interfere with the effective functioning of the group. The facilitator seeks to uncover the sabotage and lead the group through a process to work through the issues. He or she uncovers what is really going on and:

- Clarifies Stephen's promise and what got in the way of it being fulfilled.
- Requests that he recommits to have the tasks done by a certain time or, if he is unable to do this, to revoke his promise.
- Encourages other group members to support Stephen to sort out the issue himself and not get tripped up by their own 'rescuer' patterns, which will only reinforce Stephen's use of his 'victim' pattern.

150

# EXAMPLE 2

A decision needs to be made in the group. All but one person has reached consensus. Amy has been feeling angry with several members of the group because her two latest ideas were criticised and not accepted. She wants to punish the group and, although she does not have a particular interest in this specific issue, she knows the group requires agreement by everyone. She refuses to agree or propose an alternative that might be acceptable to others. She abuses some group members when they challenge her and request her cooperation. Then she walks out of the room, slamming the door: Amy is consciously sabotaging the group.

The issues for the facilitator in this example of conscious sabotage are:

- Amy's feelings of anger and alienation related to earlier incidents. This is uncompleted business that needs to be attended to.

- Amy's commitment to the group, to the group purpose and to reaching agreement is now in question and needs to be addressed. What upset is now present for the other group members, and how can this be worked through?

- What processes can be put in place to address the above issues?

In this example, a facilitator would intervene before the walk-out occurred and, with a series of questions, establish what is going on for Amy.

'What's going on for you, Amy?'

(Encourage Amy to verbalise her feelings.)

'What happened before that you are feeling angry/hurt now?'

(Establish when the upset occurred and what happened.)

'What can you say or do now to complete this for yourself?'

'How are other people in the group feeling?'

(Establish how other people are feeling and to what extent they are also triggered.)

Sabotage is usually about someone feeling powerless to influence what is happening in the present and being triggered back into earlier incidents of powerlessness—often to do with early childhood.

Soon after it is first noticed, it is useful for the facilitator to initiate a discussion on sabotage and how it shows up in a group. Each individual has ways of sabotaging themselves. In a group, these patterns are often projected onto the whole group by each individual. We act out our own patterns through others. We create our own dramas.

When our dramas are similar or complementary, it is easy for the group to become activated and upset. When these situations arise, the facilitator will encourage each person to own their own feelings:

'This is happening [description], I am feeling upset/angry/hurt/sad

[owning the feelings] and I request that [specific request for action].'

These are the skills of assertion. The facilitator can introduce these skills as needed and encourage the group to use them. She or he can also reinforce and acknowledge assertive behaviour that does occur. (See 'Uncovering sabotage patterns', Process 48.)

As the facilitator, you also need to be aware of your own sabotage patterns and how you may sabotage groups you are facilitating. By getting to know your own patterns, you will be better able to recognise them in others.

# Blaming and scapegoating

Scapegoating happens in all kinds of groups—families, children's peer groups, work groups and recreational groups. Remember the 'black sheep' who is criticised by everyone in the family?

Scapegoating occurs when one person is consistently blamed for things going wrong. This comes from thinking that, when something goes wrong, there needs to be someone (or even something) at fault, someone to be blamed. Many of us get this message from our parents as small children and tend to act it out all our lives: 'Something's wrong. Who's to blame?' go together in the same breath.

In families, children often feel powerless and at the mercy of their parents. Children are often bullied, punished or reprimanded without understanding the reason. The blamed and bullied child then repeats this behaviour and becomes the blamer and bully of younger or more vulnerable children, and eventually their own children and other adults.

Scapegoating is a persistent version of blaming, involving the bullying and victimisation of a particular person over a period of time by a group. Scapegoating always fails to honour the persons involved and their humanity. In a group it involves collusion between group members to keep scapegoating one or more other members. This can be open or covert, conscious or unconscious. Usually it is unconscious and the group will believe that they have 'right on their side'.

Scapegoating is damaging and dangerous, and a way of avoiding responsibility. 'If I focus attention on you, maybe people won't notice my shortcomings.' Have you ever felt a sense of relief when someone else is being blamed? 'Thank goodness it's not me.'

Scapegoating also occurs in reverse. Group members may scapegoat the team leader or 'boss' in an effort to diminish their power, and also their own sense of powerlessness. This happens in families when, for example, Mum and the kids gang up against Dad.

The facilitator needs to interrupt blaming and scapegoating as soon as it occurs. With blaming, encourage participants to acknowledge their own feelings, describe the behaviour they don't like in another, and make a request.

> 'I feel angry when you keep arriving late to our meetings. It disrupts the meeting and wastes time. I request that you come on time.'

With scapegoating—an accumulation of blaming that has not been attended to—there is always a history (a number of incidents over time) and this needs to be explored and worked through with the group. Have the group share, possibly in rounds:

> What really happened and what expectations weren't fulfilled?

> What does each group member need to say about it?

> What feelings have not been expressed and owned?

> 'I felt angry when...'

> 'I feel hurt when...'

Keep the group sharing until everyone has said all they have to say (is complete). Usually scapegoating is a cover-up for widespread feelings of inadequacy and powerlessness in the group. It may take some careful digging and encouragement to get through to the underlying issues.

When a culture of expressing feelings and making clear requests (assertive behaviour) is established in the group, blaming and scapegoating will diminish.

Again, a clear purpose, group culture, decisionmaking and conflictresolution  agreements are essential if scapegoating is not to recur in another form. If you are facilitating, attend to these after the conflict has been worked through.

Blaming and scapegoating may also diminish if acknowledgement is occurring in the group. A regular practice or process for acknowledging and appreciating one another establishes that everyone is valuable and worthy of respect. (See 'Affirmations and acknowledgements', Process 12.)

If a group has a purpose and culture you may like to use 'Group clearing', Process 38.

# Group factions

Related to blaming and scapegoating are the formation of fixed alliances or factions in groups. Factions are the norm within majority decisionmaking structures (democracy). Where decisionmaking is dependent on majority vote, factions have the appeal of cutting down on discussion, and allow for caucusing and quick and easy decisionmaking in the whole group. At its extreme, block voting of political parties makes parliamentary decisionmaking a formality—almost no effort is made towards distilling the collective wisdom.

Factions are another version of 'us' and 'them' thinking. Usually personalities quickly become intertwined with differing beliefs, values and points of view: *We disagree with others' beliefs.* This is similar to 'My world, your world' (see Process 22 and 'Living in different worlds'). It only takes a small step for this to become: *We dislike you as personalities.* This

156

is getting back to 'us' and 'them' thinking, with a similar outcome to blaming and scapegoating, though now the sides may be more even.

Co-operacy, with its collective decisionmaking, undermines the formation of group factions. Factions lose their usefulness in collective decisionmaking and become counterproductive to reaching consensus—when the whole group wisdom is being sought and listened for.

# Challenges within the group

Challenging one another within the group is an important skill for both group members and the facilitator. Here is a situation where a challenge is useful:

Betty is part of a six-person support group. She is very verbal and tends to dominate all the conversation. She can't seem to stop herself 'taking over'. She believes her issues are more urgent and more difficult than others', and that she really needs the support and advice of the group. Gradually, the other group members start to switch off when she speaks. They feel increasingly angry with her domination but don't want to hurt her feelings by saying how angry they are.

Often, groups gradually fall apart rather than challenge a dominating member. There is an unconscious commitment in our culture to be nice at all costs. A challenge to Betty is appropriate here. A group member can initiate this:

'I feel annoyed, Betty, that you are taking up so much group time. I want more time and I also want other group members to have more equal time. How do other people feel?'

A challenge such as this, if handled sensitively, can move the group through to greater maturity. The facilitator needs to set up a process, such as a round, which will enable a level of trust and safety to be maintained so the behaviour is challenged rather than the person. It is important to keep the process going until everyone has expressed their feelings and concerns. It is also important that Betty has the opportunity to respond at the end of the round, to express her feelings and concerns and what she has learnt about her own behaviour.

When each group member has shared, the facilitator can suggest some practices are put in place to avoid the situation arising again. Practices could include:

- An agreed time slot for each person to express their issues and get contributions and coaching from others.
- An agreement that people will take responsibility for their own feelings and challenge one another quickly rather than bottle things up.
- A round of feedback at the end of each session to clear any issues that have arisen.

Often the need for a challenge within the group will emerge in discussion outside it. Members will start to comment to one another about a person's behaviour and there will be some agreement about the 'problem'. We could criticise this kind of complaining, but we often need to verbalise our thoughts before we know what we think. Outside-the-group discussion gives members an opportunity to clarify their own feelings and perceptions without taking up group time. If there is agreement from others, then we feel more powerful and able to express ourselves in the group—we know there is some support.

However, a more powerful and empowering challenge is one that is made spontaneously in the group:

'I feel [name] when you [description of action]. Can we discuss this? I'd like to know if other people feel the same way.'

This kind of challenge is more high-risk than a challenge based on prior agreement, as the challenger is allowing themselves to be vulnerable by expressing their feelings. There may be no agreement and the challenger may feel foolish. Nevertheless, this kind of challenge happens often in high-trust groups where people are encouraged to express and work through their concerns as quickly as possible. Although group members may find it scary at first, a culture that encourages spontaneous challenging is a sign of a more mature group.

What the facilitator will consider when a challenge occurs is:

- Which process or technique will be used to work through the issue?

- What feelings are present in the group and how intense are they? If they are very intense, the facilitator will want the group to work through the issue as soon as possible.
- Can time be made available? Check this out with the group.
- What is not being said? Underlying concerns and feelings need to be brought out in the open.
- Who is the most powerless person(s) in this situation? Do they need support and how can this be provided?
- Who is the most triggered in the conversation, and by what past incidents within the group? Do these need to be identified and worked through individually?
- Have people been triggered back into their own past incidents which have no direct connection with the group—say, early childhood or experiences from other groups? They may need to be reminded to take responsibility for these.

# Challenging the group

Sometimes it is useful for the facilitator to challenge the whole group. The following are some situations where you may want to challenge the group:
- There is underlying conflict that is coming to the surface as indirect attacks.
- The energy is low (and you sense it is because people are withholding).
- Scapegoating is occurring.

- The group keeps getting off track and is lacking intentionality.
- The group is in 'group think' mode, complaining about others and making them wrong.
- The group is getting into patterned (unconscious) behaviour.
- The group is bogged down in detail and has lost sight of the vision.
- The group seems to lack commitment to reach agreement.

You, as facilitator, may first respond by drawing attention to what is happening, encouraging the group to be conscious of it and restating the purpose of the meeting. Then you may suggest a process or technique to move the group on.

'What seems to be happening in the group is...'
'The purpose of this meeting is to...'
'What we can do to interrupt this pattern is ... Do you agree?'

If the group does not respond at first, you may need to repeat the process or interrupt the pattern by:
- calling a short break;
- asking people to stand up and stretch;
- sharing in pairs;
- having a round of acknowledgements;
- choosing a trust-building exercise.

# Challenges to the facilitator

One of the fears common to new facilitators is being challenged by the group. Challenges can come in different forms, both direct and indirect. Here are some examples of challenges you might meet:

Direct:

'This process is not working.'
'You are too directive or not directive enough.'
'Your style doesn't suit our group.'
'Your interventions are inappropriate.'
'You are upsetting me or another member of the group.'
'You are too inexperienced for this group.'

Indirect:

People are slow to respond to suggestions.
People arrive back late from breaks (often).
People talk among themselves.
People ignore the facilitator.
A group member takes over the role of the facilitator without agreement.

Challenges to the facilitator are valid and need to be attended to immediately. Don't pretend it isn't happening. Listen to the challenge and, if unsure, ask for it to be restated. Then state it back to the group:

'Stephen, you feel that this process is not working.'

Check out the concern with the rest of the group:

'Do others agree with this?'

If everyone agrees, stop the process and suggest another, or ask for suggestions. If there is no quick consensus, suggest the process continue and be evaluated later in the meeting. Ask Stephen if he accepts this. If he declines, ask him to make a specific request of you (as the facilitator) or the group. He may be tripped up by baggage.

If challenges continue, stop the group and request that the whole group consider the issue. Remind them that a facilitator can only work with the agreement of the group.

'There have been several challenges to my facilitation at this meeting. I can only fulfil this role with the group's agreement. Let's have a round on what isn't working for each person. Could someone record the comments on the whiteboard as I want to listen carefully.'

When the concerns are listed, thank the group for being frank and honest. Group the concerns and then address each one in turn. You may either make suggestions or request suggestions from the group.

If a concern is unclear, ask for clarification, or ask if someone could make a specific request. You may, of course, accept or decline the request.

If the concern is general, suggest that you continue until the end of the meeting and that the group considers your continuing role as part of the agenda. Request that another person facilitates this discussion.

No facilitator can work effectively with all groups. Avoid becoming defensive. The group has the right to challenge you and request another facilitator. Retain your dignity. You are okay and so are they. One group's rejection does not mean you are not an effective facilitator.

It helps to take the attitude that you are always in training and are willing to increase your skills. Usually it works to accept the criticism and be willing to alter specific behaviour. In fact, a group will respect you for this and their trust in you will be enhanced.

For facilitator training see Processes 46 and 47.

# part 2

## Chapter 1

# facilitation and the client

When you are approached to facilitate a group process you will probably be one of the following:
- already a member of the group;
- a member of the same organisation but not in the group itself;
- an external facilitator.

There are some issues specific to each situation and some issues that are common to all. As there is some overlap, I suggest you read and consider all the following points.

## Facilitator already in the group

If you are already a member of a group and are asked to facilitate it, you will need to clarify for yourself and the group how this will work.

### *Not involved in content*

As the facilitator you will be guiding the process and will not be involved in the content of the group session(s). It doesn't work to pop in and out of the facilitator's role, trying to take part in the decisionmaking as well as facilitating.

You will need to consider whether you are prepared to forgo your involvement in the content of the group deliberations and whether you will be able to accept any group decisions, particularly if you disagree with them.

## Impartiality

You will need to check carefully with the whole group to ensure that every member can accept you as the facilitator. If you have voiced strong opinions within the group or are associated with a particular faction it may be difficult for some members to accept your ability to be impartial. You will need to check this out carefully and ensure that every group member accepts you taking on this role.

You might want to design a process that can be invoked if concerns about your impartiality arise in the group. A member of the group with a different perspective may be assigned the role of monitoring your impartiality and giving you feedback during or at the end of each session.

## Rotating the role of facilitator

The group may be able to rotate the role of facilitator between a number of people who have facilitation skills. Each group meeting could have a facilitator assigned in advance, with room for renegotiation if issues of particular interest to individual facilitators are on the agenda.

Rotating the role of facilitator is a useful way for a number of (or all) group members to share the opting out of content required, equalise the power inherent in the position, and develop the capacity of the group in facilitation. The group needs to consider its role and commitment to developing facilitation skills among its members. A group in which all members are trained in facilitation is very powerful. On the other hand weak facilitation can hold up the work of the group and lead to frustration and lack of energy in the group.

A middle way could be for the group to encourage all members to undertake basic training in facilitation skills before they facilitate the group.

# Facilitator within the same organisation but not in the group

If you work within the same organisation but are not part of the group wanting a facilitator, you will need to check out your appropriateness with all the members of the client group.

## *Confidentiality*

You will need to check out with the group their need for confidentiality—and if this applies to content only or to content and process. Assume that content is confidential anyway, but checking out is important as the group members may not have an explicit confidentiality agreement. It may be assumed, and you need to protect yourself from any future information leaks that may occur from group members. Be very scrupulous about confidentiality yourself. Your integrity as a facilitator will depend on this.

The group may also want the processes they use kept confidential. Check this out carefully and negotiate a confidentiality agreement for the whole group.

## Power relationships

The role of facilitator has considerable power. When a facilitator also has positional power they may not be the best person to facilitate a group. If you have more positional power in the organisation than all or some of the people you are facilitating, this could lead to more power being attributed to you than is needed or helpful in your role as the facilitator. It could result in some group members becoming inhibited or even mistrustful of your facilitation. Check this out carefully and be sensitive to the concerns of group members. You may prefer to decline the facilitator's role.

Alternatively, you may have less positional power than some or all of the group you are facilitating. Group members may have a decisionmaking role in terminating your contract or you may need their support to gain promotion. Check with yourself and others. Will you be willing (even if it's scary) to challenge each and every group member if you consider

168

they are sabotaging the group? If not, you will not be the right person to facilitate this group. You need to be fearlessly *for* the group achieving their purpose. If you are unsure, discuss your fears with the whole group and get their consent for you to challenge them. It is useful to record the consent in the decisions of the meeting. You can then refer back to this consent if things get sticky later.

Usually getting the group consent is sufficient to 'give permission' to the facilitator, but remember that people tend to exercise 'power over' when they feel threatened. Consider also whether you give yourself permission to facilitate and to challenge each individual and the whole group when needed.

For an internal facilitator, it is important to have a debriefing arrangement with another facilitator. Perhaps you are part of a team of internal facilitators and can offer this confidential service for one another. If not you may need an external supervisor/coach.

If you find that you need to retire from the role of facilitator it is important to share with the whole group what is happening for you before you step aside.

# External facilitator

As an external facilitator you will need to be clear on a number of issues.

# Clarifying the client group

When you are asked to facilitate a group it is necessary to first identify the individuals and groups who will be involved (your clients) and their role in the organisation.

Check carefully with the initial contact person to clarify who the primary client group is (i.e. the actual group(s) you will be facilitating). You will negotiate the purpose and required outcomes with the client group (not the initial contact person). For example, you may be approached by someone from management services to facilitate a planning session for a business unit within a large company. Ask to speak to the manager and members of the business unit, and negotiate the required outcomes with them, not the management services person.

If at all possible arrange to meet with all members of the client group individually. Try to contact as many group members as you can before the facilitation. Face-to-face or telephone contact is very good, but email is often a more convenient way to do this.

When facilitating a community group, meet with the whole group or with some of its members (representing different views) beforehand to check out the background to the group and negotiate the outcomes. Sometimes one faction of a group will approach the facilitator without consultation with the whole group. (This has happened to me.)

Always find out:

- Who is the primary client group (the group I am facilitating)?
- Who are the people in the group and what are their contact details?
- Has the whole group been consulted about my facilitation and agreed to it?

# Checking for match between facilitator and group

At the preliminary meeting or call, check for a suitable match between the group and yourself as the facilitator.

## *What is the background to the group?*

The kinds of questions you might ask are:

- Is the group from the business, public or community sector?
- Is it professional, service, retail, technical, manufacturing?
- What are the mission, vision, values of the organisation?
- What is the size of the whole organisation—large or small (ask for numbers) and at what level is the group within the organisation?
- What are the numbers and people involved in the facilitation?

- If local or central government, are politicians involved?

## How did you hear about me?

For example, by referral from a previous client or participant, through an advertisement, professional association or colleague?

## Do my values and experience match with the group goals and values?

It is helpful to have written promotional material or a website link about yourself or your business for potential clients. This material can include a statement of your own philosophy, values, code of ethics and experience. It is also helpful to include a photograph.

## What are the ages, genders and ethnic mix of the group?

Are issues around this likely to arise and affect the group's attitude to you as facilitator?

## Does the group know enough about your facilitation style and methods?

Has the group used a facilitator before? An outside facilitator, or an internal facilitator? Would the group like to talk with a previous client of a similar kind to check out your suitability? (It is good practice to offer this facility to new clients.)

# Negotiating the contract

## *What is the request?*

What is the nature of the request for a facilitator—for example, planning, team-building, clarifying issues, conflict resolution, consultative process, a public meeting?

## *What are the underlying issues?*

You may be hired for a team-building session when the underlying issue is a major conflict between a manager and staff over a specific issue, or a long-term estrangement between two groups.

## *What outcomes are required?*

What specific outcomes does the client want out of the session or workshop? How can these be measured in tangible terms? Are these outcomes achievable?

## *What other agendas do you have?*

If things go exceptionally well, what else will happen? What concerns and fears do you have? These questions will help to uncover hidden or unclear agendas.

# Is sufficient time available?

Is the client willing to allocate sufficient time to achieve the outcomes desired?

Be careful not to promise to produce results that are not possible in the time allowed. Explain to the client what time is involved, and if sufficient time is not available, lower your promised outcomes to match. How much time each process takes is learnt through training and experience. If you are unsure, ask a more experienced facilitator. If the group is new, you may want to give a provisional estimate until you have met the members and assessed the stage of group development.

# What evaluation will be included?

What feedback mechanisms can be designed both during the facilitation process and after to evaluate the extent to which the outcomes have been met? Who will be involved in the evaluation process? Will the evaluation be verbal or written? Who will design the evaluation process? When and where will it take place?

# Written confirmation

Confirm the agreements reached in a letter of confirmation to the key contact. Include:
- The group to be facilitated.
- Preparatory meetings and emails.

- The date, time and venue of sessions to be facilitated.
- The agreed outcomes and performance measures.
- Who the outcomes were agreed with.
- The agreed fee or charge-out rate and terms of payment (say, within 14 days).
- Supplementary services provided (such as typing up of notes or research).
- Follow-up services to be provided.
- Evaluation process.

# Working with an established group

If a group is already established, or will be continuing as an ongoing group, the facilitator works for the whole group. Any agreements negotiated with anyone before meeting the group must be checked out with the whole group to gain their agreement. It is useful if this has been done in writing, allowing time for anyone to request changes or make objections. In any case, it is a good practice to check your contract at the beginning of the facilitated session, whether or not you have been advised that the group has agreed to it.

It is useful to check the following for agreement:
- Your facilitation.
- The group outcomes that you have negotiated with someone before the meeting or workshop.
- The process/programme outline that will be followed.
- Follow-up.

- Evaluation process.
- Full participation by group members.
- Ground rules.

## *Your facilitation*

After you have introduced yourself and given a short background, check that all members of the group agree for you to work with them.

Keep the atmosphere light but businesslike:

I have been asked by ... (names) to facilitate this session/workshop/meeting. I have also spoken to (or emailed) ... (all of you or names of those who have been contacted). Are you all comfortable with my facilitating this session? Has anyone any problems or concerns with this?

Allow time for a response. One or more people will usually say 'yes' and others will nod their heads or smile. If the response is unclear, people seem to be avoiding eye contact with you, or you sense some underlying tension, check again:

I am unclear about that response. Is every-one okay with my facilitating this session?

If there are objections, write them all up on the board first, then go through them one at a time responding to the best of your ability. Be honest.

Objections may be on the basis of insufficient experience, being an interested party in proceedings, not being the facilitator preferred by some group members, or the fact that some participants associate you with decisions made by another group they don't agree with (a group you are in or have facilitated).

It may be helpful for you to further explain the role of a facilitator, or your own background in response to these concerns. Don't react defensively. Group members' concerns need to be addressed—they don't need to be 'reasonable' or 'rational'.

After you have addressed the concerns as best you can, check out with the group:

Are you now able to accept my facilitating this session?

If not, don't continue. It will not work for you or the group, particularly when conflict arises or you are challenged over the process. You need to be clear that you have a contract with the group to work with them.

## Checking the purpose and outcomes

Next check out the purpose and outcomes you are there to facilitate. It is helpful to have these written down on a whiteboard or large sheets of paper, or have individual copies for each group member.

*My understanding is that the group has this purpose and wants the following outcomes from this session.* (State the purpose, outcomes and measures.)

Then check for agreement (see above). When agreement is given or reached you have a contract to proceed. If changes are requested, write them up and then negotiate with the whole group for agreement.

## *Check the proposed process*

I propose to facilitate this by ... (outline the process/agenda you will use).
Check for agreement and modify if necessary.

## *Follow-up*

It is helpful to clarify at the beginning what follow-up services you will be expected to provide. This may include typing up and distributing group notes, usually from the whiteboard or large sheets of paper. Check to clarify who will be doing this. If the whiteboard is not electronic it may be easier to take all notes on paper sheets, which can then be photographed or taken away and typed up.

## *Check for evaluation process*

Explain the evaluation process briefly and request cooperation with it. It is helpful to allow time for verbal feedback at the end of each session (say 10 minutes) and an opportunity for written evaluation at the end of the series (if a number of sessions are involved).

# Check for full participation

If you are facilitating a work group, check to see if participation is voluntary or mandatory. If mandatory, allow participants to express their feelings about that. If there is resentment, suggest that it does not work for people to be present without a choice and invite them to choose to stay or leave. Usually if participants are given this choice they will choose to stay. If some participants leave you will need to check with the group whether it is okay to proceed.

# Group culture or ground rules

Ask the group how they like to work together or would like to work together (if this is the issue). Asking how they would like to work together is the question that best generates the desired group culture. If this term is unfamiliar or unacceptable use another phrase such as ground rules or group agreements. These agreements could include confidentiality, punctuality, speaking up, not interrupting, and speaking for oneself and not others ('I' statements). You may want to suggest some yourself. Remember ground rules are only useful if they are about things that matter. It is best to start with a few (not more than five) and add others later if they are needed. The group culture needs to be displayed prominently so that everyone can see it. Ask the group members to speak up immediately if they see the agreements being broken.

# Public meetings, conferences and other one-off occasions

## *One-off facilitations*

These are different to those of an ongoing group. Your client will probably be an individual or group of people acting on behalf of a larger organisation such as a local authority or city government. Here your contract will be with the organisation responsible for hosting the public meeting or conference. It is essential that you have agreement to the outcomes and processes to be followed by the key representatives. You may want to get this agreement over processes signed.

It is important that you, as the facilitator, have the mandate of the key people in the hosting organisation to proceed. If you are unsure that the people you are liaising with are the key people, you may like to discuss your concerns and ask if there is anyone else in the organisation who needs to agree to the process. Usually, someone like the city manager will be the person accountable for the conduct of a public meeting, and their signature will be on the bottom of the notice in the newspaper.

It is always a good idea to have your contract with a large organisation in writing so that you have some protection if problems arise at public meetings, as they sometimes do.

## At a public meeting or conference

Have the most senior key person you can get (the mayor, a senior politician, the city manager) introduce you and be present throughout the meeting as the host. This is very important as it gives you a stamp of approval and the mandate to proceed. If things go wrong you can then confer with them as the host or even hand the meeting back to them to close. For example, a public meeting may need to be disbanded if protesters or other angry lobby groups become unmanageable. This happened at a meeting where I was present. Don't make this decision on your own unless you have no alternative. It is better to discuss it with key senior people and recommend what action you think should be taken.

It is best for the person who introduced you to close the meeting.

## Handling disruption at a public meeting

Sometimes people come to a public meeting specifically to disrupt it. They could be protesting against the subject of the meeting, the host organisation or about some unrelated matter they want to raise in a public forum.

Before a public meeting that is likely to be disrupt-ed, check with the host and agree on a process for handling it. You may decide to:

- call a short break;
- ignore the disruption;
- evict disrupters from the meeting;
- call the police.

If you intend to evict disrupters, check the legal process for evicting people from a meeting. In New Zealand, for example, you need to ask people to leave three times, after which they can be escorted off the premises. If problems arise at a public meet-ing and people need to be asked to leave, it is the role of the key senior person to do this as the host, rather than you as the facilitator. Make sure security people are available to escort the disrupters off the premises.

# Facilitating groups of different sizes

As groups increase in size, more structure will be needed and more attention will need to be paid to timing.

## *Small groups*

Small groups of up to 15 people can work mainly as a whole group. Work in twos and threes can be useful for some sharing and trust-building. In a small group there is the opportunity for everyone to speak, and a high level of trust and participation can be developed.

## Medium-sized groups

Medium-sized groups of between 15 and 30 people tend to operate partly as a whole group and partly as a number of formal or informal subgroups. This is a practical solution that enables everyone to speak and be heard. In-depth creative work, policy development, and report writing are usually carried out by a subgroup that reports to the larger group through a nominated spokesperson.

The relationship of subgroups to the larger group needs to be negotiated by the larger group. This negotiation is part of the facilitator's role. Clarity is needed to ensure that each subgroup acts within guidelines agreed by the whole group. Time limits (even if informal and self-monitoring) can be helpful.

Listening skills become very important in medium and large groups and are the main tool for generating synergy. The energy of listening is very potent and calls forth powerful speaking.

## Large groups

Large groups (more than 30 people and up to several hundred) require more structure and two or more microphones. Part of the meeting may be held in the large group and part in smaller groups (workshops/task groups). The small groups will usually feed back their discussion and findings to the large group through a spokesperson or possibly electronically.

The process of a large meeting needs to be planned carefully to ensure that the purpose and values are clear and there is opportunity for maximum participation from those attending. A team of facilitators may be used—the main facilitator working with the large group and assistant facilitators with the subgroups.

Careful attention will need to be given to the time allowed for particular processes and the time to move between the whole and subgroups. For example, if you use a process in which everyone speaks for two minutes in a 60-person group, this will take at least two hours. It will often be necessary to impose time limits on speakers. Structure is more likely to be arbitrary, with less opportunity for collective decisionmaking.

Large groups are useful if an organisation wants to transfer information, clarify it by answering questions and get instant feedback. Large groups are less likely to be ongoing. Many people will not have the opportunity to speak in the whole group unless there are strict limits placed on speaking rights—for example, each person can only speak once or twice. As mentioned, limits on the length of time that people can speak may also be needed. Such structure needs a high degree of cooperation.

Resources such as large electronic whiteboards, polling equipment, PowerPoint facilities, overhead projectors, flip charts, newsprint sheets, name tags, masking tape, Blu Tack, felt-tipped pens and tables or easels to write on are all useful.

Graphic facilitation can be very effective in large group meetings. Here drawings are made on large sheets of paper at the sides of the room to represent the content and flow of the discussions.

Café-style set-ups with people seated around small tables for discussions can also be very effective for larger meetings. World Café is a form of meeting that combines strategic questions with discussion in shifting small groupings, with drawing or doodling on the table-top paper and often graphic facilitation on the large walls as part of a relaxed and stimulating event.[1]

See also, Large Group Interventions in Part 2 Chapter 7, 'Mapping the field of facilitation'.

# Chapter 2

# cooperative processes in organisations

Many organisations are changing from fixed and static structures to something much more fluid and virtual. Thus organisational development is focusing more and more on flexibility, responsiveness and managing changing configurations of people in many different project teams.

Short-term contracts and self-employment are becoming common as people contract in and out of organisations or hold part-time contracts with more than one organisation. All members of a project team may be on short-term contracts and required to work together cooperatively. Cooperation as equals between people with differing knowledge, experience, skill sets, world-views, cultural norms and ideologies brings many challenges.

In efforts to enhance alignment and teamwork, organisations are increasingly using group facilitators to ease the way to effective communication and relationships, and to introduce cooperative practices that will enhance teamwork and help clarify goals, outputs and accountabilities. Group facilitation skills are becoming required skills for many management and specialist positions, particularly in the people

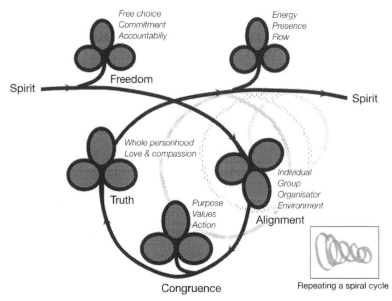

Figure 2.2 FACTS model for maintaining sustainable
cooperative processes in organisations

services (human resources) area. Training in group facilitation and other cooperative skills is becoming more available and organisations are increasingly able to choose between using in-house and external facilitators for a range of teamwork, consultative and participatory processes.

New organisational consultancies are emerging that are based within the cooperative paradigm and have the knowledge to address problems in ways that better suit the new kinds of organisation. Our company, Zenergy, is increasingly diversifying into such a cooperative paradigm consultancy, offering cooperative and 'triple bottom line' accounting advice, advice about legal structures and processes for cooperatives, and also appropriate marketing practices, as well as organisational development and facilitation, mediation, online facilitation and coaching services.

As part of my doctoral research, I undertook a cooperative inquiry with a group of facilitators on the topic of facilitating sustainable cooperative processes in organisations.[1] I wanted to find a useful way of mapping the conditions under which cooperative processes were most likely to succeed and flourish—and develop a diagnostic tool that was simple and profound and could be used while facilitating as well as for reflective learning. The model presented below developed out of the findings of that cooperative inquiry.

This model takes the form of a spiralling cycle and explains group development over time. It begins with the individual choice to be part of a cooperative process (or organisation), and the commitment and willingness this entails to take on individual accountability. The alignment of group intention follows and then the process of becoming congruent is expressed through clarifying purpose, values and action. The conflict that arises as group members seek to become congruent with their intention, purpose and values is worked through with authentic and compassionate sharing towards life-enhancing and synergistic outcomes. The model seeks to honour individual autonomy and interpersonal cooperation and shows how facilitators and groups can check for alignment of purpose and values for individuals, the group, the organisation, and the social and physical environment.

The FACTS model is illustrated on the previous page in the form of a repeating sequence of steps or spiral.

The FACTS model summarises five key factors, which are crucial to addressing the sustainability of cooperative processes. I have defined these as freedom, alignment, congruence, truth and synergy, forming the acronym FACTS. Each key factor glosses a set of related factors. The FACTS model offers a way to diagnose and guide the development of a group over time. As a diagnostic tool it can be used to uncover what is missing or needing further development for a group to flourish. The five key aspects signalled in the acronym are expanded and explained below.

## *Freedom*

Ethical facilitation uses processes that enhance free and informed choice, commitment and accountability.[2] People who take part in cooperative processes must do so freely, without coercion or fear of reprisal. Relevant information is needed for participants to make informed choices. Internal commitment to choice leads to responsibility and willingness to be accountable for one's actions.

# Alignment

For the group process to be effective, all those involved need to be aligned with the intention of the cooperative process and how it fits within the organisation or multi-organisational setting. Alignment involves the individual, group and organisation, and the consistency of the intentions of each. In addition, alignment includes connectedness with the wider social, physical and natural environment. Intentions may be expressed as shared vision, mission and goals or statement of intent. For sustainability to be achieved, the intention must extend to the health of the environment and the whole planet. The intention of the group becomes potent when it is expressed as a clear, concise, written statement of purpose containing one main idea.

# Congruence

For a group process to be effective, congruence is needed between the group's purpose (as described above), values, beliefs, assumptions, culture and actions. These can be fully conscious, partly conscious, and even unconscious. Key group values may be expressed in ground rules, group agreements, charters, actions, codes of practice, and also as images, such as logos. Actions include spoken and written words and individual and group behaviours.

Decreasing the distance between what we believe, what we say, and what we do is the domain of ethics and the 'daily delicious fight to be congruent'.[3] This aspect of group life is likely to involve self-reflection, challenging of one another, and changes in behaviour. Facilitators are useful in enabling people to receive feedback without defensiveness, and to make behavioural changes required for the group to be congruent with its purpose and values.

## *Truth*

As used here, truth encompasses whole person learning,[4] love and compassion, and collective wisdom. Personal development can provide access to embodied whole personhood by dissolving and reframing unhelpful conditioned, patterned behaviour. Experiencing all aspects of ourselves, including a wide range of emotions, without fragmentation and dissociation, allows us to connect with love and compassion to self, other persons, groups, cultures, other species, and the whole cosmos or transplanetary field.[5] Speaking individual truth and working through the conflicts that ensue takes the group to a deeper, more potent level, which in turn propels it forward towards synergy.

Sensitively facilitated cooperative processes can enhance individual access to personal truth and enable the expression of collective wisdom in the group.

## Synergy

When a group is aligned, congruent and truthful, more energy will become available. Energy will be released and enhanced. Participants will become more present, attentive and aware, and the group will experience a sense of flow and flowing with,[6] as distinct from struggling and striving. Synergy is the experience of collective energy and of the sum being greater than the parts. This energy is available to an aligned, congruent and truthful group.

## The flow of spirit

Form follows spirit.[7] Spirit can be experienced as an 'encounter with the deeper, non-material dimensions that stand behind the material world, giving it coherence and meaning'. You may refer to spirit as 'God' or 'a higher purpose', depending on your belief system. Cooperative processes are the forms that follow the spirit of cooperative endeavour or cooperacy.[8] Noticing spirit at work requires awareness. Following spirit requires intention and rigour.

Often spirit is most easily perceived through its shadow, which highlights unhelpful, conditioned behaviour, distress from the past and fear of the future. Encountering the individual, group and collective shadow material is the work of everyone who seeks awareness and consciousness. The cooperative spirit moves through cooperative processes and is an expression of the desire to experience ways of being and doing that nourish the value of the individual and the collective wisdom of the group.

If freedom, alignment, congruence and truth are present, synergy will become available, and spirit will continue to flow. The cycle of sustainability will continue and grow as a spiral. All the FACTS require on-going attention and rigour. Embodied whole persons speaking their truth with love and compassion are the prerequisite for the achievement of sustainability. If we are going to generate a sustainable world, then the fear and 'pragmatism' within most organisations must be challenged.

## Using the FACTS model for diagnosis

The FACTS model was developed for facilitators to use as a diagnostic tool while they are facilitating. To provide a deeper understanding for the reader, here are some reflections by facilitators using the model.

Using the model in an organisational workshop to assist the 40 participants understand their conflicted organisational context, Hamish Brown found that the model assisted the participants to identify their own areas of weakness. The aspects of the FACTS model identified as missing or weak in the organisation were *freedom* and *alignment.* In relation to freedom, 'people were not able to choose, given that they did not have the correct information about the management stance' regarding the issue in conflict. Brown also commented on finding the meta-model useful both as a sequential cycle and as a means of identifying how to maintain *synergy* once achieved.

Hazel Hodgkin noticed, while facilitating a policy meeting for a political party, that there was not full alignment with the purpose of the day. Early on two people expressed their unhappiness with the pre-agreed group purpose and one of them became involved in a direct conflict with another participant later in the day. Hodgkin believed the two participants' lack of *alignment* influenced their ability to participate fully and cooperatively in the meeting discussions.

Hodgkin reflected that she could have worked more on the *alignment* of the participants, particularly at the beginning of the day. She also believed that she might have usefully watched for opportunities to increase the level of honesty and emotions where appropriate. However, she believed there was sufficient *freedom, alignment* and *congruence* for significant synergy to emerge at the end of the meeting. Reflecting on synergy, Hodgkin saw this as something for which she strived:

> If it happens, it is almost always an indication of a successful facilitation. However, if it does not happen, it does not necessarily mean a lack of success. Lack of synergy may just mean that some other work was done by the group that still needs more processing before being fully worked through.

Sarah McGhee facilitated a women's collective involved in health issues and noted that the key issues here were around *alignment* and *congruence,* particularly congruence between values and behaviours. McGhee's approach to moving the group forward included naming the incongruent behaviours and invoking the spirit of the organisation:

> I stood for them being a collective of women with values (such as equity, empowerment, advocacy, love and safety) who were working on behalf of a multi-cultural community. I confronted them when I saw their behaviours didn't match what they were up to.

As there was plenty of trust built up prior to a confrontation, and there was faith in the facilitator, the group was able to move into speaking their own truth.

> By the afternoon we had named the 'elephant' as issues around power, old systems that didn't work and history of personal attacks...

Reflecting on the model, McGhee supposed that there is a skill base involved in using it—in particular, when to intervene and on what basis. She wondered how one learnt to listen for the key issues rather than little issues. She then went on to answer her own question by adding:

> Once I tapped into the spirit of the organisation as a community-based service then I was able to see what really mattered and needed to be attended to. I have learnt this from being around Maori, Pacific Island, African and Maltese cultures. If the spirit is missing then there is al-

ways a potential danger of the facilitator becoming oppressive.

In an academic setting, another facilitator, Catherine Lane West-Newman, critiqued a day-long organisational retreat she had attended as a participant. She considered it an example of an event that was not able to achieve synergy, and on reflection saw that none of the FACTS were well represented. Her vignette included the following reflections:

**Freedom.** Most people did not want to be there. Commitment to achieve cooperative processes and collective outcomes was drastically lacking in some cases and lukewarm in others—at least partly because of a history of failed meetings of this kind.

**Alignment.** No alignment existed before the meeting and none was achieved. The group decided to proceed directly to the task that the two [leaders] perceived had to be done. The facilitator was explicitly prevented from doing anything in the way of a warm-up or check-in because these are 'touchy feely' and not appropriate [for this profession]. Also, the past history of tears, tantrums, and terrorising does not allow these people to want to expose themselves to each other.

**Congruence.** Individuals at the meeting had their own purposes, values, and desires. In general each perceived that achieving their own goals and establishing themselves as the most important person there could only be done by thwarting everyone else, embarrassing, and even humiliating them if necessary in the process. It might even be said that there was an active will present to prevent congruence. Tears, accusations, complaints, dragging up past histories all contributed to the atmosphere of isolated and frustrated human entities. People claimed what they wanted. One person walked out. As the loudest complainers got what they wanted, others subsided into resentful silence. The facilitator's attempts to reframe problems and processes were simply firmly opposed and suppressed by those who had not wanted to have her there in the first place.

**Truth.** Was the victim on the day. In fact some people's truths were spoken very loudly indeed but no collective or sustainable truth was allowed to emerge. Whole personhood, love and compassion, collective wisdom? Wash your mouth out.

**Synergy.** Well, no. Energy, presence, flow? Inertia, absence, lumpy resentment and fear. A list of who would be doing what (more or less unwillingly) in the year to come. And dread that it will have to happen all over again next January. This is the very particular hell of non-co-operative processes in a large organisation.

The above critique illustrates, perhaps even more graphically than the positive previous critiques, the importance of attending to the FACTS for effective cooperative processes.

# Organisational processes

There are a great many facilitated processes that can be used in organisational settings. More are being developed and adapted all the time. Every working facilitator will experience the need to modify processes and develop their own on occasion in different circumstances.

Some of the most effective processes are also the simplest. Structured and unstructured rounds, check-ins and brainstorms are the classics, and are needed in every facilitator's toolkit. A range of these and other effective processes are contained in the Part 3 Chapter 3, 'Processes'.

## *Organisational change*

One of the most effective ways to design and implement organisational change is through internal 'vertical slice' consultative bodies. These consultative teams are made up of representatives of all levels and major groupings within an organisation and include the chief executive officer. Union or collective bargaining representatives are also often included.

The formation of such teams needs to be carefully negotiated and all key parties need to be consulted. The consultative team is typically between

10 and 30 people, depending on the nature and size of the organisation.

The team becomes the development and decision-making body for organisational and cultural change and the two-way communication channel between the different parts and levels of the organisation. This body does not replace the formal reporting structures of the organisation. It becomes an alternative structure with its own framework and rules.

The consultative body usually uses collective decisionmaking—of necessity. Majority decisionmaking can polarise the organisation and reinforce 'management versus workers' thinking, or pit one part of the organisation against another. This would weaken the value of the consultative body and the process would become counterproductive. The body can therefore correctly be described as a cooperative body and it requires the infusion of cooperative skills to be effective.

To ensure neutrality, such bodies often use a facilitator from outside the organisation, one who has no internal allegiances. The facilitator takes a key role in guiding the consultative body through the delicate setting-up phase, when it develops its purpose and identity, builds trust and commitment, establishes ground rules and boundaries, and builds its vision, goals and objectives.

Sometimes this process will include the development of an organisational charter or code of conduct, which then serves as the touchstone for further organisational reform. If a charter is involved, the consultative body will become the communication channel to involve the whole organisation in the drafting process—each consultative member communicating and holding meetings with staff groups until opportunities for input have been provided for everyone. The processes and ways of working are of crucial importance. The balance between process and task is developed over time, with process being of particular significance.

# Chapter 3

# facilitator ethics

The expansion of facilitation into the business arena has seen the term 'facilitator' often used loosely to describe managers, consultants, trainers and others who use some facilitative techniques as part of their work. This co-option of the term 'facilitator' means that there is often little distinction between the professional group facilitator and consultants or managers who have some understanding and skills in facilitation but may be unable to lead a group through chaos to consensus, or demonstrate emotional competence and resolve conflict in a volatile situation.

The use of facilitation in business (including large corporations) brings with it some interesting ethical issues, particularly around the relationships between the stakeholders and the use of consensus decisionmaking in a hierarchical organisation. Misuse of cooperative processes to 'manufacture consent'[1] and manipulate people to agree to management goals is a criticism that has been directed both at individual facilitators and the profession as a whole. These criticisms led to a desire among facilitators to clarify what was and was not ethical facilitation.

# Development of the Code

The Code project was initiated by Sandor Schuman and myself at the International Association of Facilitators (IAF) North American Conference in Toronto in May 2000, and we remained the co-champions of the project throughout. An Ethics and Values Think Tank (EVTT) was set up after the conference as an online group for IAF members, and it became the primary vehicle for the development of the Code.

The EVTT e-group of up to 85 people was most active between 2000 and 2002 when agreement was reached online. Forums addressing the Code were held at facilitator conferences in Canada, Bolivia, the USA, Malaysia, Australia and New Zealand between 2000 and 2003. The Code was finally adopted by the IAF Association Coordinating Team (ACT) in May 2004. Since that date further forums to educate facilitators about the Code have been held at many facilitator conferences and forums, including those in Europe, South Africa, Australia and Asia.

# Issues to consider

A range of issues were identified and addressed during the EVTT dialogue. In addressing and resolving these core issues, the ethics dialogue has played a pivotal role in defining the role of the facilitator. The key issues are outlined below.

## The role of the facilitator

Facilitators generally agreed that their role was that of a process expert and process guide who worked with groups to help them to be more effective. The Preamble to the Code begins as follows:

> Facilitators are called upon to fill an impartial role in helping groups to become more effective. We act as process guides to create a balance between participation and results.

These two sentences are key in describing the role of the facilitator. A facilitator is impartial (not involved in content). A facilitator helps groups to become more effective (focuses on groups rather than individuals). A facilitator is a process guide (the focus is on process not content, and on guiding not imposing). A facilitator balances participation and results (works with both rather than gives precedence to one over the other).

## Is neutrality possible?

In the literature, the facilitator's role is often described as neutral, 'content neutral', or 'substantively neutral'.[2] The facilitator competencies developed in association with the IAF include one called 'modelling neutrality'.[3] The facilitator does not contribute to content or take part in decisionmaking (unlike the chairperson of a committee who votes, and also retains a casting vote). The first draft of the Code described the role of the facilitator as 'objective' and maintaining 'neutrality'. Some facilitators were, however, concerned about the use of the word 'neutrality' to describe the facilitator role, believing that it is not possible to be truly objective.[4]

To recognise the impossibility of pure objectivity the word 'impartial' was finally agreed. There are problems, however, with this word too, as it has a static feel suggesting parts and 'parties', and is possibly more appropriate to the role of a mediator. A facilitator is more associated with collections of individuals in often shifting group configurations.

## Participation and/or results

Some facilitators emphasise the importance of enabling full participation and good relationships within the group, believing that this will strengthen trust and understanding and minimise feelings of lack of inclusion and rejection. With strong, healthy relationships, decisions are made more easily and results tend to flow.

Other facilitators consider that relationship-building in groups is time-wasting and not a priority within the often tight timeframes provided. Such facilitators prefer to concentrate on the issues, on making decisions and obtaining measurable results.

The type of group situation is obviously a factor in deciding the appropriate emphasis and the debate tends to be based on personal experience. Rather than creating a polarisation between participation and results, the dialoguers agreed that some kind of balance is needed and that this is a matter of judgement by the group and the facilitator.

## Trust, safety and equity

Some facilitators wanted clarity as to the meaning of 'trust', and Joan Firkins[5] considered that cultural difference in the use of language was involved in our understanding of 'trust'. Differing perspectives were explored in the dialogue, until the following wording was agreed in the preamble:

Our effectiveness is based on our personal integrity and the trust developed between ourselves and those with whom we work. Therefore we recognise the importance of defining and making known the values and ethical principles that guide our actions.

## Facilitator values

Discussion took place around the key values that underpin or are inherent in facilitation, and some facilitators expressed the desire for a Statement of Values as part of the Code. In the Statement of Values the debate centred on the relationship between the facilitator and the group, including to whom the facilitator is accountable, and the importance of consensus decisionmaking.

The first draft of the Statement of Values stated that:

> As facilitators we believe in the inherent value of the individual and the collective wisdom of the group *understanding that participants come with varying levels of familiarity, readiness, knowledge, and ability to engage in the process.*

This proviso (underlined) inferred that individuals and the group may not necessarily be competent, and laid open the possibility of dependency on the facilitator and their expertise. This was changed in the later drafts, to:

> As facilitators we believe in the inherent value of the individual and the collective wisdom of the group. We strive to help the group make the best use of the contributions of each of its members.

## Who is the client?

The first draft of the Code distinguished between 'clients and participants', suggesting that these might be separate categories. A spirited online debate ensued on the subject of 'Who is the client?' This led to the clarification that the participants and the group facilitated are the 'primary client' to whom the facilitator is accountable. Some facilitators in the dialogue believed that the client was the specific sponsor, project manager or other individual person who hired the facilitator.

One person went as far as to say that only one person could be the client and that identifying this person was part of the preparation for facilitation. Other facilitators were clear that the client was the group using a facilitator.

A discussion paper on the topic of 'Who is the client?' was requested from Roger Schwarz to assist the dialogue. This includes the following:

I believe that the entire group is the client—not the group leader, the group leader's manager, or some other subset of the group. I tell you this now so that you can read this essay without having to guess where I am leading.

To inform our conversation about who is the client, I need to explain how I think about what it means to be the client. Being the client means you get to decide whether you want to work with me as the facilitator. It also means that you get to decide what issues will be addressed in the facilitation. Together with me you also get to decide how these issues will be addressed.

As I mentioned above, I believe that the entire group is the client ... If you are not a member of the group being facilitated you are not a member of the primary client group.[6]

Schwarz goes on to add to his model by naming some subcategories of the client group—contact clients, intermediate clients and ultimate clients.

I consider my *primary* client to be the group that has accepted responsibility for working on the issue—the group that I may eventually facilitate ... The *contact* client makes the initial contact with the facilitator. The *contact* client may be a staff member or a secretary who is not a member of the primary client group but has been asked to contact the facilitator on behalf of the primary client. *Intermediate* clients serve as links between contact clients and primary clients and are involved in early parts of contracting ... Finally, *ultimate* clients are 'stakeholders whose interests should be protected even if they are not in direct contact with the consultant or manager'.

One response to Schwarz's paper suggested that 'we should simply refer to the GROUP as the people we facilitate and the CLIENT as the people that hire us, or get us involved'.[7] The e-group members did not agree to this definition. The final agreed wording was:

Our clients include the groups and those who contract with us on their behalf.

This is such an important issue that it is a pity we were not able to resolve it more clearly. My view is that the primary client is the group that is being facilitated. Other people related to this group who are involved in liaison or have positional power must take a secondary position and be referred back to the group if conflicts arise. It is the group's responsibility to find a way through such conflicts—with the facilitator as a resource. In a similar way, the written records of the group belong to the group (not the facilitator) and

208

the group will need to decide what to do with their documentation. The facilitator gives it back to the group, unless the group has decided otherwise.

## *Consensus decisionmaking*

Some facilitators considered consensus decision-making to be integral to facilitation, and others considered consensus as one (possibly the preferred one) of many options.

Papers on 'Consensus' were contributed to the dialogue by Freeman Marvin and John Butcher, who also commented on each other's papers. Marvin considers consensus decisionmaking essential for cooperative groups.

> I believe that consensus is at the core, at the heart, and is primary to our profession of facilitation. It is more than a technique. It is more than best practice. It is part of who we are when we facilitate. A facilitated group process without consensus is like inhaling without exhaling.[8]

Butcher argues a 'situational approach', and considers consensus to be desirable, but not essential, for a group to make durable decisions that can be fully implemented.

> Making consensus a ground rule for group decisions is unnecessary and may inhibit a group from doing good work. It may create 'false closure' by pressurising participants to publicly agree when it may be equally effective if a dissenter can say: I expressed my concern and they heard

me, but the general view was to move forward. Because I respected the significant majority of the group in its wishes, I can still have influence as this decision is implemented.[9]

The difference between these two views is really only in the definition of consensus, as Butcher's scenario could be accommodated in a more flexible definition of consensus which includes the option of expressing one's view but not blocking the group from moving forward. Marvin explains this in his response to Butcher. However Butcher is not fully convinced, believing that:

> It is not consensus decisionmaking [that] is at the heart of facilitation, as Freeman states, but the creation of an atmosphere that will permit true dialogue among the group's members, and growth in the group's capacity to manage its thinking and its internal relationships.[10]

The wording agreed for the Code Statement of Values was:

> We believe that collaborative and cooperative interaction builds consensus and produces meaningful outcomes.

## Group autonomy

Underpinning many of the dialogue discussions (such as consensus decisionmaking and the identification of the facilitator's client) was the issue of group autonomy. This issue was inherent in the discussion but not often named. Does a group have rights? How do these relate to individual rights? How do group and individual rights play out in relation to the facilitator? For a facilitator, who is in charge of the facilitated group session? To whom is a facilitator accountable? Who chooses the facilitator?

The identification of group autonomy as an ethical issue surfaced towards the end of the dialogue and was one of the last clauses added (Clause 3):

> We respect the culture, rights, and autonomy of the group.

> We seek the group's conscious agreement to the process and their commitment to participate. We do not impose anything that risks the welfare and dignity of the participants, the freedom of choice of the group, or the credibility of its work.

## Handling conflict of interest

In the initial draft of the Code it was stated in the Preamble that:

> We understand our responsibilities have the potential to be in conflict: responsibilities to the client, to the group participants; to ourselves; to society and to our profession.

As well as separating the roles of the client and the participants (see above), this wording drew attention to a possible problem (conflict of interest) without giving the facilitator any responsibility for resolving it or even attending to it.

In the final draft this issue was comprehensively addressed as Clause No. 2 in the Code:

We openly acknowledge any potential conflict of interest.

Prior to agreeing to work with our clients, we discuss openly and honestly any possible conflict of interest, personal bias, prior knowledge of the organisation or any other matter which may be perceived as preventing us from working effectively with the interests of all group members. We do this so that, together, we may make an informed decision about proceeding and to prevent misunderstanding that could detract from the success or credibility of the clients or ourselves. We refrain from using our position to secure unfair or inappropriate privilege, gain, or benefit.

# How to apply the Code

The Code is now being used by many facilitators to help them resolve difficult issues.

Some facilitators are giving the Code to all their clients as an ongoing practice. This is to be encouraged as it helps to educate clients about facilitation and what to expect from their facilitators.

Facilitator forums and conferences continue to offer workshops on the Code, often focusing on case studies or 'critical incidents'. There is continuing work to be done in training and raising awareness of ethics among facilitators and also in applying the Code to online facilitation and other new areas as they develop.

There are no enforcement measures envisaged by the IAF at this time.

*The International Association of Facilitators*
**STATEMENT OF VALUES & CODE OF ETHICS FOR GROUP FACILITATORS[11]**

This is the Statement of Values and Code of Ethics of the International Association of Facilitators (2004). The development of this code has involved extensive dialogue and a wide diversity of views from IAF members from around the world. A consensus has been achieved across regional and cultural boundaries.

The Code was adopted by the IAF Association Coordinating Team (ACT) in June 2004. The Ethics and Values Think Tank (EVTT) will continue to provide a forum for discussion of pertinent issues and potential revisions of this code.

**Preamble**

Facilitators are called upon to fill an impartial role in helping groups become more effective. We act as process guides to create a balance between participation and results.

We, the members of the International Association of Facilitators (IAF), believe that our profession gives us a unique opportunity to make a positive contribution to individuals, organisations, and society. Our effectiveness is based on our personal integrity and the trust developed between ourselves and those with whom we work. Therefore, we recognise the importance of defining and making known the values and ethical principles that guide our actions.

This Statement of Values and Code of Ethics recognises the complexity of our roles, including the full spectrum of personal, professional and cultural diversity in the IAF membership and in the field of facilitation. Members of the International Association of Facilitators are committed to using these values and ethics to guide their professional practice. These principles are expressed in broad statements to guide ethical practice; they provide a framework and are not intended to dictate conduct for particular situations. Questions or advice about the application of these values and ethics may be addressed to the International Association of Facilitators.

### Statement of Values

As group facilitators, we believe in the inherent value of the individual and the collective wisdom of the group. We strive to help the group make the best use of the contributions of each of its members. We set aside our personal opinions and support the group's right to make its own choices. We believe that collaborative and cooperative interaction builds consensus and produces meaningful outcomes. We value professional collaboration to improve our profession.

### Code of Ethics

*1. Client Service*

We are in service to our clients, using our group facilitation competencies to add value to their work.

Our clients include the groups we facilitate and those who contract with us on their behalf. We work closely with our clients to understand their expectations so that we provide the appropriate service, and that the group produces the desired outcomes. If the group decides it needs to go in a direction other than that originally intended by either the group or its representatives, our role is to help the group move forward, reconciling the original intent with the emergent direction.

*2. Conflict of Interest*

We openly acknowledge any potential conflict of interest.

Prior to agreeing to work with our clients, we discuss openly and honestly any possible conflict of interest, personal bias, prior knowledge of the organisation or any other matter which may be perceived as preventing us from working effectively with the interests of all group members. We do this so that, together, we may make an informed decision about proceeding and to prevent misunderstanding that could detract from the success or credibility of the clients or ourselves. We refrain from using our position to secure unfair or inappropriate privilege, gain or benefit.

*3. Group Autonomy*

We respect the culture, rights and autonomy of the group.

We seek the group's conscious agreement to the process and their commitment to participate. We do not impose anything that risks the welfare and dignity of the participants, the freedom of choice of the group, or the credibility of its work.

*4. Processes, Methods and Tools*

We use processes, methods and tools responsibly.

In dialogue with the group or its representatives, we design processes that will achieve the group's goals, and select and adapt the most appropriate methods and tools. We avoid using processes, methods or tools with which we are insufficiently skilled, or which are poorly matched to the needs of the group.

*5. Respect, Safety, Equity and Trust*

We strive to engender an environment of respect and safety where all participants trust that they can speak freely and where individual boundaries are honoured. We use our skills, knowledge, tools and wisdom to elicit and honour the perspectives of all.

We seek to have all relevant stakeholders represented and involved. We promote equitable relationships among the participants and facilitator and ensure that all participants have an opportunity to examine and share their thoughts and feelings. We use a variety of methods to enable the group to access the natural gifts, talents and life experiences of each member. We work in ways that honour the wholeness and self-expression of others, designing sessions that respect different styles of interaction. We understand that any action we take is an intervention that may affect the process.

*6. Stewardship of Process*

We practice stewardship of process and impartiality toward content.

While participants bring knowledge and expertise concerning the substance of their situation, we bring knowledge and expertise concerning the group interaction process. We are vigilant to minimise our influence on group outcomes. When we have content knowledge not otherwise available to the group, and that the group must have to be effective, we offer it after explaining our change in role.

*7. Confidentiality*

We maintain confidentiality of information.

We observe confidentiality of all client information. Therefore, we do not share information about a client within or outside of the client's organization, nor do we report on group content, or the individual opinions or behaviour of members of the group without consent.

*8. Professional Development*

We are responsible for continuous improvement of our facilitation skills and knowledge.

We continuously learn and grow. We seek opportunities to improve our knowledge and facilitation skills to better assist groups in their work. We remain current in the field of facilitation through our practical group experiences and ongoing personal development. We offer our skills within a spirit of collaboration to develop our professional work practices.

# Chapter 4

# a sustainable society

Facilitation includes balancing and harmonising the rhythms of nature.

—Zenergy programme participant

Facilitation is not value-neutral. The inherent value of the individual, the collective wisdom of the group, cooperation, choice and consensus are all key values in facilitation (see the Code of Ethics). These are also key values in peaceful social change. This similarity is not surprising, as the history of facilitation stretches back into civil rights and workers' movements, the women's movement, community development, the peace movement, and grass-roots protest movements of many kinds. In addition, consensus and facilitation have been used by some intentional communities and cooperatives for many years.

## Choosing the facilitation work we do

As group facilitators, we make choices about the work we do, what clients we work with, and when, where and how we work. These choices are based on personal (and professional) values, beliefs, relationships, commitments and needs—our own context.

Consider the diagram Figure 2.4.1 Context awareness diagram. Locate yourself at the centre of the diagram. Choose an issue of interest to you personally, then see how far you can go in noting your awareness of that issue from the perspective of each band. Note how your perspective alters as you extend yourself into the outer bands of the map.

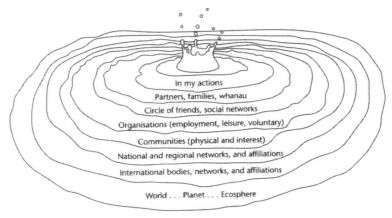

Figure 2.4.1 Context awareness diagram

Now locate a group relevant to you towards the centre of the diagram. Consider the group purpose and an issue it is facing. Envisage the context of the group. Note how your view of the group alters as you consider the group's place within the whole organisation of which it is part, then community, national and regional affiliations, and the world or ecosphere.

Now imagine an organisation with a number of groups that are internal and also external to it, all interacting with and influencing one another and forming and re-forming in dynamic interplay. Consider how an expanded awareness of these dynamics might influence your presence in, and approach to, relating to or working with these groups.

# A sustainable context for organisations

Facilitators often work with groups that are part of larger organisations. Most organisations are experiencing increasing pressure to become more socially and environmentally responsible. Organisational responses to these challenges have included the development and introduction of 'triple bottom line' accounting systems, where social and environmental effects are factored into profitability along with economic considerations.[1]

Contributing to new thinking for a sustainable society, L.W. Milbrath argues that top priority must be given to the good functioning of the whole ecosystem, and second priority must be given to the good functioning of our society. Only when these two are viable is it permissible to seek quality of life in individualistic ways we may choose. Milbrath also argues that it is a mistake to give top priority to economic values, because this would lead to sacrificing vital life systems at a time when the increasing world population needs those life systems even more. The core values he affirms are love and compassion, justice, security and self-realisation.

A sustainable society extends love and compassion not only to those near and dear but also to people in other lands, future generations and other species. It recognises the intricate web of relationships that bind all living creatures into a common destiny. Life is not mainly conflict and competition between creatures; rather a sustainable society emphasises partnership rather than domination; cooperation more than competition; love more than power.[2]

As can be seen in the illustration overleaf, this model places life in a viable ecosystem at its centre. The viability of the ecosystem underpins the core social values and is a necessary prerequisite to the good functioning of society. The outer rings further elaborate on the core values.

Futurists such as Barbara Marx Hubbard, Hazel Henderson and Sohail Inayatullah are developing a context for conscious ethical evolution in which we can all play a part in a co-creative society.[3] Hubbard believes that sustainable, life-affirming designs will emerge through the efforts of those who are part of the social potential movement. In the area of business, she describes the goal as conscious evolution, and she calls on businesses and entrepreneurs to apply their genius to the development of socially responsible businesses and investment. In her book *Conscious Evolution* she says:

> The goal is a sustainable, regenerative economy that supports restoration of the environment, preservation of species and the enhancement of human creativity and community, including ex-

panded ownership, network marketing, community-based currencies, micro credit loans and other such innovations.

Henderson stresses the need to redesign all our systems in a bottom-to-top design revolution. We should, she says, reshape our production, agriculture, architecture, academic disciplines, governments and companies to align them with nature's productive processes in a new search for suitable, humane and ecologically sustainable societies. Henderson discusses the important role of reliable sustainability indicators to assist with this transition.

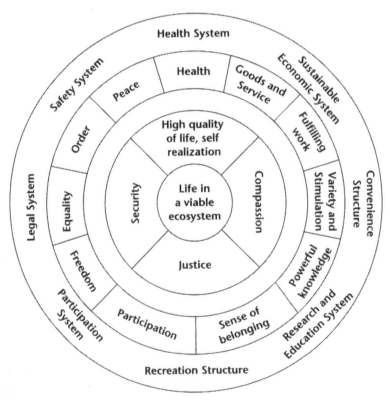

Figure 2.4.2 A proposed value structure for a sustainable society[4]

Jared Diamond explores such indicators in his book *Collapse: How Societies Choose to Fail or Survive.* This in-depth analysis of a number of ancient and modern societies and why they failed identifies 12 significant environmental factors that need to be addressed. Diamond believes that present societies can survive if humans have the courage to practise longterm thinking, and are willing to make bold, courageous, anticipatory decisions at a time when problems become perceptible but before they have reached crisis proportions. He also identifies that another crucial choice is the courage to make painful decisions about values. In *Collapse* he asks:

Which of the values that formerly served a society well can be continued to be maintained under new changed circumstances? Which of those treasured values must instead be jettisoned and replaced with different approaches?

# Personal values

The developing vision of a sustainable society, described above, can be taken as a context for facilitators and others working collaboratively.

Collaborative processes can be used in a wide variety of ways, both for good and for ill. There is ample historical evidence that people can, and do, work cooperatively to wage war, pursue genocide and destroy the environment. This raises important questions for both facilitators and participants, such as what is the purpose of using a particular collaborative process and how will the outcomes be used. For example, if a group process was used to damage a person or the social fabric, or diminish the ecological sustainability of an environment, then it may be unethical to use it.

Individuals, whether group facilitators, leaders or members, need to check the alignment of their personal values with the purpose and values of the groups and organisations with which they work. Without such alignment checking, congruence issues may remain unconscious, and anxiety and uneasiness may not be recognised as symptoms of deep disquiet. Purpose and values determine acceptable behaviour, and this is what ethics is about—the alignment of purpose, values and action. Because ethical use of processes involves making judgements about what and where one takes some action, and when and how one does it, it can be regarded as limiting for some. Also, it can mean that one needs to become engaged in issues that are not clear cut. Indeed, one recognises many areas as grey.

Facilitators' understandings, definitions, values and contexts differ, and so different choices will be made regarding the meaning of sustainability and social responsibility. But this does not mean that we should or can avoid action. Most activities involve ethical issues of some kind, whether we are conscious of them or not. We can become more conscious of such considerations and act on our developing understanding (see Part 2 Chapter 3, 'Facilitator ethics').

# Social change

Although it is possible to work with a group without taking into account its wider context, if we do so we miss the opportunity to be fully effective. It would be like gardening by attending only to the readily visible parts of the plants and ignoring the roots, soil, water, air flows, adjacent plants, and adjacent species. The garden environment (including all the plants) is an ecosystem and the study of the relationships of organisms to their environment is known as ecology. The discipline that concerns itself with the relationships of human society and with the rest of the planetary ecology is known as 'social ecology'.[5]

Social ecology is closely aligned with the permaculture principles of 'care of the people, care of the planet, and share the resources'. These principles can be also applied to organisations, and when applied to money flows in business, for example, can create a paradigm shift in thinking. Transforming profit and loss to surplus and deficit has been called the main difference between traditional and cooperative accounting.

For future generations to survive and flourish on the planet there will need to be a rapid increase in the ability of people and nations to communicate, cooperate and find peaceful solutions in areas such as water, pollution, energy, climate change, transport and food safety. To enable cooperative decisionmaking in these areas, ready access to all aspects of cooperative technology is needed, including facilitation skills. As facilitators we need to develop, refine and invent this technology so that it is sufficient to the tasks at hand. We also have a responsibility to quickly  disseminate this knowledge throughout the world and at all levels of society. It is important that we resist the temptation to keep expertise locked up in professional silos.

This book has been written to inspire you to further develop your own understanding about facilitation. As part of growing this understanding I encourage you to become aware that everything we do is always within a larger context, and that every group exists within a context. Every action we take as a person and facilitator has reverberations over a wider area and with people that we do not yet know. If there are only seven degrees of separation on the planet we have a wonderful opportunity to co-create a peaceful, sustainable world.

Chapter 5

# facilitation and therapeutic groupwork

Hamish Brown

## Introduction

This chapter explores the differences between group facilitation and individual therapeutic work undertaken in a group context, and presents some of the features of group psychotherapy. There are some important differences between group facilitation and group psychotherapy, and some useful ways in which group psychotherapy can contribute to group facilitation.

In group facilitation, the purpose will have an external focus which then requires the people in the group to work together to achieve it. The purpose of therapeutic groups is the development of individuals within the group. In therapeutic groups the development of the group is necessary to support the development of the individuals, while in facilitated groups the development of the group is necessary so that the group can be effective in achieving its purpose.

Although many different methods have been developed over time to create therapeutic change in the participants of a therapeutic process or group, these methods have several things in common. Therapeutic methods tend to have a theory of human development and change underpinning them; similarly, group therapeutic methods often also have an underpinning social theory.

This is somewhat different from group facilitation methods, which do not necessarily have an underpinning theory of human development, although they often have a theory of social development. This chapter explores the theories underpinning the psychodrama method, and uses this method as a departure point for considering therapeutic methods and processes more widely.

The author holds that therapeutic methods are not only for use with people who have a diagnosable psychological illness, but that every person can gain great value from engaging as a participant in personal development or psychotherapy. Group facilitators can also benefit from understanding how personal, as well as social, change happens. In addition, they have a special need to engage in their own development because of the personal nature of the demands of being a group facilitator.

# Psychodramatic theory

This section briefly presents the theory underpinning the psychodramatic method. Psychodrama was developed by Jacob L. Moreno in the early twentieth century. It has been developed and grown around the world by many hundreds of practitioners since. Moreno coined the terms 'group psychotherapy' and 'role-play' in the 1920s; at that time psychodrama was unique in that it was a group-centred therapeutic method. Moreno envisaged a world in which therapeutic work with individuals was not separated from the daily work of living and creating—a world in which our communities were holistic, connected and integrated. He believed that in this respect individual development cannot and should not be separated from community development or social development.

The central psychodramatic concepts are creative genius, spontaneity, warm-up and role theory. The notion of creative genius is at the heart of the psychodramatic method. Moreno believed that every person has within them potential for creative genius and he suggested that spontaneity is the catalysing agent of this creativity. Thus, spontaneity is Moreno's central therapeutic notion. In *Psychodrama Volume 1* he describes it in this way:

> The infant is moving, at birth, into a totally strange set of relationships. He has no model after which he can shape his acts. He is facing, more than at any other time during his subsequent life, a novel situation. We have called this response of an individual to a new situation—and the new response to an old situation—spontaneity. If the infant is to live, this response must be positive and unfaltering.[1]

Spontaneity is the human capacity that liberates creativity, which in Moreno's view is abundantly present, though possibly latent, in every individual. In describing creative genius and spontaneity, he creates a theory of human development that is grounded in possibility and potential.

Spontaneity and creativity are positive and primary phenomena...

...From the way in which men [and women] of creative genius warm up with their whole organism in status nascendi [the moment] to creative deeds and works, we can get the clues of how every infant, in miniature, warms up and maintains itself from the moment of birth on.

...The first basic manifestation of spontaneity is the warming up of the infant to a new setting.[2]

Moreno created the notion of warm-up to describe the process of people becoming involved with other people, things and events. The more involved we are, the more warmed up we could be said to be. However, the notion of warm up also includes the nature of our involvement. Moreno continues:

The warming-up process is a phenomenon which can be measured. Its expansion depends on the kind and degree of novelty to be met.

Warm-up is the first manifestation of life.

In a situation that is common or recurring for you, you can notice the nature of your warm-up to the situation by tuning in to the first inklings of experience you have in the situation. You will notice that you probably warm up the same way each time, and this is likely to result in the same sort of experience and outcomes. Spontaneity is the capacity to utilise our creativity to change the warm-up we experience.

The psychodramatic method explicitly provokes, stimulates, trains and tests out this creative response, this new action, into generative capacity in people, using role-play and other dramatic methods. Generative ways of being (roles) occur through engaging with the warm up the person has towards what is new and creative for them. As creativity is experienced the desire to create becomes stronger than the desire for safety, self-protection or domination. Generative roles are the natural result of a process of warming up. As warm-up increases, the person becomes able to create a new response out of nothing, their creativity and their desire.

Role theory is the theory of human development and change developed by Jacob L. Moreno. By role Moreno intended the 'whole way of being' a person has at a specific moment in time. Role is the whole expression and experience of the person, as they are, in a specific situation or context in the present moment[3]. A role has thinking, feeling and action components, is contextual, and has values, beliefs and motivation. The self (personality) can be described in terms of the range of ways of being (roles) that are lived out by a person in all aspects of their life.

People have a wide range of different roles (ways of being) which are accessed in different aspects of their lives. These ways of being can be characterised as generative, coping or fragmenting.[4] A person will experience different degrees of agency in different situations; sometimes they will find they can choose how they want to be in a situation and sometimes not. The psychodramatic method involves using action and dramatic methods in groups to assist individuals to make progressive developments to their role repertoire, such that greater agency, creativity and satisfaction are experienced.

When we use role theory in describing human development, trauma and damage to people can be understood in terms of the effect on the functioning of the person as it is lived out (as enacted roles) in the present. Creativity and generativity will also be lived out in the present. Role theory provides an excellent approach for understanding people in groups because groups only happen in the present. What has happened in the past or what may happen in the future can only be influenced by facilitation through the present moment. The facilitator can only work in the present moment, with some appreciation for what has gone before and what may follow.

Role theory enables us to see the process of the group as a system of role relationships that unfold in relation to each other as the group progresses—role and counter role. Thus a generative role is a role that literally consciously creates what the person desires with the others in the group; a coping role copes with the situation that exists in the group, and a fragmenting role is affected by the situation that exists in a way that is experienced as negative by the person.

In perceiving a system of role relationships in the group, both the role being enacted by each person and its impact on the ways of being (roles) of others can be described. Thus it is possible and helpful to understand how the system of relationships in the group is maintained, and we can formulate interventions that will assist people to find more satisfying ways of being with each other and thus create change in the system of relationships and the individuals.

This approach to groups and development is supported by what has been said about organisations as social systems by such authors as Stacy and Senge.[5] However, it also provides a specific developmental context that allows one to view emerging issues as personal or social depending on the purpose of the group and what will be of most value to it and its participants. This developmental context opens up a wide range of interventions to the facilitator or group therapist.

# Generative capacity

We humans have extraordinary capacity to envision the world we want to be a part of, and the potential capacity to create the world as we imagine it could be. These capacities are tempered by the kind of society we live in and the resources that are available for their development. The world, our communities and organisations, our families and ourselves are all interrelated. As we create ourselves as we want to be, so we cannot resist creating the world as we have envisioned it. We begin to build relationships and communities that respect and honour us as we are and within which our visions for the world begin to be fulfilled. Conversely, as we grow societies in which people are valued, the people become more able to connect with each other, envision the future together and create a better world. This has been described as the development of generative capacity.[6]

Groups provide a rich context in which change and development can happen. As individuals in the group develop, so this development can be tested out and further expanded in the context of the system of relationships in the group. As each individual develops, the group develops, and through this participants have mirrored back to them the effects of the change they are experiencing. Also, as the group develops, so it becomes easier for it to assist the individuals within it to develop.

In the following sections these ideas are looked at more broadly, and consideration is given to human development and change as an aspect of living.

# Tuning in

More and more, people are tuning in to what it is to live fully, tuning in to what it is like to be themselves, and tuning in to the experience of others. As we tune in, we begin to notice many subtle micro events and experiences. As we tune in, the world around us becomes richer, our experience of ourselves deepens and our awareness of the contrasts that exist between things develops. Also, as we tune in, we may begin to become present to strong emotions in ourselves—things long forgotten may awake as we notice that actually, it was not all okay. We may begin to notice how much we are just coping with life. But if we do not tune in we will never know what it is to really live.

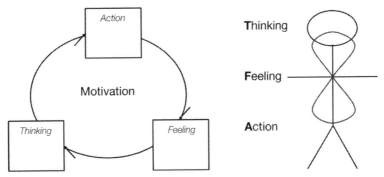

Figure 2.5.1 The change process

# *The change process*

Personal change, and perhaps all change, involves thinking, feeling and action within the context of motivation. It is possible for people to become deeply and profoundly different from how they currently are, if they desire this. Different therapeutic methods work with different elements of this change process.

For example, Cognitive Behaviour Therapy seeks to change thinking associated with dysfunctional behaviour. Feelings are not seen as central in this thinking–behaviour (action) relationship, however as behaviour changes, the emotions experienced as negative often change with it.

Psychodynamic Psychotherapy seeks to assist the client to feel into and become conscious of the feeling tones in themselves and the therapeutic relationship, and to make sense of this experience. As feeling is understood and changes, so the person becomes able to act in ways that were previously too painful, or required more robustness than the person had.

Existential Psychotherapy seeks to find, create or change the meaning people attribute to themselves, their experience and the world. As the person finds meaning, so an authentic motivation to be, act and think in a manner congruent with this meaning develops.

In the psychodramatic method change generally occurs in action first, but these elements of thinking, feeling, action and motivation in a specific context are understood as interconnected. Role development is the development of new ways of being. As new ways of being are developed, so old, overused, or dysfunctional ways of being are used less. There is a notion that the person is functioning the best they can with the role development they have.

Each of these methods has an extensive methodology and underpinning developmental theory (or theories) which have been developed over time. My intention here is not to give a full description of these methods; rather to suggest some relationship between them.

Many ideas and processes from these methods have been applied in organisational contexts other than the therapeutic. Approaches broadly similar to Cognitive Behaviour Therapy in particular inform a range of approaches to organisational change, including *The Fifth Discipline,* according to Stacy.[7,8] Bion introduced group psychoanalytic ideas into organisational contexts.[9] In addition, several of the psychodramatic methods have been widely applied in organisational contexts such as the use of role-play.

## *Action*

> To throw one self into the middle of life, to express one self freely in the moment without regard to whether this is exhilarating or scary is the action of a heroic person.[10]

The behaviour is described as heroic because by acting this way we enter a dynamic relationship with life in which we cannot help being affected. As we risk living, so life lives with us, in a dance in which each partner creates new steps that the other then flows into. As we create, so we are ourselves created.

Figure 2.5.2 illustrates the context for individual and group development, in that people experience themselves in relationship with other people. This could be described as a relational context for living that exists whether we are interested in change or not. As we act, others respond to us and we then respond to them—our experience is created by a dynamic series of actions and interactions. If we find that we always seem to have a particular sort of experience, then we can tune into how we are functioning in our relationships and notice what creates the dynamic experience that is happening. We may find we want to change something about ourselves or that we want to be better able to affect the other(s), to create change in them, or in the network of relationships—all of these things involve our learning and development.

Figure 2.5.2 Relational context

The way this integrated theory is used by a person-centred facilitator is different to how it may be used by a group therapist. This integration of theory and practice, person and group enables facilitators to work with awareness and elegance as they make choices in the moment about how to intervene to assist the group to move towards its purpose.

## Relevance to facilitation

As we have seen, facilitation can be distinguished from group psychotherapy through consideration of the purpose to be achieved by the group. However, facilitators are also involved in individual change with people, as social change and individual change are inextricably linked.

# Chapter 6

# facilitation online

Stephen Thorpe

Groups are now working across time and space using Internet technology, and facilitators are being used to facilitate online meetings of many different kinds. This chapter explores the evolving area of online facilitation.

## Online groups

Groups form online around work, specific interests, communities of practice, and shared intention. They use email, e-groups, chat rooms, blogs, Internet Relay Chat (IRC) and other new forms of communication technology.

Nationally, regionally and globally dispersed teams save time and travel by using the Internet to share information, discuss issues and coordinate input. Virtual organisations, without a physical home other than a collection of laptops, do their work in different parts of the world in different time zones and hemispheres.

Areas of e-ducation, the virtual classroom, distance learning and online training have all embraced the Internet for their management and delivery. Similarly, online conferences, seminars and trade shows have become increasingly popular venues for people to network and conduct business. IBM's world jam online event saw a mind-boggling 50,000 people take part in a one-day meeting.[1] Outsourcing of call-centre and help-desk activity is also dispersed, with UK and USA companies outsourcing to India, New Zealand, Australia, the United Arab Emirates and the Philippines, among other countries.

# Differing space and time

Online, many people in different places at the same time (or differing times) across the world can communicate and cooperate in ways never before possible. With synchronous (same-time) communication, everyone can work together in the same context. Using video, audio, text and web tools a discussion can be focused on work that needs cooperation. With asynchronous (different-time) communication, everyone can see what everyone else is writing, and respond as and when they choose. Multiple conversations on multiple topics often occur in the thread of this kind of group discussion. Using visuals, documents and text, a discussion can be built up over time and space. The table below illustrates synchronous and asynchronous activities.

|  | Synchronous (same-time) | Asynchronous (different-time) |
|---|---|---|
| Same place | Face-to-face meetings | Kiosk |
|  | Group decision support |  |

|  | Synchronous (same-time) | Asynchronous (different-time) |
|---|---|---|
|  | Electronic meeting systems | Interactive portals |
| Different place | Internet Relay Chat | Email |
|  | Web collaboration | Forum |
|  | Tele & web conference | Web collaboration |
|  | Online events | Online communities |
|  | Global Virtual Teams | Global Virtual Teams |
|  | Virtual organisations | Virtual organisations |
|  | E-ducation | Blogs E-ducation |

Table 2.6.1. Time and space matrix of online facilitation

# The facilitator online

Several new roles have emerged to improve group cohesion and online group effectiveness. These are the roles of the moderator, facilitator, instructor, technology mediator, domain expert, discussion leader, listserv owner and administrator. Of these new roles, the roles of moderator and facilitator have the greatest impact on a group's effectiveness.

## *Moderator*

In the online environment, the moderator is the role that ensures an online group system is functioning. This may include monitoring discussion boards to ensure all postings meet guidelines and standards of behaviour, and organising discussion material. Moderators are usually responsible for many of the technical tasks required in assisting the group to participate, such as adding new members and fixing bouncing addresses. Moderators may also review posts to ensure they are in alignment with the group purpose before they are approved for the group to see. Small changes are sometimes made, and some postings may be rejected if they do not meet the group's guidelines. Although this role can include some process suggestions, this function is increasingly being performed by a facilitator.

## Facilitator

The role of the facilitator online is to guide the group process, help a group generate its purpose and culture, address conflict, and make interventions to keep the group working towards its purpose. In this sense, it is similar to the facilitation of face-to-face groups. However, facilitators online experience some new challenges that relate to the less tangible nature of the medium.

Not being able to see participants means that body language, tone of voice, posture, mood and energy levels are difficult to assess, making it harder for a facilitator to gauge the subtleties of the group dynamic. There are also additional tasks required of an online facilitator. For example, there is often a need to act as technology guides as well as facilitators, and knowledge of technology and familiarity with an online set-up are imperative.[2] Often there is a lot of preparation involved, and the processes used may not be that effective, or may only work well for some participants. For example, participants who do not have access to computers, are unable to type, are unfamiliar with the language used, or have special needs such as dyslexia or illiteracy, will be disadvantaged.

Working online can be an effective form of meeting, sharing and working with others. The benefits become more obvious as people gain skills, experience and confidence in using online technology. As usage of online media grows, the possibility of richly diverse cultural communication in a connected world becomes a reality.

## Technology benefits and issues

| Asynchronous technology (different-time) | Benefits | Drawbacks |
|---|---|---|
| Email (webmail, MS Outlook, Eudora, Groupwise) | Easy to learn and use, file attachment, broadcast to many, platform independent, written record of conversations. | Slow response, easily misinterpreted, poor context, no visual or audio cues, lack of acknowledgement or feedback, long emails difficult to respond to. |

| Asynchronous technology (different-time) | Benefits | Drawbacks |
|---|---|---|
| E-groups (list serv) (yahoogroups) | One email address, quick and easy to set up, choice of communication style (i.e. emails, daily digest, web only, etc.), builds group knowledge over time, provides time for making thoughtful, in-depth responses, efficient knowledge sharing. | Tends to have few very active members and many silent listeners, large volume hard to manage, public misunderstandings, out-of-office replies can cause disruption, advertising imbedded in e-group systems. |
| Discussion forum (PhpBB, others...) | Threaded discussion, convenient, searchable, good for information dissemination and archive, file attachment, easier to manage multiple conversations. | Public misunderstandings, interfaces can be confusing, lack of visual and audio cues, poor context. Hard to follow multiple discussions. |
| Blogs (blogger.com, wordpress, bloglines, moveable type, drupal, multiply, w.blogger, buzznet, flickr) | Good for information dissemination and archive, thoughtful and in-depth postings, searchable, blog tagging assists finding conversations, builds narrative over time, tagging and linking of blogs helps people keep track of current conversations on topics of interest. | Discussion more controlled by owner, can be less relevant or less factual. |

Table 2.6.2 Some specific communication tools

| Synchronous technology (same-time) | Benefits | Drawbacks |
|---|---|---|
| Internet Relay Chat (ICQ, MSN messenger, Yahoo messenger, PalTalk, AIM, AOL) | Efficient and immediate response, easy to see who is online, good for side conversations (back channel) and informal conversation, useful for ad-hoc informal conversations, often include additional tools (whiteboard, games, avatars). | Available times may inconvenience one or more group members, poor context, lack visual cues, can have one dominate the conversation, interface can be confusing, irrelevant information, multiple conversations occurring simultaneously. |
| Audio conferencing (Skype, freeconference, hotconference) | Real-time interaction, richer context with voice cues, greater sense of connection than text, familiarity with telephone interaction, immediate response, can include special features (file sharing, profiles and built-in IRC). | Cost, voice lag or echoes, best with broadband connection for everyone, unequal participation, low stability (as yet), participants need plenty of advance notice, meeting times constrained by participant time zones. |
| Video conferencing (Skype, Yahoo messenger, MSN messenger) | Real-time interaction, richer context with voice and non-verbal cues, greater sense of contextual setting. | Video can lag behind voice or voice echoes, unfamiliarity, requiring adjustment, difficult to read visual cues, requires high-speed broadband connection for everyone, special facilities, low stability (as yet). |
| Web collaboration (WebIQ, WebEx, Facilitate 4.0, hotoffice) | Same time and place can be combined with different time and place, can make meetings more structured, can have anonymous feedback and voting, increased creativity, more participation in decisions, outputs in electronic formats (txt, MS Word, MS Excel, audio). | Unfamiliarity of interfaces, can force decision making down one path, can limit creativity, linear data entry modes (choosing, polling, preference scales) tendency to group think, requires clear facilitation, often required to teach tool and facilitate meeting at same time, requires preparation. |

# Specific issues

## *Group beginnings*

As with any group, emphasis is needed on the initial relationship development process. Strong relationships between members mean more effective groups, and this is even more important online. After introductions, it is valuable to use Internet Relay Chat (IRC) software or to share Skype addresses. Using these can create opportunities for informal, spontaneous communication between team members and the facilitator. These informal encounters create a common context and perspective that support group interaction and group work.[3] Other useful approaches are to create peer or buddy systems, share personal stories, share photographs and images of personal objects, discuss hobbies, create sports groups, and share family stories or other aspects of members' lives. These all help to build a picture of each other that is helpful when interacting.

## *Group support*

The online facilitator is often required to fill the extra tasks of preparing specialised technology for group access and training participants in its use. A learning curve is involved, and participants' abilities to use and learn complex online tools differ. Other tasks identified for the online facilitator can include mentoring, mediating, coordinating, monitoring, innovating and directing.[4] It can be useful to create illustrated 'How to' documents for using tools, such as showing members how to create mail rules and folders within MS Outlook, or how to set up Skype, and online 'field trips' or tutorials can also be organised. It is also good practice to create an alternative mode of communication in case the technology doesn't work.

## Purpose and culture

Purpose and culture are as important in online groups as they are in face-to-face groups. As online groups begin, they tend to orientate to an initial task focus and participants will be looking for clear structure from the facilitator. It is important to be clear about what the purpose of the group is and for everyone to align on it. Include the group's purpose in any documents you email to members. You can also put the purpose in your email signature each time you email the group. This keeps it uppermost in participants' minds.

It is important that everyone is actively involved in creating and aligning on creating a culture that will enable all to participate fully. Particular things you may want to address in the culture of an online group are:

- Appropriate timeframe for responses.
- Notice period for real-time events.
- Cultural differences.
- Assuming goodwill from others.

- Checking out assumptions.
- Appropriate netiquette.
- How acknowledgements will be done—individually or in a group.
- Notice for upcoming events.
- Confidentiality.

## Cultural differences

Cultural differences are likely to be more significant online, and they are not always obvious due to the lack of emotional cues and feedback. Team members and facilitators will interpret the group language through their own cultural understanding and perspective. Sometimes different participants will use the same words, but they will have a range of understandings.

## Always assume goodwill

Messages and their meanings can easily be misinterpreted online. Inflamed conversations can erupt based on the words that were said, argued and justified rather than what was intended (this is known as 'flaming'). Assuming goodwill is a good counter to these triggering conversations. People are likely to have differing assumptions about behaviour, and different expectations. Conversations that are normal in your own context may be alien or offensive to others in their context. Assuming goodwill interrupts this type of flaming conflict and assists the group to move forward.

## *Tools and processes*

As the facilitator you will need to choose appropriate tools and adaptable processes so that all participants can be involved in creating the purpose of the group and its culture. If the group cannot meet at the same time you may need to use asynchronous email or a discussion forum as the tools. Some things may take longer to do asynchronously. There may be a need to offer a combination of ways in which the group can contribute to the conversation. For example, some members may not have strong textual skills and may prefer to use audio or video conferencing.[5]

Chapter 7

# mapping the field of facilitation

To help provide an understanding of the diverse influences on facilitation, this chapter outlines a range of approaches that have contributed to the development of the field.

## Consensus-building

Many indigenous peoples have used, and continue to use, consensus-building approaches to decision-making. The following are a few examples.

## *Wisdom circles—Americas*

A wisdom circle is a way for small groups of people to create a safe space within which to be trusting, authentic, caring and open to change. A wisdom circle is designed to encourage people to meet in small groups, and to listen and speak from the heart in a spirit of inquiry. The circle is opened and closed with a ritual of the group's choosing, using a talking object, and inviting silence to enter the circle. The wisdom circle is held spiritually and energetically, and creates a space for deep listening and connection.

Wisdom circles are discussed in detail in the book *Wisdom Circles: A Guide to Self-Discovery and Community Building in Small Groups,* by Charles Garfield, Cindy Spring and Sedonia Cahill. In it they outline the 10 'constants' or guidelines for creating and holding wisdom circles.

## Traditional Maori decisionmaking—New Zealand

Traditional Maori decisionmaking is characterised by the following:

- Consensus is preferred even if it takes time. It is important to allow time in which to consult well, as once a decision is made things are actioned quickly and decisively.
- Emotion is expected, vented and tolerated, especially when mana (authority or prestige) is challenged. Reconciliation is then part of the way forward to the consensus decision.
- Strategic withdrawal may occur and leave the 'take' (the subject of discussion) on the floor. People may turn to te reo Maori (the Maori language) and tikanga Maori (Maori customs) in conflict situations.
- Speakers and waiata (songs) are important. Whakapapa (genealogy) determines the order of the speakers. More than one person is likely to be involved in the consultation process. Participants should also be prepared to sing a waiata.

- Silence is important and does not mean consent. What is not said is noted.[1]

## The Religious Society of Friends—Quakers

Consensus decisionmaking has been a centrepiece of the Religious Society of Friends since its beginnings in 1660. At times it has seen them through extremely difficult decisions and divisions.[2]

Each member of the meeting is expected to listen to the voice of God within themselves and, when led, to contribute it to the group for reflection and consideration. A decision is reached when the meeting as a whole feels that the 'way forward' has been discerned. This may mean that those who are informed on or passionate about a given issue are willingly deferred to. However, in other cases some members of the meeting will 'stand aside' on an issue, meaning that while the meeting has achieved a sense of unity, for their own personal reasons they are unable to agree with the result. In still other cases a meeting may reach a sense of unity notwithstanding that some members remain opposed, although the meeting would probably proceed only after considerable time was spent in discernment to ensure that the concerns of the dissenting members had been heard and the sense of the meeting was clear.

# *Women's movement—Starhawk*

Consensus decisionmaking played an important role in the women's movement in the 1960s and onwards. Participative processes were encouraged and consensus was strongly favoured because it provided an equal voice for all women and was an alternative to hierarchical ways of doing things.

In her book *Truth or Dare,* Starhawk, a feminist and activist from the USA, distinguishes 'power with' from 'power over' and describes ways of reaching cooperative decisions. On her website she describes consensus as a process for people who want to work together honestly in good faith to find good solutions for the group.

Consensus cannot be used by people who do not, can not or will not cooperate. It should not be attempted in a group where there are people who want to maintain their wealth and privilege, or want to dominate or control others. In these situations, non-violent struggle would be more appropriate.

# Radical education

Education that challenges the status quo and uses facilitated strategic questioning has also been influential. The following are some examples.

# Conscientisation—Paulo Freire

Paulo Freire was a Brazilian educator and policymaker who is credited as the source of many of the concepts that make up Development Education. Freire wrote several books, his most famous being *Pedagogy of the Oppressed.* While initially concerned with the problem of illiteracy in Latin America, this book is now extremely well-known for its assertion that education can conquer oppression and is a means for liberation and social change.

Conscientisation is a process by which the learner advances towards critical consciousness. Its objective is to empower the knowledge and resources of groups, by facilitating a learning process that becomes critical, transitive and raises consciousness, with the potential of liberation. Open questions, which help to uncover embedded social and political oppression, are used by the learning facilitator.

# Strategic questioning—Fran Peavey

Fran Peavey, a social-change activist from the USA, wanted to talk to people in other parts of the world and develop in herself what she called a 'global heart'. Fran's method of working in sensitive areas of social-change involved listening and asking questions, often obvious ones that people were reluctant to ask for fear of appearing stupid. Fran called her way of working 'strategic questioning', and she developed the skills of asking questions that would make a difference. Strategic questioning is a powerful tool for personal and social change as it helps people to discover their own strategies and ideas for change. It is a process that changes both the listener (or questioner) and the person being questioned.

## Heart politics

Fran Peavey's book *Heart Politics* inspired a group of people in New Zealand to call their network by the same name. This social change network began a relationship with Fran, and she visited one of their gatherings at Tauhara Retreat Centre, Lake Taupo, in the central North Island of New Zealand. Tauhara Centre is a place where people from all spiritual and peaceful traditions can come together to meet and learn.

The Heart Politics network, which grew from some earlier festivals of cooperation, had its first gathering in 1989, and since that time the network has grown and developed in New Zealand, Australia and the USA. Two main residential gatherings are held in New Zealand each year, and one in Australia. Heart 'Politicians' also meet in their local cities and towns, at various men's and women's gatherings, and those dedicated to dialogue, leadership and cultural change. Circle sharing, home groups, use of open space techniques and dialogue on social-change issues are all features of the gatherings. Some Heart Politicians refer to the gatherings as an opportunity for soul work. The purpose of the Heart Politics gatherings was recently defined by the trustees as 'conscious and intentional culture building for sustainability and the common good'.[3]

# Alternative conflict-resolution

The following are examples of alternative methods of conflict resolution that do not rely on litigation, but use facilitation.

## *Alternatives to Violence Project (AVP)*

The AVP programme began in 1975 when a group of inmates at Greenhaven Prison (New York) were working with youth who were coming into conflict with the law. They collaborated with the Quaker Project on Community Conflict, devising a prison workshop. The success of this workshop quickly generated requests for more, and AVP was born.

AVP is dedicated to reducing the level of violence in society by introducing people to ways of resolving conflict without needing to resort to violence. The project is designed to create successful personal interactions and transform violent situations.[4] AVP programmes now take place in many countries around the world.

## Alternative conflict resolution—Chris Moore

Formal negotiation, mediation and facilitated problem-solving as an alternative means of dispute resolution are now widespread and well developed. Chris Moore and his colleagues at CDR Associates in Boulder, Colorado were significant contributors to this development. Moore's publications include *The Mediation Process: Practical Strategies for Resolving Conflict.*

# Group work involving individual therapy

Group work for individual therapy uses a variety of facilitated methods.

## T-groups—Kurt Lewin

In its origins the T-group is the principal tool of a particular form of education, the Human Relations Laboratory. Here traditional educational power and authority relations are abandoned, albeit within tightly organised limits, and anarchy is experienced. The learners become their own subjects, and no longer objects to be filled with packages of knowledge. The learner in the T-group learns from his or her own and others' immediate experience by researching it, giving and gaining accurate and open information about it, and engaging in a shared process of making sense of events.[5] Kurt Lewin, who emigrated to the USA from Germany in the 1930s, is considered one of the founders of social psychology and coined the term 'action research'.

## *Encounter groups—Carl Rogers*

Encounter groups are facilitated groups whose members authentically encounter each other (and themselves). An environment of (supposed) safety and trust is created that enables members to express their feelings and accept themselves for what they are. Encounter groups most often have a leader who is experienced at getting people to open up. The group may meet for several hours a week over a period of months, or it may meet continuously as a marathon group for 24 hours or more, with individuals dropping out for naps.

The thinking is that the intensity and prolonged time of the marathon group will break down social resistance faster, and accomplish as much as groups whose meetings are interspersed over longer periods of time. The goals of encounter groups include examining one's behaviour and values, learning about people in general, becoming more successful in interpersonal relationships, and developing conflict-resolution skills.[6]

# Open encounter—Will Schutz

Developed at Esalen, California in the 1970s and 1980s, open encounter is an approach that combines group therapy, psychosynthesis, bioenergetics, psychodrama, Gestalt, and other group methods 'in the moment'. The approach encourages openness and honesty in all human relationships. Schutz believed in stripping away every last vestige of convention, secrecy, defensiveness and social conditioning until finally the pure and shining gem of unadorned human nature would be revealed for all to behold.[7]

Encounter can be experienced as a somewhat blunt instrument as participants often work through their issues by projecting them onto others. The recipient is then triggered into their own issues, but may also feel somewhat clobbered in the process.

# Psychodrama and sociodrama—Jacob Moreno

Psychodrama is the name given by Moreno to the method he developed for helping people become more creative in day-to-day living. It has applications in many different areas in which people are learning, changing and relating to others, in training, education, healing, spiritual life, business, performing arts and organisations. Practitioners of this powerful method integrate all levels of a human being: their thinking, their intellect, their imagination, their feelings and their actions in their social context. In this way, learning can be applied directly in actual living situations at work, outside the home, in other organisations and in close relationships.

Under the guidance of a trained practitioner known as the director, the method involves improvisational dramatic action. The script for this drama is 'written', moment by moment, out of the purposes and concerns of an individual, or the group where the method is being applied. Group members take active part in one another's dramas, so that they bring them as close to life as possible. In this way group members may generate and practise new behaviours and ways of thinking, and test them out for their impact on those around them before they do this in the actual work or life situation. The consequences can then be examined, and new decisions be made about to how to apply the learning.[8]

# Group development

Methods focusing on the development of the group include the following.

## *Tavistock method—Wilfred Bion*

The Tavistock method originated with the work of the British psychoanalyst Wilfred R. Bion. Convinced of the importance of considering not only the individual but also the group of which the individual is a member, in the late 1940s Bion conducted a series of small study groups at London's Tavistock Institute of Human Relations. He reported his experiences in a series of articles for the journal *Human Relations,* and later in the book *Experiences in Groups.*

The theory is that groups have a manifest, overt aspect and a latent, covert aspect. The manifest aspect is the work group, a level of functioning at which members consciously pursue agreed-on objectives and work toward the completion of a task. Although group members have hidden agendas, they rely on internal and external controls to prevent these emerging and interfering with the announced group task. Tension always exists between the two; it is balanced by various behavioural and psychological structures, including individual defence systems, ground rules, expectations and group norms.

The method is formally applied in a group relations conference to study the ways in which authority is vested in leaders by others, the factors involved as they happen, the covert processes that operate in and among groups, and the problems encountered in the exercise of authority. A consultant confronts the group by drawing attention to group behaviour by means of description, process observation, thematic development and other interventions, some of which are designed to shock the group into awareness of what is happening.

## Community building—Scott Peck

M. Scott Peck wrote several books on group work, and as part of his work he developed a model of the four stages of community. This model, which is outlined in his book *The Different Drum,* is a very helpful way of describing the natural development of a group over time. The four stages of community are:

- **Pseudo-community**—when people meet and are being very nice to each other, avoiding any kind of conflict.
- **Conflict and chaos**—where members have moved through being nice and begin to challenge one another. Individuals struggle to win, and have their norm prevail.
- **Emptiness**—this stage requires members to give up something to allow the group to move on towards achieving its purpose.
- **Authentic community**—people begin to speak with vulnerability and authenticity. There will be sadness, joy and extraordinary individual healing. Community is born.

# Community development

Community development, which involves the wider community, evolved out of social work practice in the UK from the 1950s onwards. Community development uses facilitation in many ways and has been an important influence in developing the theory and practice of facilitation.

# ICA Technology of Participation—Brian Stanfield

In the 1970s the Institute of Cultural Affairs (ICA), based in Chicago, began to create community development projects around the world. Initially 24 were created, one in each time zone. These demonstration projects were followed by Human Development Training Schools in which the local people, working with the institute's staff, explained to people in surrounding communities how progress had been made in the first community.

The methods developed by the ICA to conduct its planning and training programs are now called the Technology of Participation (ToP). These methods have been used by businesses, government agencies, schools and private voluntary organisations to encourage reflection, conduct participatory planning and problem-solving, and guide systematic implementation. They have been used to build leadership capacity and to institutionalise teamwork as organisational practice.

The basic group facilitation methods include the Focused Conversation and Consensus Workshop methods and a short-term Action Planning process. ICA books include Laura Spencer's *Winning Through Participation: Meeting the Challenge of Corporate Change with the Technology of Participation,* and Brian Stanfield's *The Art of Focused Conversation: 100 Ways to Access Group Wisdom in the Workplace* and *The Courage to Lead: Transform Self, Transform Society.*

# Organisational development

The use of facilitation in organisational development grew from the 1980s.

## *Appreciative Inquiry—David Cooperrider*

Appreciative Inquiry was pioneered in the 1980s by David Cooperrider and Suresh Srivastva, two professors at the Weatherhead School of Management at Case Western Reserve University, USA.[9] Appreciative Inquiry is used widely to bring about collaborative and strengths-based change in thousands of profit and nonprofit organisations and communities in many countries.

Appreciative Inquiry is a way of being and seeing. It is both a worldview and a process for facilitating positive change in human systems, such as organisations, groups and communities. The main assumption of Appreciative Inquiry is simple: every human system has something that works right—things that give it life when it is vital, effective and successful. Appreciative Inquiry begins by identifying this positive core and connecting to it in ways that heighten energy, sharpen vision, and inspire action for change.

## *Systems thinking—Peter Senge*

Systems thinking allows people to make their understanding of social systems explicit and improve them, in the same way that people can use engineering principles to make explicit and improve their understanding of mechanical systems. This broad view helps people to identify the real causes of issues and know where to work to address them. There are certain principles of systems thinking that guide one to see this broad view. Systems thinking is the basis for the approach to developing the learning organisation.

Peter Senge's book *The Fifth Discipline,* and its companion, *The Fifth Discipline Fieldbook,* are seminal works about systems thinking and its application to organisations. Senge identifies five 'component technologies' that are the basis for building learning organisations (and systems thinking in individuals): vision, teamwork, personal development, mental models, and systems thinking. The five disciplines are all very important for facilitators.

# Large Group Interventions

In 1992, Billie Alban and Barbara Bunker edited a special issue of the *Journal of Applied Behavioural Science* that was dedicated to exploring what they saw as an emergent social technology—Large Group Interventions. They wrote the book *Large Group Interventions: Engaging the Whole System for Rapid Change* in 1996. In it they present a comprehensive overview of the main methods that had emerged at that stage. They began many of the conversations about this new field of change practice in that book and at many organisational development conferences and workshops around the world.

Approaches within Large Group Interventions include: Search Conference, Future Search, Real Time Strategic Change, ICA Strategic Planning Process, The Conference Model, Fast Cycle Full Participation Work Design, Real Time Work Design, Participative Design, Simu-Real, Work-Out and Open Space Technology.

# *Search conference—Merrelyn Emery*

The search conference method grows out of the socio-technical systems theory and practice work of Eric Trist and Fred Emery; it is most clearly articulated in Merrelyn Emery and Ronald Purser's 1996 book *The Search Conference: A Powerful Method for Planning Organizational Change and Community Action.*

Search conferencing is a participative planning event that enables a large group to collectively create a plan that the members themselves will implement. They search for the most desirable future of a system.

The phases are:

- **Phase 1 (The Past):** Participants share their perception of changes over the past five to seven years.
- **Phase 2 (Appreciating the Environment):** The environment is 'appreciated' by focusing on the system's past, present and future.
- **Phase 3 (Reality):** Constraints are addressed and groups of participants select a strategic goal

and work in self-managed teams to develop action plans.

- **Phase 4 (Implementation):** The final phase of the conference occurs after the conference itself, and focuses on implementation. It usually includes changing the organisation's way of working.

In the words of Emery and Purser:

The desirable future for the world as it has been envisioned by people from hundreds of Search Conferences expresses a set of common ideals. The world people wish to bring into being is a world in which they can

- Work together
- Be joyful in their daily lives
- Make wise decisions

## World Café—Juanita Brown

World Café, which was designed by Juanita Brown and David Isaacs, is a useful method for discussing issues in a relaxed and informal way.

In World Café a focus question is chosen, people discuss the question at small tables, then they move between tables sharing thoughts and building on one another's insights; as they go they are also writing and doodling on the paper tablecloths. The key to creating a successful World Café conversation is employing seven guiding principles, which when used in combination foster courageous conversations and collective intelligence.

The World Café process is particularly useful when you want to generate input, share knowledge, stimulate innovative thinking, and explore action possibilities around real life issues and questions. The method works well for large groups (see www.theworldcafe.com).

# Public participation

Facilitation is now used at many community forums and public meetings. The new-style public meeting will be led by facilitators rather than a chairperson, and the aim will be to maximise public participation using facilitated processes. There may be discussion and dialogue in both small and large groups, and there may also be some computer-assisted recording and polling of views, priorities and points of agreement and difference. This is in contrast to the old-style public or town meeting which took the form of a heated public debate with a few voices dominating, tempers becoming frayed, and motions and amendments put and voted on using majority voting.

Public participation processes are becoming so popular that an international network of practitioners has formed the International Association of Public Participation, known as IAP2. Their website is www.iap2.org. The IAP2 homepage states that:

The International Association for Public Participation, working through its members, helps organisations and communities around the world improve their decisions by involving those people who are affected by those decisions.

IAP2 has over 1000 members in 16 countries. Resources listed on its website include related organisations and networks.

# Graphic facilitation

Graphic facilitation by visual practitioners can be a very effective way of recording large group meetings. Drawings are made on large sheets of paper at the sides of the room as the group dialogue unfolds. The drawings reflect both the content and flow of the discussions. The drawings help to focus the group on what has taken place, and over time they can form a visual history of a group. A useful website is http://www.visualpractitioner.org/education/featured/value1.htm.

# Online facilitation

Facilitation on the Internet is a growing area of facilitation practice. Online facilitators use email, voice and video conferencing, and a variety of computing tools. For more on this see Part 2 Chapter 6, 'Facilitation online'.

# Further information

A useful book that helps to map the field of facilitation is *The Tao of Democracy: Using Co-intelligence to Create a World that Works* by Tom Atlee. The book covers collective intelligence, democracy and whole-ness, consensus-making, cooperative and holistic politics, dialogue methods and citizens' deliberative councils.

## The developing field

Although the methods covered above are all impor-tant in the development of the field of facilitation, this is by no means an exhaustive list. See what other methods you can find, perhaps by searching on the Internet.

# part 3

## Chapter 1

# facilitator education

This chapter explores aspects of facilitator education and introduces the Zenergy approach to training facilitators.

At Zenergy we describe our facilitator training as 'whole person' (or holistic, person-centred, and multi-sensory).

Working with groups of people without manipulation, coercion or reliance on charisma requires an embodied awareness of self, others and the group within the wider social and physical environment. Such awareness is grown over time as a whole body experience, called integrated learning. The ability to be centred, grounded and self-reflective, and to connect with others in constructive ways, is asking a lot from aspiring facilitators. Yet at the same time it is a wonderful personal development journey.

In addition there are conceptual models, skills and a toolkit of processes to gather through lots of experiencing and practice. To meet the needs of our trainee facilitators we have gradually developed an integrated modular training programme that can be completed over a two-year minimum period. However, most trainees take four years to complete the programme, and value the practice time between the intensive four-to five-day modules as a way to practise, question and integrate the learnings. Many participants take as much of the training as they want without completing the whole Diploma of Facilitation. A few of our diploma graduates later become interns and facilitators with our cooperative company Zenergy.

# The holistic approach

The organic and holistic approach to an emerging universe described in the work of David Bohm recognises that the whole cannot be separated from the parts.[1] Something may be distinguished by separating it temporarily from the whole, after which it will fall back naturally into the whole.

Francisco Varela, in dialogue with Joseph Jaworski in his book *Synchronicity: The Inner Path of Leadership,* says:

Our language and our nervous system combine to constantly construct our environment. The world is open—non substantial. We exist in language. It is by languaging and recurrent actions or human practices that we create meaning together...

We lay the path down by an accumulation of recurrent human practices. This is literally what it means to be human—to exist in a world of distinctions such as community, families, our work, and objects like spoons—all of which exist

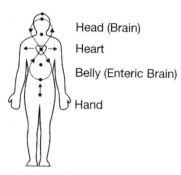

Head (Brain)

Heart

Belly (Enteric Brain)

Hand

Figure 3.1.1 Whole person learning

nowhere except in this accumulation of bodily actions and human practices, this network of actions and languaging...

...it is through language that we create the world, because it's nothing until we describe it. And when we describe it, we create distinctions that govern our actions. To put it another way, we do not describe the world we see, but we see the world we describe.

Facilitator education, which is primarily learning a toolkit of techniques and processes, does not do justice to the ever-changing, organic, fluid nature and subtleties of the group dynamic and the work of a facilitator. An understanding of the interconnectedness of all things and the growing capacity to be aware of oneself, others, the group and the environment are also a necessary part of becoming a facilitator.

One of the models we use in our training programmes illustrates how whole person learning happens. In our whole person or integrated learning approach we use the idea of a head brain and an enteric (belly) brain. The head understands and the belly experiences. The two 'knowledges' flow together and are integrated in the heart.

# 1. Understanding—head

Understanding is a function of thinking. A concept is considered, understood and accepted or rejected by the rational, thinking mind. It is logical, it makes sense.

# 2. Experiencing—belly

Experience is of the body—something happens, it is experienced. Where did I experience it in my body? What did I see, hear, sense? Was it pleasant or unpleasant? What did the experience suggest to me?

Understanding (head) and experiencing (belly) do not necessarily occur in that order—they can occur in the reverse order, or mixed together.

# 3. Integrating—heart

Concept and experience are then checked for relatedness and congruence. Do they fit together? Do they make sense? If they do, they can and will be integrated. This then can be named as a distinction that can be used. An integrated distinction will be *spoken from the heart*—it has both thought and experience to back it up.

# Embodied learning

The whole person model illustrates that learning takes place in the whole body (it is literally embodied). This approach has been confirmed in the work of neuroscientist Candace Pert.[2] She has identified peptides as key biochemical components of a psycho-somatic network that operates throughout the body and reinforces the close relationship between thought and emotions as a whole body experience. In the same way, whole personhood is very much an embod-ied phenomenon. It can only be experienced in the physical body and is fully dependent on having a physical body.

Awareness of the integrated nature of the body/mind has been recognised in many spiritual and cultural traditions such as yoga, Sufism and other forms of sacred dance, martial arts such as tai chi, holistic health methods, energy work and many kinds of body work, such as rebalancing and Heller work.[3]

In the Zenergy facilitation training programmes, practitioners are encouraged through simple exercises and practices to bring their energy into the body, and especially into the belly and heart, as this seems to assist facilitators to connect more easily with the energy of the whole group and individual members.

# Multisensory approaches

Working with groups of people can be greatly en-hanced by the use of multisensory stimulation. This is related to embodied learning, as we learn by using all our senses. Multisensory experiences can usefully become part of the experience of every group and every facilitator training experience.

# Using the senses

Here are a few of an unlimited number of creative approaches you can try when using the differing senses of sight, sound, smell, touch, taste, movement, and the subtle senses associated with being in nature and other special environments.

| | |
|---|---|
| Drawing | Can you draw it? Try drawing the idea on paper. This is useful to help clarify confused or complex ideas and feelings and see them from another perspective. The line, the colours and the patterns all suggest new possibilities. |
| Painting | Painting is useful for getting into the feel, or sense, of something. The sensation of using paint helps to access flow and texture. The colours are vibrant and the movement is flowing. |
| Non-dominant hand | When drawing or painting try to use the nondominant hand as well as the dominant hand. This will give a different look and feel, and suggest different possibilities. |
| Movement | Use a gesture to illustrate an idea. Take a step—by standing and taking a step. Experience the physical and emotional effect of this. |
| Tension | Create tension through holding a scarf or string oneself (with an end in each hand), between two or more people, or between a person and a firm object. |
| Sound | Sing, whistle and make sounds to express a feeling or idea. Chant, sing (out of tune, in tune), yodel, harmonise or bang a rhythm with found objects. |
| Symbol | Find an object (in the room or garden) that symbolises in some way the idea or feeling. Put it in a special place in the room. |

| Sensation | Find something with a similar texture to the idea or feeling. |
| Story | Make up stories. Create scenarios, steps and outcomes. Find many different possibilities for developing a story. |
| Drama | Dramatise the event; try understatement, overstatement, melo-drama, farce, opera and comedy. |
| Imagination | The sky is the limit—or is it? What about the galaxies, the cosmos, black holes, space travel, inner space, the tiniest particle, the biggest creature? |

# A comment on our approach

A colleague in Australia, Glyn Thomas, writing in the *IAF Handbook of Group Facilitation* in a chapter called 'Dimensions of Facilitator Education', outlines a four-dimensional model of facilitator education. Thomas found that many of the approaches to facilitator education in the literature on this subject seemed to fit into one of the following broad frameworks (which he then refers to as dimensions):

- Technical facilitator education approaches, which are skills-based and formulaic in style.[4]
- Intentional facilitator education approaches, where practice is grounded in theory and justifications, and particular interventions are provided.[5]
- Person-centred facilitator education approaches, which specifically emphasise the attitudes, personal qualities and presence of the facilitator.[6]

- Critical facilitator education approaches, which emphasise awareness of the political nature of facilitation and the effects on all participants.[7]

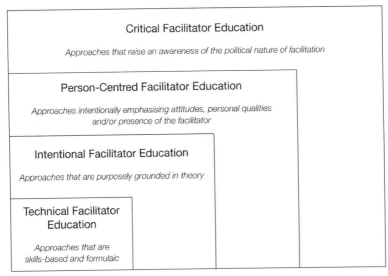

Figure 3.1.2 The dimensions of the facilitator education (Thomas's model)

Thomas's model uses nested boxes to describe the four key dimensions. This model is shown below.

The dimensions portrayed in the larger boxes are considered to be extensions of the dimensions portrayed in the smaller boxes nested inside them. In this respect, the model implies that a dimension portrayed in a larger box covers much (but not necessarily all) of the content or foci of the preceding dimension, but there is also an implied progression in the depth and complexity of the facilitator education process. Thomas found that many of the approaches to facilitator education tended to focus on the content of a single dimension portrayed in the model. He considered our Zenergy facil- itation approach to be one of a few exceptions to this approach, emphasising the importance of skills, processes and knowledge across a number of dimen- sions presented in the model. He noted that our ap- proach was person-centred, in that it recognises that an effective facilitator is 'more to do with who you are and who you are being for the group you are working with—the relationship you develop with the group is the key'.[8]

# Other training programmes

As well as the Zenergy facilitator education ap- proach there are many other approaches. Here are two other methods.

## *ICA ToP facilitator training*

Trademarked as the Technology of Participation, the ICA basic group facilitation includes the 'Focused Conversation' and 'Consensus' workshop methods and a short term 'Action Planning' process. Focused Conversation aims to conduct purposeful, productive, focused conversations, capture the wisdom of the group, stimulate feedback and reach shared aware- ness in meetings. The Consensus workshop enables a group facilitator to weave everyone's wisdom into a practical plan. Participants become familiar with a five-step process that moves from the collection of data and ideas, through the organisation of the data into meaningful groupings and to a point of consensus, resolution, and product. The Action Planning process enables participants to more effectively apply ToP methods in their own situations.

## *Skilled Facilitator approach—Roger Schwarz*

The Skilled Facilitator approach developed by Roger Schwarz is a values-based systems approach to facilitation that focuses on creating highly effective groups and organisations.[9] It uses a set of core values (valid information, free and informed choice, internal commitment and compassion) and principles, as well as specific techniques and methods that follow from them. Designed to facilitate fundamental change, the approach is central to creating empowered organisations, self-managing teams, and learning organisations. Because of its guiding principles, participants can also use the approach to improve their effectiveness in almost any setting or role.

## Zenergy training leading edges

Towards the end of the Zenergy Diploma of Facilitation, participants take part in two four-day master classes. Participants identify areas of growth and development they wish to explore, and the programme is co-created around their individual requests. Recent requests have included areas such as transformation, emergence, resonance, collective consciousness, presence and expanded consciousness.

We have been experimenting with accessing expanded consciousness, also known as the 'zero point field', the 'field', and the fourth dimension. We work with expanded consciousness because it seems to be a way of accessing more intelligence than we can access in other more individual ways—it seems to be a way of accessing collective intelligence in a direct and profound way.

In her book *The Field,* Lynne McTaggart writes about this phenomenon and documents the work of frontier scientists in proving the existence of this all-encompassing energy field that connects everything in the universe. We are all part of this dynamic interplay, which includes time, space and thought. Frontier scientists such as Pribram, Laslo and Braud have become convinced that the brain is simply a retrieval and read-out mechanism of the ultimate storage system—The Field.

In *The Field,* McTaggart quotes Karl Pribram as he explains that we are ultimately vibrations:

> We perceive an object by resonating with it, getting 'in synch' with it. To know the world is literally to be on its wavelength ... Think of your brain as a piano. When we observe something in the world, certain portions of the brain resonate at certain specific frequencies. At any point of attention, our brain presses only certain notes,

which trigger strings of a certain length and frequency.

We pick up this information in the electrochemical circuits of the brain, then project a virtual image out in space and 'see' it with our eyes as something existing in time and space. This means that the world we see is a virtual creation of projected images. Through his experiments on cats Pribram also found that our thoughts and memories are not stored in our brains and that there is no such thing as the individual mind. All very tantalising stuff, with interesting ramifications for group activity and facilitation.

# Peer facilitation training programme

The following chapter covers a peer facilitator training programme designed for a group of six to 12 aspiring facilitators. This is held over a period of 12 to 15 weeks, with one three-hour period per week. The advantages of such a peer programme are that it can be run anywhere a group of aspiring facilitators can get together.

The facilitators at Zenergy (www.zenergyglobal.com) are also available to lead training programmes and workshops in facilitation skills throughout the world and online. We are also available by email to discuss particular issues that come up during peer training programme sessions (email zenergy@xtra.co.nz).

# Chapter 2

# training programme

## Introduction

This chapter describes a facilitators' training programme that you can use with a group of colleagues. It is designed as a peer training programme, which means you will all be learning together, without an expert to guide you. The purpose of the programme is to develop facilitation skills through experiential learning.

The programme works well with a group of six to 12 participants. If there are six people, there will be time for plenty of practice and dialogue. If more than 12 people take part, the programme will need to be modified by extending the timeframes or breaking into two smaller groups for some processes.

Each of the 12 sessions is based on one or two chapters of this book. Session 11 will be designed by the participants. Session 12 is for self-and peer-assessment, completion and planning for further training.

## Programme outline

**Preparatory session**

Session 1: Facilitation and the role of the facilitator (Part 1 Chapters 1–2)
Session 2: Purpose and culture (Part 1 Chapter 3)
Session 3: Facilitating yourself (Part 1 Chapter 4)

**Review**
Session 4: Facilitating another (Part 1 Chapter 5)
Session 5: Facilitating a group (Part 1 Chapter 6)
Session 6: Making interventions (Part 1 Chapter 7)

**Review**
Session 7: Shifting levels (Part 1 Chapter 8)
Session 8: Dialogue and storytelling (Part 1 Chapter 9)
Session 9: Getting to consensus (Part 1 Chapter 10)

**Review**
Session 10: Addressing conflict (Part 1 Chapter 11)
Session 11: Applications (Part 2)
Session 12: Self-and peer-assessment, evaluation, completion

## Resources

- Whiteboard (plain, electronic or digital), flip charts or large sheets of plain paper. Whiteboard pens, felt-tipped pens, pastels, paints (from school art supplies).
- A copy of this book and a personal notebook for each person.

- A large room in which you can move around easily. Set up chairs in a circle, with space for the whiteboard.

## Sessions

A two-hour preparatory session is followed by 12 three-hour sessions.

Some groups may like to occasionally hold two sessions on the same day as a whole-day event. A half-to one-hour break should then be programmed between sessions.

## Preparatory session

The two-hour preparatory session is held so that proposed participants can:
- Meet one another.
- Share their specific purpose for taking part in the programme.
- Arrange where and when the training sessions will be held.
- Familiarise themselves with the overall programme outline (above).
- Address any questions and concerns.
- Commit to full participation and attendance at every session.
- Set some preliminary ground rules—such as confidentiality, punctuality, willingness to be coached and receive feedback.

- Address any housekeeping issues that need to be organised in advance.
- Clarify and confirm who will be in the programme.
  **Homework:** Read Part 1 Chapters 1 and 2 of this book.

At the preparatory session, decide who will be the primary facilitator for the first session.

It is suggested that one person be the primary facilitator for each session. There will also be plenty of opportunities for participants to facilitate sections of particular sessions. The primary facilitator will ensure that sections of their session have facilitators allocated from among the participants. The primary facilitator will also set up the space for the group, start the session, facilitate the check-in, ensure continuity, and facilitate the last section of the session.

## *Facilitator feedback*

An opportunity for giving and receiving feedback to each facilitator can be built in to each session; take six minutes for this within the time allowed at the end of each exercise for reflection, and self-and peer-assessment. You may like to choose a timekeeper and a recorder.

The feedback process gives two minutes for the trainee facilitator, who completes the sentences:

One thing I could improve is...
One thing I did well is...

This is followed by two minutes for the participants, who complete the sentences:

My constructive criticism is ... (2 minutes)
My acknowledgement to you (the trainee facilitator) is ... (2 minutes).

Encourage short, pithy comments. Discourage stories, discussion or justification. Encourage trainee facilitators to receive feedback as a gift, whether they agree with it or not. Encourage participants not to repeat feedback already given.

To complete the process, the trainee facilitator chooses one constructive criticism and one acknowledgement as their 'gems' for learning.

## Some feedback guidelines

- Speak with honesty and good intent.
- Set aside labels and judgements (avoid 'ought', 'should' or 'must').
- Separate the person from the behaviour.
- Be specific, with both constructive criticism and acknowledgement. Tell people exactly what they said or did.
- Check readiness to receive feedback, and appropriate time and space.

- Focus on what's missing that will make a difference, not what's wrong.
- Present feedback so that it is perceived as an opportunity, not a threat.

## Criteria for effective facilitation

Criteria for effective facilitation will be developed as part of Session 4 of this training programme. These criteria can then become a checklist for facilitator feedback for the following sessions, and the basis of a self-and peer-assessment process in Session 12.

# Session 1: Facilitation and the role of the facilitator

## Purpose of session

To develop a conceptual understanding of facilitation.

## Objectives for session

- To understand the concepts in Part 1 Chapter 1, 'Preparing the ground', and Part 1 Chapter 2, 'The role of the facilitator'.
- To explore the development of facilitation.
- To explore the role of the facilitator.
- To understand the difference between facilitation and facilitative.

# Session outline

## A: Welcome
## (25 minutes) (primary facilitator)

Welcome everyone to the first session and introduce yourself, giving a short background of your experience and sharing something personal.

Remind the group of the purpose of the programme—to develop facilitation skills through experiential learning.

Outline the purpose and programme of Session 1.

Choose a timekeeper for the session.

## B: Check-in
## (15 minutes) (primary facilitator)

This is a structured round in which people introduce themselves in turn and share a story about their involvement in facilitation, either as a facilitator or as a participant. Allow three to five minutes for each participant. See Structured rounds, Process 1.

End with feedback to the facilitator. See Facilitator feedback, Process 52.

## C: Understanding Part 1 Chapter 1
## (40 minutes) (section facilitator)

Have someone introduce Part 1 Chapter 1 and give a summary (10 minutes). Use an unstructured round, with each person speaking on what they got out of the chapter. Then have a free-flowing discussion on the chapter.

End with feedback to the facilitator.

Take a 15-minute break for refreshments.

## D: Energiser or game
## (15 minutes) (section facilitator)

Choose a physical energiser or game someone knows, or refer to Games and energisers, Processes 32–34.

End with feedback to the facilitator.

## E: Understanding Part 1 Chapter 2
## (30 minutes) (section facilitator)

Have someone introduce Part 1 Chapter 2 and give a summary (10 minutes). Again use an unstructured round, with each person sharing what they got out of the chapter. Then have a general discussion on the chapter. Use the whiteboard to clarify the difference between a facilitator and facilitative managers, trainers and leaders. Consider the implications of co-facilitation for your training programme.

End with feedback to the facilitator.

## F: Energiser
## (10 minutes) (section facilitator)

End with feedback to the facilitator.

## G: Organisation details
## (10 minutes) (primary facilitator)

Organise the roster so that one person is the primary facilitator for each of the programme sessions. If the group has six participants, for example, each participant will be the primary facilitator for two sessions.

Give homework for the next session: read Part 1 Chapter 3, 'A framework for facilitation'.

The primary facilitator for the next session will negotiate the facilitation of the session sections. Ask participants to first nominate the section they want, then negotiate the double-ups and gaps. Use consensus decisionmaking for this.

## H: Feedback
## (10 minutes) (primary facilitator)

Feedback for the primary facilitator, who asks for feedback on the session.

Aspects to consider in the feedback:
- Were time limits kept, including starting and finishing on time?
- Did everyone participate fully?
- Was the group purpose clarified?
- What level of trust has been generated?
- What was the key learning for each person?

- What were the strengths and areas for improvement of the facilitation?

**I: Completion**
**(10 minutes) (section facilitator)**

Share anything that would complete the session for you (including things you might say to someone else about the group afterwards).
Acknowledgement and affirmations: share these.
End of session.

# Session 2: Purpose and culture

## *Purpose of session*

To establish the framework for the group.

## *Objectives for session*

- To understand the concepts in Part 1 Chapter 3, 'A framework for facilitation'.
- To align on a group purpose for the programme.
- To develop the group culture.

## *Session outline*

**A: Welcome**
**(5 minutes) (primary facilitator)**

Welcome everyone to the second session.
Outline the session purpose and programme.

Choose a timekeeper for the rest of the session.

## B: Check-in
## (15 minutes) (primary facilitator)

See Structured round, Process 1.
End with feedback to the facilitator; see Process 52.

## C: Sharing on Part 1 Chapter 3
## (30 minutes) (section facilitator)

Have someone introduce Chapter 3 and give a summary (10 minutes). Use a round, structured or unstructured, with each person speaking (possibly with a time limit), on what they got out of the chapter. Then have a general discussion on the chapter.
End with feedback to the facilitator.

## D: Energiser
## (10 minutes) (section facilitator)

See Games and energisers, Processes 32–34.
End with feedback to the facilitator.

## E: Clarify the purpose
## (40 minutes) (section facilitator)

See also Group purpose, Processes 6 and 7.

Use a round in which each person speaks the purpose for the programme in their own words. Write up key words from each person on large sheets of paper.

At the end of the round, identify any agreement and disagreement, and align the group on a common purpose.

Acknowledge your successful alignment with a physical activity—a whoop, clap, cheer, etc.

Write the purpose up and display it prominently during each session.

End with feedback to the facilitator.

Take a 15-minute break for refreshments.

## F: Group culture
## (30 minutes) (section facilitator)

Develop the group culture. How do we want to work together?

See Developing the group culture, Process 8. Include any ground rules that were set at the preparatory session. Draw or write the culture for display, as was done for the group purpose.

End with feedback to the facilitator.

## G: Organisation details
## (10 minutes) (primary facilitator)

Give homework for the next session: read Chapter 4, 'Facilitating yourself'. Organise the roster for one person to be the primary facilitator for each of the sessions of the programme. Then have participants choose a section from the next session to facilitate.

## H: Feedback
## (10 minutes) (primary facilitator)

Feedback for the primary facilitator, who asks for feedback on the session.
- Aspects to consider in the feedback:
- Is everyone present?
- Were time limits kept, including starting and finishing on time?
- Did everyone participate fully?
- Was the group purpose clarified?
- What level of trust has been generated?
- What was the key learning for each person?
- What were the strengths and areas for improvement of the facilitation?

## I: Completion
## (5 minutes) (primary facilitator)

Share anything that would complete the session for you (including things you might say to someone else about the group afterwards).
Acknowledgements and affirmations: share these.
End of session.

# Session 3: Facilitating yourself

## *Purpose of session*

To understand and practise the skills of self-facilitation.

## *Objectives for session*

- To understand the concepts of Part 1 Chapter 4, 'Facilitating yourself'.
- To deepen the group connection.
- To self-assess a level of self-facilitation.
- To create a buddy system among group members.

## *Session outline*

### A: Welcome
### (10 minutes) (primary facilitator)

Welcome everyone to the third session.
Outline the session programme.
Choose a timekeeper.
*Note:* Remember to allow six minutes for feedback before the end of each facilitated session.

### B: Check-in
### (20 minutes) (primary facilitator)

Is there anything you would like to share to be fully present in the group now? (Two to three minutes each).

End with feedback to the facilitator; see Process 52.

## C: Sharing process
## (40 minutes) (section facilitator)

My precious possession, Process 11.
End with feedback to the facilitator.
Break for refreshments (15 minutes).

## D: Sharing on Chapter 4, 'Facilitating yourself'
## (30 minutes) (section facilitator)

Have someone introduce the chapter and give a summary (10 minutes). Then have a round, with each person speaking (3 minutes) on their response to the chapter.

Follow with a general discussion.
End with feedback to the facilitator.

## E: Self-facilitation
## (30 minutes) (section facilitator)

Have the group divide into pairs. In turn, the members of each pair explore the questions below. The other person listens without comment, taking notes if requested.

Questions (5 minutes each):

In what areas of my life am I the most self-facilitative? (3 minutes each)

In what areas of my life am I the least self-facilitative? (2 minutes each)

What is one area in which I could be more self-facilitative? What will this look like? What's one step I can take toward this within the next 24 hours?

Bring the whole group together and ask participants to share their discoveries (10 minutes).

End with feedback to the facilitator.

## F: Buddy system
## (10 minutes) (primary facilitator)

Participants contract in pairs to coach one another, by telephone or in person, at least once before the next session.

Have them arrange times and write them in their diaries.

## G: Homework
## (10 minutes) (primary facilitator)

Homework reminder: read Part 1 Chapter 5, 'Facilitating another'. Confirm the next primary facilitator. People choose sections of the next session to facilitate.

## H: Feedback

**(10 minutes) (primary facilitator)**

Feedback for the primary facilitator: ask for feedback on the session.

**I: Completion**
**(5 minutes) (primary facilitator)**

Share anything that would complete the session for you (including things you might say to someone else about the group afterwards).
Acknowledgement and affirmations: share these.
End of session.

# Session 4: Facilitating another

## *Purpose of session*

To become aware of key aspects when facilitating another.

## *Objectives for session*

- To understand the concepts of Part 1 Chapter 5, 'Facilitating another'.
- To experience process around valuing difference.
- To practise being present to another person.

## *Session outline*

### A: Welcome, check-in, and review of buddy system

**(20 minutes) (primary facilitator)**
Outline the session programme.

Choose a timekeeper.
Check in: structured or unstructured round, Process 1 or 2.
Review the buddy system:
- How is it working?
- What's missing?
- Any requests and promises?

## B: Being with
**(20 minutes) (section facilitator)**

Being with another, Process 20 (2 or 3 minutes each way). Do this twice, with brief sharing in pairs before the second time. Share in the large group, with a round on:

What I learnt from this process was...
Feedback for the facilitator; see Process 52.

## C: Sharing on Part 1 Chapter 3 in the whole group
**(20 minutes) (section facilitator)**

Feedback for the facilitator.

## D: Identity check
**(25 minutes) (section facilitator)**

Identity check, Process 43.

Participants choose a partner to whom they have a strong response, positive or negative. Allow up to five minutes each way. Some people may need more time.

Repeat the process with a new partner (if time is available), then ask participants to share in the whole group.

Feedback for the facilitator.

Break for refreshments (15 minutes).

## E: Differing perceptions
## (50 minutes) (section facilitator)

My world, your world, Process 22.

Or:

## Listening skills

Mining the gold, Process 26.

Feedback for the facilitator.

## F: Organisation details
## (15 minutes) (primary facilitator)

Homework reminder: read Part 1 Chapter 6, 'Facilitating a group'.

Also remind participants about contacting their buddies.

Confirm the next primary facilitator. People choose sections to facilitate for next session.

**G: Feedback
(10 minutes) (primary facilitator)**

Feedback for the primary facilitator: ask for feedback on the session.

**H: Completion
(5 minutes) (primary facilitator)**

Share anything that would complete the session for you (including things you might say to someone else about the group afterwards).
Say these now.
Acknowledgements and affirmations.
End of session.

# Session 5: Facilitating a group

## *Purpose of session*

To understand the role of a facilitator with a group.

## *Objectives for session*

- To understand the concepts in Part 1 Chapter 6, 'Facilitating a group'.
- To be able to identify group baggage.
- Prioritise the characteristics of an effective facilitator.
- To explore group synergy.

# *Session outline*

## A: Welcome
## (20 minutes) (primary facilitator)

Welcome everyone to the fifth session.
Outline the session programme.
Choose a timekeeper.

## B: Check-in
## (40 minutes) (section facilitator)

Sharing withholds, Process 36.
*Note:* By this session there will be plenty of 'baggage' emerging in the group. Revise the session programme if more time is needed.
Feedback for the facilitator; see Process 52.

## C: Sharing on Part 1 Chapter 6
## (45 minutes) (section facilitator)

Brainstorm in the whole group:
What are the characteristics of an effective facilitator? Prioritise the resulting list (see Process 4).
*Note:* Keep this list and use as criteria in Session 12.
Working in pairs or threes and using the prioritised list, have participants address the following questions:
What are my strengths as a facilitator?
What are my weaknesses?

What are my areas of training and development?

Ask participants to design some specific actions to advance their training and development for this week.

Feedback for the facilitator.

Break for refreshments (15 minutes).

## D: (30 minutes) (section facilitator)

Share in the whole group, as an unstructured round, answers to this question:

What experiences have I had of synergy?

Ask participants to consider all the group experiences they have had—family, school, work, recreation, community, spiritual.

Feedback for the facilitator.

## E: Organisation details
## (15 minutes) (primary facilitator)

Review the buddy system.

Homework reminder: read Part1 Chapter 7, 'Making interventions'.

Confirm the facilitator for the next session.

## F: Feedback
## (10 minutes) (primary facilitator)

Feedback for the primary facilitator: ask for feedback on the session.

**G: (5 minutes) (primary facilitator)**

Share anything that would complete the session for you (including things you might say to someone else about the group afterwards).
Say these now.
Acknowledgements and affirmations.
End of session.

# Session 6: Making interventions

## *Purpose of session*

To understand and practise making group interventions.

## *Objectives for session*

• To understand the concepts of Part 1 Chapter 7, 'Making interventions'.
• To explore the attitude of a facilitator in a group.
• To practise making interventions as a facilitator.

## *Session outline*

**A: Welcome and check-in
(25 minutes) (primary facilitator)**

Welcome everyone to the sixth session.

Outline the session programme.

Choose a timekeeper.

Check in; see Being with a group, Process 21.

## B: Sharing on Chapter 7
## (25 minutes) (session facilitator)

Ask participants to share with the whole group their answers to this question:

What is the attitude of the facilitator when using interventions?

In other words, where are they coming from/who are they being?

Feedback for the facilitator.

Break for refreshments (15 minutes).

### C: (1 hour) (session facilitator)

Working as a whole group, ask participants to choose three sections in the chapter and develop role-plays based on them.

Allow 20 minutes for each role-play, including setting up, presenting, deroling and sharing in the whole group. (See Role-plays, Process 25).

Feedback for the facilitator.

## D: Acknowledgement
## (30 minutes) (session facilitator)

Affirmations and acknowledgements, Process 12.

Feedback for the facilitator.

**E: Organisation details
(10 minutes) (primary facilitator)**

Homework reminder: read Part 1 Chapter 8, 'Shifting levels'.

Confirm the facilitators for the next session.

**F: Feedback
(10 minutes) (primary facilitator)**

Feedback for the primary facilitator: ask for feedback on the session.

**G: Completion
(5 minutes) (primary facilitator)**

Share anything that would complete the session for you (including things you might say to someone else about the group afterwards). Say these now.

Acknowledgements and affirmations.

End of session.

# Session 7: Shifting levels

*Note:* From now onwards for the rest of the training programme, give facilitators feedback after each session.

## *Purpose of session*

To be able to facilitate different levels in a group.

# Objectives for session

- To develop awareness and comfort with the different levels available to a group.
- To be able to design a ritual with a group.
- To understand the concepts in Part1 Chapter 8, 'Shifting levels'.
- To conduct the halfway programme review.

# Session outline

## A: Welcome
## (25 minutes) (primary facilitator)

Bring a welcoming ritual to start the session (10 minutes).
Welcome everyone to the seventh session.
Outline the session programme.
Choose a timekeeper.
Check in.

## B: Sharing on Chapter 8
## (25 minutes) (session facilitator)

Have participants share their thoughts on Part1 Chapter 8, 'Shifting levels'.
Then ask participants to address these questions in pairs:

Which levels do I feel most comfortable with?
Which levels do I feel the least at home with?

Are there any levels which I would remove or add?

Finish with a round of sharing in the whole group.

Feedback for the facilitator.

## C: Continuums
## (30 minutes) (session facilitator)

Process 24.
Break for refreshments (15 minutes)

## D: Mind expander
## (20 minutes) (session facilitator)

Process 21.

## E: Changing energy levels
## (10 minutes) (session facilitator)

Ask participants to share in a round what they have noticed about changing energy levels during parts C and D above.

## F: Halfway review of the training programme
## (30 minutes) (primary facilitator)

Use the soft evaluation model in Part 3 Chapter 4, 'Design frameworks'.

Have participants work in pairs or threes, writing down their responses.

Finish with a group sharing.

## G: Organisation details
## (10 minutes) (primary facilitator)

Homework reminder: read Part 1 Chapter 9, 'Dialogue and storytelling'.

Confirm the facilitators for the next session.

## H: Feedback
## (10 minutes) (primary facilitator)

Feedback for the primary facilitator; see Process 52.

Ask for feedback on the session.

## I: Completion
## (5 minutes) (primary facilitator)

As a group, design and carry out an ending ritual. Have one that reflects the uniqueness of your group.

End of session.

# Session 8: Dialogue and storytelling

## *Purpose of session*

To explore dialogue and storytelling.

# Objectives for session

- To understand the concepts in Part 1 Chapter 9, 'Dialogue and storytelling'.
- To practise dialogue.
- To practise storytelling.

# Session outline

## A: Welcome
## (25 minutes) (primary facilitator)

Bring a welcoming ritual to start the session (10 minutes).

Outline the session programme.

Choose a timekeeper.

Check in or Being with a group, Process 21.

## B: Sharing on Chapter 9
## (25 minutes) (session facilitator)

Have participants share their thoughts on Part 1 Chapter 9, 'Dialogue and storytelling'.

## C: Dialogue
## (40 minutes) (session facilitator)

Use an unstructured round, Process 2, and continue the round for as long as needed to reach depth and meaning. Practise powerful listening (see Mining the gold, Process 26).

Break for refreshments (15 minutes).

## D: Storytelling
## (40 minutes) (session facilitator)

Choose one of the processes in storytelling processes 28–31.

## E: (20 minutes) (session facilitator)

Ask participants to share in a round what they have noticed about dialogue and storytelling during parts C and D above.

## F: Organisation details
## (15 minutes) (primary facilitator)

Homework reminder: read Part 1 Chapter 10, 'Getting to consensus'.
Confirm the facilitators for the next session.

## G: Feedback
## (10 minutes) (primary facilitator)

Feedback for the primary facilitator; see Process 52.
Ask for feedback on the session.

## H: Completion
## (5 minutes) (primary facilitator)

As a group, design and carry out an ending ritual. Have one that reflects the uniqueness of your group. End of session.

# Session 9: Getting to consensus

## *Purpose of session*

To be able to facilitate group decisionmaking.

## *Objectives for session*

- To understand the concepts in Part 1 Chapter 10, 'Getting to consensus'.
- To address 'group think'.
- To use a variety of techniques to enhance consensus.

## *Session outline*

### A: Welcome
### (25 minutes) (primary facilitator)

Welcome everyone to session nine.
Outline the session programme.
Choose a timekeeper.
Check in: have participants complete with their existing buddy, then choose a new buddy who will be rigorous in interrupting their patterns.

### B: Sharing on Chapter 10
### (25 minutes) (session facilitator)

Have someone introduce the chapter and give a summary (10 minutes). Follow with a general discussion.

## C: Getting to agreement and barriers to agreement
## (40 minutes) (session facilitator)

Ask participants to plan an event or outing for the group to be held this week. Remind them that they will need to agree on what is done, the date and time, cost, and where they will meet. Stress that everyone must attend as part of the training. Have two people monitor the barriers to agreement that arise, and write the barriers up on the whiteboard as they occur.

For the last 10 minutes of this section, debrief on the process and how any barriers were dismantled.

## D: Group think
## (15 minutes) (session facilitator)

Brainstorm:
   What is special about this group? (3 minutes).
Next ask participants to choose another group to compare themselves with and brainstorm:
   We are better than (the other) group because ... (3 minutes)
Finish with a round on what the group noticed. (For example, had they already decided they were

better during the first brainstorm? Where is the line between being special and being better?)

Discuss the issues raised in the section of Chapter 10 on group think.

Break for refreshments (15 minutes).

## E: Consensus decisionmaking using non-verbal cues
## (40 minutes) (session facilitator)

Practise using hand signals (see the Zhaba Facilitators Collective hand signs in Appendix B) or coloured cards (see Eco-neighbourhood Consensus Decisionmaking process in Appendix A).

## F: Organisation details
## (5 minutes) (primary facilitator)

Homework reminder: read Part 1 Chapter 11, 'Addressing conflict'.

Confirm the facilitators for the next session.

## G: Feedback
## (10 minutes) (primary facilitator)

Feedback for the primary facilitator; see Process 52.

Ask for feedback on the session.

## H: Completion

**(5 minutes) (primary facilitator)**

As a group, design and carry out an ending ritual. Have one that reflects the uniqueness of your group.
End of session.

# Session 10: Addressing conflict

## Purpose of session

To learn how to address conflict.

## Objectives for session

- To understand the concepts in Part1 Chapter 11, 'Addressing conflict'.
- To be able to recognise sabotaging behaviour.
- To be able to interrupt blaming and scapegoating.
- To practise facilitating different kinds of challenges.

## Session outline

**A: Welcome**
**(25 minutes) (primary facilitator)**

Welcome everyone to the tenth session.
Outline the session programme.
Choose a timekeeper.
Check in.

**B: Debrief**
**(15 minutes) (session facilitator)**

Conduct a debriefing on the ending. Include a variety of individual reflection, pairs, small groups and whole group.

Address the following questions:
What behaviours did I notice?

...Facilitating myself.
...Facilitating one another.
...Facilitating the group.
...Disempowering myself, others and the group.
...Giving advice, blaming, coaching without agreement.

How does my behaviour within the group differ from my behaviour outside the group?

## C: Sharing on Chapter 11
## (20 minutes) (session facilitator)

Have someone introduce the material and give a summary (10 minutes). Then have a round, with each person sharing their reflections on the chapter. Follow with a general discussion.

## D: Sabotage
## (25 minutes) (session facilitator)

Use Process 48, Uncovering sabotage patterns. Have a timekeeper monitor the times.

Have participants work in pairs, taking five minutes each way to coach one another on how they sabotage themselves every day. Stress to participants that they should be intentional. Do not allow any time extension. Do not share in the whole group.

Go straight on to a round in the whole group addressing the question:

How do I sabotage this and other groups?
(We all have our ways and means.)

*Note:* If a person has trouble identifying sabotage patterns, coach them. This will be a breakthrough for you. Be rigorous yet light. Look back to patterns you have noticed in earlier sessions. (Divide 25 minutes by the number of people in the group and set individual time limits.)

Break for refreshments (15 minutes).

## E: Challenges
## (1 hour) (session facilitator)

Have participants move into three subgroups, with each group taking one of these topics:
- Challenges within the group.
- The facilitator challenging the group.
- Challenges to the facilitator.

Ask each group to design processes or roleplays so that the whole group can practise these scenarios. Allow 10 minutes. Encourage rotation of roles so that several people get the opportunity to be in the key roles. Give each subgroup 15 minutes to work with the whole group. Include a five-minute debrief to draw out the learning (45 minutes).

See also Role-plays, Processes 45 and 46 (or 25).

## F: Organisation details
## (5 minutes) (primary facilitator)

Homework reminder: each person to choose a chapter from Part 2 to read and summarise for the next session.

Also read the workshop design process in Part 3 Chapter 4, 'Design frameworks'.

Remind participants to contact their buddies.

Confirm the facilitators for the next session.

## G: Feedback
## (10 minutes) (primary facilitator)

Feedback for the primary facilitator; see Process 52.

Ask for feedback on the session.

## H: Completion
## (5 minutes) (primary facilitator)

The closing ritual.

End of session.

# Session 11: Applications

## *Purpose of session*

To consider aspects of the facilitator at work.

## *Objectives for session*

- To understand the issues a facilitator will face when facilitating groups.
- To design a theme-based session together.

## *Session outline*

### A: Welcome
### (25 minutes) (primary facilitator)

Welcome everyone to the eleventh session.
Outline the session programme.
Choose a timekeeper.
Check in.

### B: Sharing on Part 2
### (60 minutes) (session facilitator)

Each person introduces their chosen chapter and gives a summary. Discuss (10 minutes each, or allocate the time according to your group numbers).
Use energisers as needed.
Break for refreshments (15 minutes).

## C: Workshop design
## (60 minutes) (session facilitator)

Form into two subgroups. Each group will design a one-day workshop.

Refer to the section on workshop design in Part 3 Chapter 4, 'Design frameworks'.

Each subgroup decides on a scenario and develops a written design on a large sheet of paper, clearly outlining the sections and giving processes and times.

Share the designs, and the design process. Give feedback to each group.

## D: Organisation details
## (5 minutes) (primary facilitator)

Homework reminder: read Self-and peer-assessment, Process 35, and confirm the facilitators for the next session.

## E: Feedback
## (10 minutes) (primary facilitator)

Feedback for the primary facilitator; see Process 52.

Ask for feedback on the session.

## F: Completion
## (5 minutes) (primary facilitator)

The closing ritual.
End of session.

# Session 12: Self-and peer-assessment and completion

## *Purpose of the session*

To practise self-and peer-assessment and achieve completion.

## *Objectives for session*

- To experience a self-and peer-assessment process.
- To complete and celebrate the training programme.

## *Session outline*

### A: Welcome
### (15 minutes) (primary facilitator)

Welcome everyone to the twelfth and last session.
Outline the session programme.
Choose a timekeeper.
Check in.

### B: Self-and peer-assessment
### (90 minutes) (session facilitator)

Self-and peer-assessment, Process 35.

Reconsider the effective facilitator criteria developed in Session 5. Add to or change the criteria as needed.

This exercise can be done in groups of four people.

Set time limits for each person's self-and peer-assessment.

Break for refreshments (15 minutes).

## C: Follow-up and action planning session
## (30 minutes) (session facilitator)

The questions below can be addressed in several ways—in pairs, in threes and in a whole group discussion.

What are our key learnings from the programme?

Where do we go from here?

What further training opportunities are there?

Do we want to continue meeting as a self-directed peer group of facilitators?

## D: Completion
## (30 minutes) (primary facilitator)

Final thoughts.
Acknowledgement and affirmations: share these.
Getting complete, Process 39.
Celebrate yourselves together.
The training programme has ended.

# Chapter 3

# processes

## Group processes

The processes in this chapter are grouped by category. Read each process carefully before using it, so that you understand it fully. It helps to describe the process and seek group agreement to use it. If there is opposition, provide an opportunity for people to express this and listen for natural apprehension about new ways of doing things. After concerns have been expressed, respond to these and encourage the group to give the process a try. However, don't force the group to do a process against its will—it won't work without agreement. Processes work best if they are used with a light touch.

In this chapter, we will cover the following processes:

Rounds

Brainstorming and sorting

Group culture

Growing the vision

Relationship deepening

Consensus

Addressing conflict

Being with

Listening skills

Interrupting disempowering conversations

Storytelling processes

Games and energisers

Peer assessment

Clearing processes

Completion processes

A space for the sacred

# Rounds

Rounds are basic techniques for groups. They can be used:

- as a 'check in' at the beginning of a meeting;
- to share emotions and build relationships;
- to explore and develop an issue;
- to identify areas of agreement and difference;
- for debriefing and evaluation;
- for conflict resolution.

The potency of rounds comes from collective sharing. Listening deeply to one another grows understanding and appreciation of self, other, the group and the many and varied ways of being in the world that make up the whole of human experience. It is rather like viewing, turning and polishing a diamond.

The most common use of rounds is as a check-in at the beginning of a meeting. This gives participants the opportunity to presence themselves, find their voice and establish their right to speak. This is also an opportunity to share any important personal news (as considered appropriate).

Rounds are also useful in dialogue and conflict resolution because they will bring out the full range of views and, when everyone listens attentively, help to reveal a way forward. Participants stay in the circle for the whole process and endeavour to create a safe and respectful environment.

As with all exercises and techniques, begin by describing the process and getting group agreement.

# Process 1: Structured rounds (also called Go-rounds)

**PURPOSE:** To enable sharing, thoughtful contribution and full participation.

**MATERIALS:** Chairs set up in a circle. Optional: watch, whiteboard.

**TIME:** Optional. Check how much time is available. Even if not using strict times it is helpful for the facilitator to do the maths mentally: calculate the number of group members multiplied by the time allocated for each person (say 3 minutes each) plus a few minutes for setting up and completing. For example: 10 people x 3 minutes=30 minutes+10 minutes setting up and completing=40 minutes total time.

**PROCESS:** Clearly identify the purpose for the round. Call for a volunteer or ask someone to begin, and nominate the direction the round will go. Group members take turns to speak without interruption and without response or comment. Other group members give their full attention and deep listening to each speaker. The timekeeper (if needed) gives a signal when the allocated time is up. Group members may say 'Pass' or indicate in some other way if they do not wish to contribute.

*Note:* At first you may need to coach the participants not to interrupt or respond (unless this is an agreed part of the group culture). You may also need to gently encourage shy members to speak. If rounds are used more than once, it may be useful to begin with a different person each time.

## VARIATIONS

- If the purpose involves exploring specific issues the facilitator (or participant) may summarise the range of views at the end of the round, including the main points of similarity and difference, then check this with the group. If clarity is needed and not reached after one round, a second round can be held to see if views have changed or developed.

- If the aim is to seek agreement, the facilitator may check out emerging agreements with the group, saying, for example: 'I sense the group agrees on these points..., and needs to clarify these...'

- In an issues-or topic-related round you may want to ask someone to write (or draw) the key words (or ideas) from each participant on a large sheet of paper or whiteboard as the round progresses.

It is also useful to write up the main summary points after the round as part of the summing-up process. To complete the round, agree on and record any follow-up action.

# Process 2: Unstructured rounds (also called Popcorn)

**PURPOSE:** To encourage in-depth contribution and sharing.

**MATERIAL:** Whiteboard (optional).

**TIME:** Variable.

**PROCESS:** Describe the purpose of the round. It is similar to a structured round, except there is no speaking order. People speak when they feel ready or moved to speak. There may be times of silence between speakers. Stay relaxed and present to yourself and the group. Breathe.

Each person 'checks in' or addresses the focus or issue without interruption. There is no time limit or order of speaking. Other group members listen attentively, without responding or commenting. There is only one opportunity to speak (optional).

## VARIATIONS
- See variations for Process 1.
- A second round may be useful (particularly for conflict resolution).

- To complete, draw out the themes and agreements or ask for the participants to help with this. Record any follow-up action.
- For dialogue, continue the rounds for as long as needed to reach depth and meaning. Practise powerful listening (see Mining the gold, Process 26).

# Brainstorming and sorting

## *Process 3: Brainstorming*

**PURPOSE:** To generate a large number of ideas quickly and encourage creativity and flexible thinking.

**MATERIALS:** Whiteboard or large sheet of paper.

**TIME:** Choose a specific time period, say five or 10 minutes.

**PROCESS:** Choose an issue that requires development. Request participants to say whatever idea comes into their head, without censorship and as fast as possible. Write all ideas on the whiteboard.

It may be necessary to have two people writing at the same time to catch all the thoughts. Notice how people's thinking is sparked by others' comments and encourage this. Make sure people do not evaluate or comment on each other's suggestions; remind them about this if necessary. If the response is sluggish, get people to stand up or even hop on one foot.

## VARIATIONS

- Have group members go to the whiteboard to write up their own ideas. Although this can appear chaotic, it keeps the energy moving and builds ownership in the group.
- 'Solution-storming': brainstorm solutions to a problem or conflict.

# Process 4: Priority-setting

**PURPOSE:** To identify priorities after a brainstorm or other similar exercise.

**MATERIALS:** Brainstorm sheets or lists of previously generated alternatives on a whiteboard or sheet of paper.

**TIME:** 10 minutes.

**PROCESS:** Using marks (such as ticks or crosses), invite participants to choose two preferred ideas or alternatives from the brainstorm or list and write them down individually on a piece of paper. (This minimises the influence of others.) Next ask people to go to the board and put a mark beside their choices. Add up the marks beside each choice and prioritise accordingly. This priority list can be used as a shortlist for further research and development.

### Using Post-its

Give out Post-its and ask people to write each of their preferences on a separate Post-it. Two preferences usually works well. Collect the Post-its and attach them to the board close to the original choice. Add up the Post-its beside each choice and re-prioritise the list accordingly. This priority list can be used as a shortlist for further research and development.

### Electronic

Electronic tools can also be used to collect preferences. This can include electronic polling devices or Internet-based tools.

# Process 5: Criteria-setting

**PURPOSE:** To produce a list of key criteria.

**MATERIALS:** Whiteboard and whiteboard pens; or flipchart and markers.

**TIME:** 35–50 minutes.

### PROCESS

*Step 1* Have the group discuss the criteria they want to use in meeting the group or project purpose. Record the contributions on a flipchart or whiteboard. Do not exclude any contributions at this stage.

*Step 2* Invite participants to mark their most important criteria. Suggest each person choose two or three only. People put their marks (such as ticks or crosses) on the flipchart or whiteboard next to their choices.

*Step 3* Rub out any criteria that have no marks beside them.

*Step 4* Discuss any duplication and reduce the list further. See if you can reduce the list to five or fewer criteria. (Three to five is a manageable number against which to measure the achievement of a purpose.)

# Group purpose

Every group needs a purpose. Introduce the idea of aligning on a group purpose that is short (12 words or fewer), specific (one main idea) and inspiring. The purpose will set a direction and identify 'what' will be accomplished as distinct from the 'how' (this will be the group culture). The purpose is likely to begin with 'To...'. Here are two ways of developing a group purpose.

# *Process 6: Finding the group purpose*

**PURPOSE:** To align on a group purpose.

**MATERIALS:** Whiteboard.

**TIME:** 30–40 minutes.

**PROCESS**

*Step 1 (3 minutes)*

Introduce the idea of aligning on a group purpose that is specific, short and inspiring.

*Step 2 (5 minutes)*

In groups of three to four find a sentence or phrase, symbol, drawing, mindmap or combination that expresses the purpose of the group. As each group finds their purpose, they write it up on the whiteboard.

*Step 3 (5–15 minutes)*

In the whole group, invite everyone to allow their thinking to extend beyond any attachment to their own ideas. This is about working together to achieve an inspiring outcome without any sense of compromise.

Create a purpose using the ideas presented as a springboard. It may be that one of those presented, or a combination, is the one.

If no agreement occurs, there may be a new purpose that emerges out of the common elements, or someone may have a brainwave.

*Step 4 (5 minutes)*

Write up the agreed purpose. Check for alignment—if this is present people will be 'lit up' and ready for action.

Celebrate reaching an aligned group purpose.

*Step 5 (optional)*

If no aligned purpose is forthcoming have a session on sharing withholds (see Process 36); it may be that people have underlying concerns or there may not be a clear purpose for the group.

# Process 7: Developing the purpose

**PURPOSE:** To develop and align on a group purpose.

**MATERIALS:** Whiteboard, pens, paper.

**TIME:** 60 minutes (variable).

**PROCESS**

*Step 1* Have the group divide into subgroups of about three or four, with the instruction: 'In your small group start to uncover the group's purpose.'

*Step 2* After the groups have been working for a few minutes, ask one or two of the members to swap to another group. This keeps cross-fertilisation happening and stops groups getting into 'group think'. Swap two or three times. Then merge small groups together into bigger subgroups to align on a purpose until the large group is back together. During this process help the groups distinguish purpose statements from culture statements. Also suggest that the group intention is held by the group purpose, so it is worth taking on something that is important and inspiring to them.

*Step 3* Bring the groups back together and have them put the work they have been doing face down in the group.

Give the instruction: 'Someone in the group will now recognise that they know what the purpose is. If you notice it is you, please get up and write it on the board. Don't worry too much, because we will all immediately know if that's "it", "not it" or "sort of it".' As people get up and write the purpose on the board, discussion will emerge as to whether this is the purpose, and if not, why not. This needs to be facilitated so it results in greater alignment. Do not get into the content at all.

*Step 4* At some point you will most likely notice that people are generating more ideas without truly appreciating what has already been expressed. Intervention about this will generate a shift; you may invite people to listen more deeply to each other, or to listen for where they are in alignment with what is being said rather than where they are different.

*Step 5* As the group has almost reached alignment, people may notice that alignment is a choice. It is helpful for the leader to introduce the concept of 'Are you really aligned?' as distinct from 'Are you giving in?' This will result in a purpose to which group members are genuinely aligned.

# Group culture

Group culture answers the question: 'How are we going to work together?' or 'How are we going to be together?' Sometimes group culture is known as guidelines, ground rules, group agreement or the group charter.

# Process 8: Developing the group culture

**PURPOSE:** To develop a group culture.

**MATERIALS:** Flipchart, pens, paints (optional).

**TIME:** 30–40 minutes.

**PROCESS:** If you are following on from developing a purpose, it is likely that some culture statements emerged in the purpose session.

*Step 1* Ask people to give some thought to what is most important to them to participate fully in the group. They may like to discuss their thoughts in pairs for a few minutes. If so, give a timeframe of three minutes.

*Step 2* Ask people to write down their contributions on the flipchart or whiteboard. If their wording or meaning is the same as someone else, they can just tick the existing statement.

*Step 3* Check for clarification and alignment with the statements that have been expressed. Ask if there is anything that is really important that is not expressed, and add it. Remember, less is more, and it is easier to remember five culture statements than 10.

*Step 4* The culture is a living document. It can be added to or changed. Ask for a volunteer to create a drawing or painting of the group culture, including the words. Place it prominently in the room so that it can be referred to easily and often.

*Step 5* Have the group members start to *be* the culture and also help monitor it.

# Growing the vision

## *Process 9: Speaking your vision*

**PURPOSE:** To develop powerful speaking.

**MATERIALS:** None.

**TIME:** 40 minutes total (for 10 people):
5 minutes introduction, including a short
 demonstration;
10 minutes for coaching in pairs (5 minutes x 2);
20 minutes (2 minutes each) in the whole group;
5 minutes debrief.

## PROCESS

In pairs; A=speaker, and B=coach. After 2, swap roles.

A speaks their vision on a theme of their choice. B listens and coaches A:

1. To remove all limiting/qualifying words. For example:

'I would quite like to see...'
'Fairly important...'
'I suppose that...'
'I might be able to do it...'
'It would be great if...'
'I would love that but...'
'If only...'

The coaching needs to be direct: 'Say that again without the "but".'

2. To enlarge the picture and speak expressively. For example:

'Can you say that more expansively?'
'Can you show your enthusiasm with your face and tone of voice?'
'Can you describe that more fully?'
'Can you say that in a way that lights you up?'

Come back to the whole group. Each person now speaks their vision to the whole group, expressively and without qualification, and uninterrupted.

## VISION FOCUS

Suggestions for vision focus:

- My ideal living environment.
- World peace.
- Healing the planet.
- The perfect team to be part of.
- My children's future.
- My brilliant career.
- My work for the world.

## VARIATIONS

- Work in threes with a coach and a listener—5 minutes each.
- Work in twos but allow 8–10 minutes for each person.
- Work in the whole group; the facilitator coaches the participants until the vision is powerful.

# Process 10: Building the group vision

**PURPOSE:** To develop a common vision.

**MATERIALS:** Large sheets of paper, markers.

**TIME:** Variable, say 60 minutes.

**PROCESS:** Invite people to sit or stand at one end of the room and project their thoughts forward in time to the successful realisation of their dreams for the group.

Ask people to move forward and stand in a place in the room that represents a five-, 10-or 20-year gap from where they are currently standing. Once they have moved, interview different people, asking them to describe what the future they have stepped into is like.

As different people speak have someone writing down what is said. More people will stand together around some ideas, and fewer around others. As people speak a collective sense of vision for the future will emerge, with highly significant aspects and less significant aspects.

Next ask the group to develop an inspiring sentence that encapsulates the essence of the vision. Keep this short and punchy (12 words or fewer, so that everyone can remember it easily). This sentence is the vision of the group. Refer back to it often and display it in prominent places so the group is constantly reminded of it.

# Relationship-deepening

## Process 11: My precious possession

**PURPOSE:** To deepen group relationships through sharing.

**MATERIALS:** Participants' precious possessions (or a representation such as a drawing or photo).

**TIME:** Drawing time (say 10 minutes) plus five minutes per group member.

**PROCESS:** Ask participants to bring an item of personal value to the group. Participants share about their precious possession in a structured round. Other members listen attentively without speaking. Sharing about things that we value is an effective way of moving the group forward through deepening relationships.

After the sharing round, allow time for integration and appreciation. Remember to thank people for the gift of sharing themselves.

# Process 12: Affirmations and acknowledgements

**PURPOSE:** Giving and accepting acknowledgement.

**TIME:** 10 minutes.

**PROCESS:** Have participants pair up and share for 2 minutes each way what they appreciate about each other. After each acknowledgement the listener says 'Thank you', and makes no other comment. Have the participants repeat the process in different pairs. It can be helpful if the first pair know each another already.

# Consensus

Here is a way of making decisions that encourages people to be proactive and positive. See also Part 1 Chapter 10, 'Getting to consensus', where there are two other processes.

## Process 13: Proactive consensus

**PURPOSE:** To develop consensus.

**MATERIALS:** Paper, pens or whiteboard.

**TIME:** Variable.

**PROCESS:** This process encourages participants to remain proactive and keep suggesting possible solutions rather than remaining attached to a particular outcome.

*Step 1* Clarify the purpose and need for the decision.

*Step 2* Identify the issues—use a Popcorn round (Process 2) or brainstorm (Process 3)

*Step 3* Request proposals from the group. All proposals are written up without alteration or debate.

*Step 4* Provide an opportunity for each person to speak to their preference or suggest modifications. Encourage listeners to centre themselves, breathe, and listen deeply to the words and the emotions expressed. Encourage speakers to speak

344

for their preference rather than against someone else's.

*Step 5* Ask each group member to indicate the wording that best reflects their view. Mark each preference. Write up modifications to each proposal using differently coloured pens. After everyone has spoken, remove or cross out proposals that have no support.

Check for agreement. There may be part agreement at this stage. Mark the agreement by circling or underlining the agreed words. Rub off or cross out proposals and modifications that are not now supported.

*Step 6* If agreement has not been reached, request new proposals or modifications that capture the wisdom of the group and meet with general agreement. Record these. Check for agreement.

*Step 7* If a decision is being held up by disagreement from one or two people, ask the dissenters to propose a solution. (This helps them to remain proactive.) Also, check with them to see if they are directly affected by the outcome. If not, see if they will allow the decision to be made anyway.

*Step 8* When agreement has been reached, check that everyone is actively in agreement. A round in which each person says 'Yes' or 'No' is useful for this.

Do not assume silence means assent.

*Step 9* If agreement is not reached encourage the people who feel most strongly to meet together separately and come back to the whole group with an agreed proposal.

# Process 14: Listening for agreement

**PURPOSE:** To listen for agreement.

**TIME:** Variable.

## PROCESS

*Step 1* During rounds, or a free-flowing discussion, the facilitator listens for agreement and encourages group members to do the same. As rounds continue, agreement may begin to emerge. Listen for this. There will be moments when agreement happens, when everyone unconsciously agrees on a solution.

Someone will express their own view, which will also be the group agreement, as yet unspoken. This is the moment to listen for. Everyone will relax slightly, like a group 'Aha—yes, that's it.' Agreement has occurred. It can be 'heard' by a carefully listening facilitator. Often it is like a bell being struck. This is the time for the facilitator or group member to intervene. Say straight away:

'I think we have agreement. Let's check it out.'

*Step 2* Say what you hear as the agreement and ask the group for confirmation. If the group does not confirm the agreement, continue the round or discussion.

These moments are important—if not captured, the group may move past agreement and go off on a tangent.

Sometimes a partial agreement can be captured.

'I think we all agree on X. Can we confirm this? Now let's continue with Y.' Using this technique, a number of partial agreements can be established which together lead to a group decision.

# Process 15: Consensus decisionmaking using criteria

**PURPOSE:** To reach consensus using criteria.

**MATERIALS:** Whiteboard and/or flipchart.

**TIME:** Variable.

**PROCESS**

*Step 1* Ask the group to generate a list of criteria that are important to them and which underpin the decision outcomes they want. Do not introduce time limits or a limit to the number of criteria.

*Step 2* Negotiate over criteria to ensure alignment. Normally agreement can be reached through people being more specific about their criteria.

*Step 3* Ask the group to suggest possible options which they believe meet the criteria. Do not limit the number of options or discuss whether or not they meet the criteria.

*Step 4* Ask people to speak to their option and how it meets the criteria.

*Step 5* Have people reconsider their preference and indicate it with a mark. Ask people to speak to their option and how it meets

*Step 6* Delete any options that are not chosen. Discuss options that are chosen. Ask if any of the options would be unacceptable to anyone because they do not meet the criteria. Mark these. Review the criteria to see if there are any unexpressed criteria, and if so, add them to the list of criteria.

*Step 7* Repeat steps 3–6 until agreement is reached.

# Addressing conflict

People in conflict need to be held, heard and healed—the 3 H's. The holding refers to energetic holding by a group of people who create a safe space in which to address the conflict and stay until the process is complete. Hearing refers to deep listening. Healing most often comes from the first two and happens from within each person as they are held and heard.

# *Process 16: Conflict resolution using rounds*

**PURPOSE:** To provide a clear framework and safe environment to work through conflict.

**MATERIALS:** Whiteboard or large sheets of paper.

**TIME:** Most conflict-resolution processes take time. Allow between one and two hours depending on the size of the group. The minimum time for three rounds would be 6 minutes per person, plus 15 minutes.

**PROCESS:** Structured rounds are particularly effective for working through conflict as they provide a clear framework and a safe place for expressing strong feelings. In this process each person speaks in turn, uninterrupted, for as long as they need. Then the next person speaks, and so on around the whole circle. All present are encouraged to listen respectfully and actively. This round can continue for one or two whole circuits of the circle, or for as long as is needed. So far we have found that groups rarely need to go round the circle more than twice before the solution has been worked out or the conflict is seen as lacking substance.

What happens during this whole process is that the *group* expresses its hurt or upset, clarifies the issues, and finds a solution—it is the *group* working through the conflict. The job of the facilitator is to empower the group by providing a structure for the group process.

*Step 1* Encourage people to express their feelings and clarify the issue in the first round.

*Step 2* Have a second and possibly third round to suggest solutions. Discourage people from suggesting solutions before feelings have been expressed and really heard—this is often all that is needed. Quick-fix solutions can have the effect of ignoring feelings, and upset people will remain upset even though the solution is agreed.

In the second and third rounds, encourage people to develop their thinking each time, to build on each other's thoughts and not get stuck in a fixed place. Contribution by non-triggered people is important as they tend to see the conflict more objectively.

*Note:* Remember the facilitator does not need to have a solution. Trust the group to work the issues through.

*Step 3* Write up the issues and suggested solutions as they are clarified.

*Step 4* When different solutions have been listed have a round where people state their preferences.

## VARIATIONS
- Unstructured rounds can be used in a similar way.
- If the group is large—say, more than 30—the participants who feel personally involved in the conflict are invited to come into a central seated circle. The others stand behind them and provide active and powerful listening. A listener may join the seated circle if they feel a strong need to contribute, and people can leave the circle if they are fully resolved and have no more to contribute.

# *Process 17: Fishing for agreement*

**PURPOSE:** To resolve conflict where participants seem to be stuck in rigid positions.

**TIME:** 30 minutes (variable).

**PROCESS**

*Step 1* Have the participants who are key to the conflict sit facing each other in a small circle, with the others seated in a large circle around them. This is called creating a fishbowl.

*Step 2* Have someone restate the purpose and values of the group, the results promised and the time constraints. This will help ground the exercise in reality.

*Step 3* Encourage the key players to speak directly to each other. Have them speak one at a time, in such a way as to enrol the others in their own perspective. Have a time limit of, say, five minutes each. Allow a further two minutes per person for questions of clarification—not debate—from other key players.

*Step 4* Ask the key players to swap chairs (or move one chair to the right if there are more than two viewpoints) and speak from the perspective of the person who was sitting in their chair previously. Encourage them to really get into role and argue passionately for the other's view.

*Step 5* Ask the key players if anything has shifted. 'What have you seen?'

'Has your view changed and can you suggest a solution?'

Continue until each of the key players has spoken from every viewpoint.

*Step 6* If there is still no solution, ask the outer circle to make suggestions and proposals.

*Step 7* If no solution emerges ask the key players to meet as a subgroup after the meeting and come up with a proposal for the whole group to consider at its next meeting. The next process may also help.

# *Process 18: Bottom-lining*

**PURPOSE:** To resolve conflict that acknowledges and honours people's limits.

**TIME:** 30 minutes (variable).

**PROCESS**

*Step 1* After a round, discussion or fishbowl, when a solution has not yet been reached, ask the key players to nominate an unaligned partner from the group—preferably one with facilitation skills. Have them meet the partner, who will explore the key player's bottom-line—that is, find out what is not negotiable in the issue as distinct from a preference or want that is not essential.

*Step 2* Have the unaligned partners meet and develop a solution that honours the bottom-lines.

*Step 3* The partners then check the solution with the key players. Ask the key players:

'Can you accept this solution?'

'Can you agree with it although you are not getting everything you want?'

*Step 4* Whether a solution has been found or not, bring the findings back to the whole group. The facilitator may like to ask the question:

'What is the cost of reaching—or not reaching—agreement, to the project and the group?'

# Process 19: Proposing and counter-proposing

**PURPOSE:** To resolve conflict by concentrating on what can be done rather than what can't.

**TIME:** 30 minutes.

**PROCESS**

*Step 1* During rounds or discussion ask the key players in the conflict, and others in the group, to keep proposing and counter-proposing solutions—building on or sparking off one another—until a solution comes up that people generally like. It will have a 'ring' to it. Encourage people to be creative and to step outside their normal thinking patterns.

*Step 2* Note this solution down for fine-tuning later. Encourage the group—particularly the key players—to continue proposing solutions and not get stuck in a particular position.

# Being with

## *Process 20: Being with another*

**PURPOSE:** To experience being fully present to yourself and another person.

**TIME:** 20 minutes.

## PROCESS

*Step 1* In pairs, sit facing one another and bring all your available attention to being with the other person. Take up soft eye-contact (slightly unfocused, not staring) if culturally appropriate.

Notice your thoughts, feelings and body sensations without attachment to them.

Notice any embarrassment and laughter and let that pass.

Notice your connection with your chair and the earth. Note them and let them go.

At the end of 3 minutes, share your experience with the other person in your pair.

*Step 2* Repeat with different pairs, this time for 5 minutes.

*Step 3* Debrief in the whole group.

## VARIATIONS
- Increase the time with each pair—up to 40 minutes.
- Practise this exercise by yourself, looking into a mirror.

354

- Practise this exercise with other forms such as trees, stones and the sea.
- Practise this exercise without direct eye contact
- Practise this exercise to allow your breathing to synchronise.

## Process 21: Being with a group

**PURPOSE:** To experience being fully present to yourself and the other members of the group.

**TIME:** 5 minutes.

**PROCESS:** The group stands or sits in a circle, facing one another. If sitting, uncross your arms or legs. Become aware of your breathing. Centre your attention in your belly and imagine you are like a tree, with a root system deep within the ground and branches reaching towards the sky.

Be aware of your physical body, your energy and the space around you. Now allow yourself to also become aware of the other group members. Focus your attention on each group member in turn. Observe their physical body, their energy and their relationship to the space around them. Move your attention around the group. Be with each group member in turn for a short period (say 10 seconds). Do not seek out eye contact or avoid it either. Do not linger long with any one person.

Keep your attention moving so that you become present to everyone in the group. Continue to pay attention to your breathing. Have it be relaxed and deep. Become aware of the group as a whole. Be with the group and each person in it. Include yourself in this. Bring the purpose and the vision of the group to mind. Allow any feelings and thoughts to come and go. Stay with being with the group.

The exercise will end naturally or can be ended by the facilitator, who will thank the group.

**VARIATION**
- Do this exercise while holding hands, left-hand palm up, right-hand palm down. Be present to the energy in the group and between your hands.
- Do this exercise while standing with arms around each other's shoulders (if appropriate).
- Immediately after this exercise, while in the same positions, chant or sing together.
- Do this exercise with your eyes closed (imagine or sense each person rather than looking at them).
- This exercise can also be done by any individual group member at any time.

# Valuing difference

## Process 22: My world, your world

**PURPOSE:** To illustrate our different worlds through a visual display (for two or more people).

**MATERIALS:** A large sheet of paper (such as newsprint) each, and an assortment of coloured pens.

**TIME:** 50 minutes.

**PROCESS**

*Step 1* Take a sheet of paper each. Individually and without conversation divide it into a number of sections, one for each category of your own choice. You may like to work in different rooms.

Suggestions for categories: work, home, relationships, physical, emotional, mental, spiritual, play, recreation, the world, the universe, making a difference, other beings, garden, environment, creativity, wellbeing, training and development, politics.

Choose the six categories that have the most interest for you.

In each section on the sheet write the name of the category, then your responses to the following questions.

In this category:

- What are the most important things to you?
- What are your hopes and fears?
- What do you want more of and less of?
- What are your areas of development?
- What is one action you intend to take in the next week?

You may like to use particular colours, shapes, symbols or words that have meaning for you. Work/play through each in turn. After you have completed all the categories you may want to mark some connections between them, or other insights.

*Step 2* Come back together when you are finished, or at a prearranged time (say after 30 minutes) and share your 'worlds' one at a time. Go into detail. Allow others to ask for clarification on your picture. Avoid assessment and judgement about one another's worlds. Accept them as a display of who each person is.

When this process is completed compare your pictures for differences and similarities. If done as a group exercise you may like to pin them up on a wall. Share your perceptions and insights.

Thank one another for revealing your worlds.

# Process 23: Mind expander

**PURPOSE:** To share and appreciate difference and expand the mind.

**TIME:** Up to 30 minutes.

**PROCESS:** Invite participants to sit comfortably and relax their breathing. Suggest that they allow their minds to stretch 'sideways'. Invite them to respond verbally to each of the following questions in their own time. Allow several minutes for each question. Suggested questions are:
- What is the colour of soft?
- What is the sound of fur?
- What is the feel of music?
- What is the smell of blue?
- What is the taste of happiness?

- What does warm sound like?

Have fun making up your own questions. After the exercise, ask the question:

'Is there anything you'd like to share about the exercise?

# Process 24: Continuums

**PURPOSE:** To physically show the range of feelings or responses on any topic and open it up for discussion.

**TIME:** From 15 to 30 minutes.

**PROCESS:** Define a curved line in the room, with one end being an extremely positive feeling and the other being an extremely negative feeling. Ask people to place themselves along the continuum according to how they feel about the topic.

Examples of the topic might be:
- How well you feel you are supported in your work.
- How well you feel you are listened to in the group.

Invite people to share with someone near them on the continuum, then in the whole group.

**VARIATION**
- To explore complex issues ask the first question and have people place themselves on a continuum in a straight line on one side of the room. Then ask a second, related question and have partici-

pants move perpendicularly to the original line; this will result in people placing themselves in relation to an X and Y axis. Follow with discussion about the placings.

# Process 25: Role-plays

**PURPOSE:** To try out different behaviours in a safe environment where assistance and feedback are available.

**TIME:** Variable.

**PROCESS**

*Step 1* When a situation occurs where a different behaviour may be useful a role-play can be suggested. Ask the person:

> 'Would you like to try out some different ways of responding in that situation? Are you willing to do a role-play?'

If they are willing to proceed, invite the person to move to a new place (say, in front of the group) and sit/stand alongside them.

*Step 2* Check the purpose of the person doing the role-play.

> 'What do you want to accomplish out of this situation?'

The person (primary player) responds.

*Step 3* Have the primary player briefly describe the situation and the people who are part of it. Allow no more than 2 minutes.

*Step 4* The primary player chooses people to take the other roles, and where they will sit or stand. They move to each of these positions and model each person's part.

'Sit how that person sits and say what that person says.'

*Step 5* After this briefing the primary player returns to their role-play position and chooses who starts and exactly what they say. The other players respond within the roles described.

*Step 6* If the primary player gets stuck, the facilitator can:

- invite feedback from the group;
- invite the primary player to swap places with a member of the group not involved in the role-play, and observe the situation being acted out in front of them;
- invite the primary player to take on a coach from the observers and have them stand/sit alongside them and make suggestions.

It is best to keep the role-players in their roles once the role-play is set up, as the role-play will change if the roles are changed. If the role-play participants want to give feedback to the primary player, ask them to do it from their role in the role-play, speaking the perspective of the person they are playing.

*Step 7* The primary player practises one or more different ways of handling the situation until they find one that feels 'right'.

*Step 8* It can be useful to have some sharing and reflection from the group. Avoid letting the group get into evaluating the primary player or giving feedback.

*Step 9* Debrief from the roles.

All players must derole, i.e. separate themselves from the role they were playing.

'I am not like ... I am ... and I...' (Outline differences.)

Make sure participants are deroled before you continue. If unsure, get them to describe the room or add up numbers in their head. This will help them to shift their attention.

# Listening skills

## *Process 26: Mining the gold*

**PURPOSE:** To develop listening skills in distinguishing the 'gold' in another's speaking.

**TIME:** 50 minutes.
8 minutes for each focus (4 minutes x 2 people).
3 minutes introduction and 10 minutes sharing in the whole
group at the end of the exercise. The facilitator will act as timekeeper.

**PROCESS:** Working in pairs, choose an A and a B, where A is the listener and B the speaker. B speaks for 2 minutes on any topic, while A listens for the concerns of B (spoken or in the background). B should not speak about their concerns; rather they should just talk randomly about the topic.

> A then reflects back to B the concerns they 'heard' for 1 minute.
> B listens for recognition of being really heard.
> B gives feedback on how well they were heard for 1 minute:
> 'Yes, you got my concerns.'
> 'Yes, that rang true.'
> 'You recognised concerns that were unspoken or that I was unclear about.'
> 'I felt really heard.'
> 'You didn't hear my concerns.'
> 'I didn't feel listened to.'
> 'You put in some concerns that don't ring true (maybe your own).'
> Swap roles and repeat.

## Listening focus for four sections
1. Concerns of the speaker.
2. Commitments of the speaker.
3. Contribution of the speaker.
4. Magnificence of the speaker.

## Possible topics for speaker
Any topic of interest to the speaker will work equally well. If speakers are stuck for a speaking focus encourage them to choose a topic that they have energy for. Give examples such as:
• a work project;

- family;
- a relationship;
- a hobby;
- starting the day;
- favourite weekend activities;
- work problems;
- a political issue.
  Complete the exercise with sharing in the whole group.

*VARIATION*
- Change partners for each listening focus.
- Change the listening focus when pairs swap roles. This will halve the time of the exercise.

# Interrupting disempowering conversations

## *Process 27: Empowering interpretations*

**PURPOSE:** To invent an empowering interpretation of a problem or conflict.

This exercise builds on the skills developed in the two previous processes.

**TIME:** 35 minutes. 10 minutes x 2 people, plus 5 minutes introduction and 10 minutes sharing in the whole group at the end.

364

**PROCESS:** In pairs, A speaks about a problem, area of concern or conflict he or she is currently involved with (3 minutes). B listens for the concerns, commitment, contribution and vision of the speaker. B then feeds back what he or she heard through his or her powerful listening (3 minutes). A now invents a new and empowering interpretation of the problem, building on the feedback from the listener. B can also add coaching at this point (3 minutes). The pair finishes by debriefing (1 minute).

Swap roles and repeat.

Bring the whole group back together and invite one or two people to share their new interpretations.

## VARIATION

- As part of the introduction the facilitator works with a participant in front of the group to demonstrate the process. Allow an additional 5 minutes.

# Storytelling processes

## Process 28: The talking stick[1]

The talking stick is a tool that helps to create a sacred space for exchanging ideas. The tradition is to carve or decorate a special piece of wood that becomes a ritual object for the group. The stick is passed around the circle. Holding the stick confers on a person the authority to be heard; it is time to speak their truth and have it listened to without being interrupted.

**PURPOSE:** To speak the unspoken.

**TIME:** 5–10 minutes each.

**PROCESS:** In a circle, the first person takes the speaking stick and speaks.

Three guidelines for speaking are:
- Speak briefly.
- Speak about yourself.
- Speak from the heart.

While the person is speaking others are silent and listen. When the first person finishes, they pass the stick to the next person, and so on around the circle.

If you have remarks you feel you can't contain and you don't have the stick in hand, you contain them anyway.

If you have nothing to say, or if it has been already spoken, just pass the stick to the next person.

### VARIATION
- When they finish speaking each speaker returns the speaking stick to the centre of the circle. Whoever is ready to speak next will step forth and claim it.

## Process 29: Exploring the group story

This process explores the story of a group (its birth, its milestones, context and events, the key players and challenges faced). It can reveal what is available next and provides a blueprint for further action.

**PURPOSE:** To explore the group story.

**MATERIALS:** Flip charts and markers, paints, pastels and crayons.

**TIME:** 30–45 minutes.

## PROCESS
*The beginning of the story*

Invite the participants to describe the beginning of the group. Describe the birth of the group, its characters and the setting for the story.

What were the first things that happened?
Who were the initiators?
What was their vision?
What did they do?

*The middle of the story*

Invite the participants to introduce the current opportunities or challenges facing the group. Ask:

Who are the key characters?
What is happening now?
How does the present embody the vision?
What are the paths we could take now?

*The end of the story*

Invite the participants to speak as if they are in happily ever after and the story is ending. Ask:

What happened?
How did you get to a positive outcome?
What were the first steps?
What was let go?
How is the vision fulfilled?

## VARIATION

- Create a timeline of the events and people from the beginning to the end. Then extend it further, both before and after the beginning and the end of the group.
- Use graphic facilitation (drawing) to illustrate the group's story.

# Process 30: Once upon a time

This story process is a light approach to describe a group's story in a simple and non-threatening way.

**PURPOSE:** To describe the group story.

**MATERIALS:** Flip chart and markers.

**TIME:** 20–30 minutes.

**PROCESS:** The facilitator begins a structured round (or Go-round) of story with the group by asking the first person *'Once upon a time...?'*

The first person then adds an event or people at the birth of the group or its vision. A scribe takes down the responses on a flip chart.

The facilitator asks the next person *'and every day...?'*

The second participant fills in one thing or event that also occurred. The third person is asked *'and then every day...?'* and so on until the group runs out of events and issues.

The facilitator then asks *'Until one day...?'*

The group then describes their current problem, opportunity or challenge.

The facilitator then asks the group *'Because of that...'*

The group then describes the impact of the change or challenge.

The facilitator then asks the group *'Until finally...'*

The group then describes possibilities for action, alternative options and steps to take.

Finally the facilitator asks, *'And the moral of the story is?'*

This provides the following information for the group:

> *Once upon a time ...* History and context of the group
>
> *Every day ...* Description of problems and issues

*Until one day ...* Catalyst for change/movement
*Because of that ...* Impact that the
  change/movement creates
*Until finally ...* Steps to be taken/goal
*And the moral of the story is ...* Group learning.

# Process 31: Exploring the group context

Exploring the group context helps uncover the wider environmemt within which the group is operating and the influences that impact on the group.

**PURPOSE:** To explore the wider context of the group.

**MATERIALS:** Flip charts and markers, paints, pastels and crayons.

**TIME:** 45 minutes to 1 hour.

**PROCESS:** Ask people to explore the group context using the 'context awareness' diagram (see Part 2 Chapter 4) as a prompt.

Invite participants to use markers, paints, pastels and crayons, and to work in pairs or individually.

Bring the group back together to present what they have recorded.

Look for the common stories, see if patterns emerge and where the stories are different. Ask questions such as:

What does the group notice?
What does the group want to change in their story?
What are the opportunities to develop more potency?
What needs to happen next?

# Games and energisers

## *Process 32: Quick games and energisers*

Here are a variety of exercises to try:
- Have the group stand up and stretch.
- Do star jumps.
- Throw a ball round the group or throw two or three balls around the group at once.
- Cross-body touching: elbow to opposite knee, 20 times, fast.
- Rapid tapping with three fingers on the breast-bone.
- Tap head and rub stomach simultaneously, then swap movements.
- In pairs, one person moves forward while the other taps them with the fingertips—from the top

of their head down their back, buttocks and legs. Then swap over.

## Process 33: Touch blue

Everyone sits on a chair in a circle, except one person who stands in the middle. The person in the middle calls something like *'Everyone who has something blue on'*, and all those with blue have to move to another chair. While they are all moving, the person in the middle needs to try to find a chair too. The person left without a seat is the new caller. The person in the middle may only describe something that is true for them too.

*Note:* this game is fast and potentially hazardous. Stress the importance of taking care of one another.

## Process 34: Wizards, gnomes and giants

**PURPOSE:** A fun game with lots of hilarity.

**MATERIALS:** Requires some space in which to walk/run.

**TIME:** 5–15 minutes.

**PROCESS:** This is a version of the game 'Paper, scissors, rock'. Form two teams facing each other. For each action the teams will first need to form a huddle and choose what to be from the following three characters:

*Wizards*—who stretch their hands out in front, wiggle their fingers and make a whooooooo sound.

*Giants*—who put their hands above their heads, jump up and down and make a low ho-ho-ho sound.

*Gnomes*—who get down close to the ground with their hands by their ears and make a high ning-ning-ning sound.

Tell the participants that wizards win over giants, giants win over gnomes and gnomes win over wizards.

Teams line up facing each other, about 2 metres apart, with each having a 'safe' zone behind, say, the wall. The facilitator starts each action off by saying: 'One, two, three, go.' Each team then acts out its chosen character and the winners chase the other team to 'tag' them before they reach the safety zone. Anyone tagged before reaching the safety zone joins the winning team. If teams both choose the same character, nothing happens (except hilarity).

# Peer assessment

## *Process 35: Self-and peer-assessment*

**PURPOSE:** To receive feedback from peers.

**TIME:** 10 minutes to prepare and 15 minutes per person.

**PROCESS:** This is a group process for self-and peer-assessment. It is for use by an individual or individuals wanting feedback for their own learning, or as part of a more formal performance review. It can also be used for a review of a team project.

*Step 1* Individual(s) wanting feedback develop criteria for this—what they want feedback about. Keep the criteria simple and concise—no more than five or six key areas. Take 10 minutes for each person to assess themselves against the criteria.

*Step 2* A group meeting is set up—small groups of four or five are best. Choose a person to act as a facilitator/timekeeper, someone to record the comments of the peers (revolve these roles each round) and someone to be 'IT'. All feedback needs to be considered, but do not get attached to the feedback. It will include non-relevant comments and projections.

*Step 3* The person who is IT shares their self-assessment with the group (4 minutes).

*Step 4* The individuals in the group then share their constructive feedback with the person who is IT. This can include devil's advocate, areas for growth and development, niggles and concerns (4 minutes).

*Step 5* The individuals in the group then share their positive feedback with the person who is IT (4 minutes).

*Step 6* The person who is IT reviews their self-assessment in light of the feedback they have received (2 minutes).

*Step 7* Rotate roles.

# Clearing processes

Clearing processes are about letting go of blocks, withheld communications and patterned behaviour that get in the way of our being fully present both to ourselves and to others. The advantage of clearing processes is that they provide a space for rich, authentic relating and the presencing of love and cooperation. Clearing processes require commitment and the courage to break through our comfort zone and our own ideas about others and ourselves. They seem scary, take time, and can't be hurried, although facilitation can help to quicken the pace.

# Indications for a clearing session

Indications that a clearing session is needed could be one or more of the following:

- a recurring feeling of discomfort with someone or the group;
- a reluctance to participate fully in the relationship/group;

- avoiding eye contact with someone (or a number of people);
- not having much fun together;
- low energy;
- often feeling irritable with someone (or a number of people);
- a certainty that you are right about something and someone else is wrong;
- a feeling of resignation or hopelessness about your relationship with someone (or the group);
- a feeling of alienation from others;
- yawning not related to lack of sleep;
- inability to reach agreement on specific issues.

Clearing processes are always voluntary.

Most people have little or no experience of being clear with other people and react to each other out of old patterns and unfinished business—usually from their parents and families of origin. So these processes are revolutionary. If used regularly they would alter the way we related to one another. The main thing to watch for is people projecting distress onto others (making it their fault) and stopping the process much too soon, before all have reached the bottom of the pile.

## *Process 36: Sharing withholds about ourselves*

**PURPOSE:** To free up group energy.

**TIME:** 30–60 minutes.

Here are three types of withholds, presented as A, B and C. You may use these together or separately.

**PROCESS:** A Introduce the value of sharing withholds as a way of freeing up energy in the group. Let people know that withholds are things that are their unexpressed truth, as opposed to the truth. Suggest that the recipient of a withhold may get some value from receiving it, and equally may let it go by without owning it for themselves. Let people know that the only response to make to the person sharing a withhold with them is 'Thank you.'

Have a round in which each person shares something about themselves that they have been withholding from the group—something they may have been thinking but not saying. Suggest some starting phrases such as:

'You would understand me more if you knew...'
'Sometimes I ... [behaviour] when I feel ...
[feeling]'
'I would contribute more to the group if I...'

This process works best if you go round the group several times until people are brave enough to say what they are really withholding.

**PROCESS:** B Some withholds can be directly with another person, such as:

'I think you presented your report last week really
 well.'
'I admire the way you handled our meeting this
 week.'
'I find you very attractive.'
Or they can be challenging, such as:
'I thought you dominated our last meeting, and
 I was annoyed about it at the time.'
'I haven't heard you say anything at our team
 meetings, and I wonder why.'

The purpose of sharing withholds like this is to
free up the person sharing the withhold; the other
person may or may not get value from receiving it.

Check if people are willing to try this exercise, and
get agreement before continuing.

Standing up and milling around the room, invite
participants to move to one person at a time and
share anything that they have been withholding. The
person who receives the withhold makes no response
other than 'Thank you.'

**PROCESS:** C Have a round in which each person
shares something they have been withholding from
the group. Withholds are usually to do with judgements and assessments about ourselves, others, or
what the group is doing. The facilitator can assist by
suggesting a starting phrase:

'You would understand me more if you knew...'

'Sometimes I ... [behaviour] when I feel ... [feeling].'

'I would contribute more to the group if...'

'If I could wave my magic wand and alter one thing in the group right now, it would be...'

This process works best if you go round the group several times until people are brave enough to say what they are really withholding.

End the session by thanking the participants, and remind them not to go up to people afterwards to discuss the withholds they received from them.

*Note:* Lack of energy is usually to do with withholding—that is, failure to communicate. We are alive to the extent that we are prepared to communicate. Remember that we withhold our fear, and the group climate needs to be one of trust and generous listening for participants to share their withholds. The more pressing the withhold, the scarier it is to share it. There needs to be a level of trust in the group for this exercise to be effective.

# *Process 37: One-to-one clearing*

One of the participants invites another to have a clearing session.

'I'm feeling uncomfortable around you. I'm not sure exactly what it's about. Can we meet to have a clearing session? Are you available now?'

If the other person is willing but unavailable right then, arrange a time and place. You may want to negotiate to have a facilitator present, or agree to call on one if you get stuck.

Start the session by each declaring what you are committed to in the relationship, yourself and the other person. For example:

> 'I am committed to our friendship (or good working relationship) and want to be relaxed around you. And I want you to be comfortable around me too.'

Then describe the feeling or behaviour that you have noticed in yourself. Seek to identify the incident. There always is one.

> 'I noticed that I was uncomfortable (or annoyed) when ... happened.'
> 'Having said that, what I now see is that...'
> 'And what's underneath that is...'
> 'And the feelings I have about that are...'

The hard things to say are usually feelings that we don't like to experience in ourselves or admit to others. They often seem petty and despicable, such as feelings of jealousy, anger, meanness (not wanting to lend or share things), feelings of being invaded or taken advantage of, or being subjected to too many demands.

The feelings often don't fit with our own image of ourselves as generous and tolerant. They often seem to relate more to our childhood than to the present. Own all the feelings as your own and tell the other person what behaviour triggered them, without judgement of right or wrong, good or bad, of either yourself or the other person. This is often the hard bit.

You may also be reminded of past incidents with that person or someone else where something similar happened. Say this too.

'Another situation I remember is...'
'And when that happened I felt...'

Keep speaking, uninterrupted, until you can go no further. After that the other person has a turn to do the same. There may be requests and promises you both want to make along the way or at the end.

'I request that when that situation happens again you...'
(be specific)

When the second person has finished, have further turns each until you get to the bottom of the pile.

If you get stuck or it is too scary to continue, either person may call time-out and renegotiate to meet again with a facilitator. Relationships, particularly close working and personal ones, will bring up all our old unhealed patterns from the past, many to do with our parents and siblings. You almost certainly will have touched on deep hurts and strong feelings. Personal therapeutic work may be needed.

**Indications that clearing is complete**

You will know when you reach the bottom of the pile because you will feel empty, complete (there is nothing left to say) and you are freed up to be with yourself and the other person. You have the space to appreciate, recognise and love them.

When the process is complete, thank one another and acknowledge your own and their courage and magnificence.

*VARIATION*

- After each turn, the second person reflects back the essence of what was said as a checking process. The first person needs to be satisfied with the reflection before the second person has their turn.
- Use this variation all or part of the time. It is most useful when one or both people are becoming very triggered. When we are triggered, we tend to remember only the trigger phrase and not the other things said.

# *Process 38: Group clearing*

This is a similar process to one-to-one clearing, and it can involve some or all members of the group. The indications that a clearing session is needed are the same as for one-to-one clearing and are listed above. If only two participants or a small section of a group are involved the clearing session may be best done outside group time. Use the one-to-one clearing process and adapt it to two or more people.

If most of the group are involved you may choose to have a clearing session (preferably straight away), or schedule a special group-clearing session if it appears likely that a longer time is needed. (Read Process 37, One-to-one clearing, as a preparation for this process.)

*Note:* If the group is a cooperative group they will usually have a commitment to reach agreement. If the group is a hierarchical or adhoc group they will now need to consider whether they are prepared to make a commitment to get clear and reach agreement. This will need to include considering if there is sufficient safety (confidentiality and power balance) for people to allow themselves to be vulnerable. This process is not appropriate for uncommitted groups.

**PURPOSE:** To refocus the group.

**MATERIALS:** Whiteboard.

**TIME:** Variable—anything from 30 minutes to 3 hours. There needs to be a commitment to see the process through.

**PROCESS:** Declare the need for a clearing session.

Check for agreement to have a clearing meeting. If there is agreement, continue as follows.

Have someone speak the purpose and the vision of the group.

'Our purpose is ... Our vision is...'

*Note:* If the purpose and vision are unclear this may be the issue.

Then invite participants to identify what is getting in the way of their full participation in the group.

'What is getting in the way for me is...'

Take turns in uninterrupted rounds. Listen generously to one another. Continue with the rounds until the group reaches the bottom of the pile.

Encourage group members to own their own feelings and thoughts rather than project them on to others. If requests are made in the rounds, write them up on a whiteboard to address after the rounds are completed. (See One-to-one clearing, 'Indications that clearing is complete'.)

Now ask for any further specific requests and add these to the whiteboard. Address requests one at a time. Have members accept, or decline and counter-offer. If no counter-offer is acceptable, ask the whole group to suggest solutions.

If the group cannot come to agreement, this is an indication that the group is still not clear. Before going any further, do Process 20, Being with another, or Process 21, Being with a group.

Then go back to the beginning of this exercise and repeat the process. Do not finish the session until the group is complete.

If you have repeated the exercise three times and the group is still not clear, ask each person to choose whether or not to remain in and recommit themselves to the group. Provide a generous opening for people to choose.

When the process is complete, thank and acknowledge one another for your courage and magnificence.

## VARIATION

• As for Process 37, One-to-one clearing.

# Completion processes

These exercises are powerful as ongoing processes, as well as being essential for completing a project.

# *Process 39: Getting complete*

**PURPOSE:** To stay clear and focused with a group.

**TIME:** Up to 5 minutes per person.

**PROCESS:** Ask each person a relevant question such as:

'What do you need to say to be complete for this week?'

'What do you need to complete your involvement with this group.' Then ask:

'Is there anything else?'

'Any niggles, thoughts, feelings, unmet expectations, requests, promises?' (Suggest as appropriate.)

'Is there anything you might say to someone after the group is over? I request that you say it now.'

The person should think carefully to see if they have left any 'baggage' behind—anything they would like to say to someone else after the group.

After everyone has had a turn ask:

'Are there any acknowledgements that anyone would like to make to themselves or others?'

The only response from those acknowledged is a 'Thank you.'

# Process 40: Getting complete—project

**PURPOSE:** For ongoing review of a project.

**TIME:** Up to 5 minutes per person.

**PROCESS:** Hold a completion meeting at the end of each week during the project to review progress and clear up any misunderstandings. Each person in turn reviews their part in the project, including:

• what they have achieved;

- any commitments made that have not been completed—new commitments can be made or agreements revoked;
- any interpersonal niggles—these are spoken and cleared;
- any acknowledgement of self or others.

Anyone may ask for feedback on work done, and the facilitator may check to see if that person has said everything they want to say.

# A space for the sacred

## *Process 41: Creating a sacred space*

**PURPOSE:** To encourage a sense of the sacred.

**MATERIALS:** A carpet, cloth, table or area to put things on.

**TIME:** 3 minutes per person.

**BEFORE THE PROCESS**

Invite each person to bring an item of personal value to the group. Let people know that they will be speaking about it to everyone.

**PROCESS**

*Step 1* Sitting in a circle, people take turns to tell the story of their item and place it in a chosen place—on the carpet, cloth, table.

*Step 2* Allow silence at the end of this process.

*Step 3* The objects can be left in the sacred place for the whole of the meeting, seminar or workshop, or in the workplace—as the participants wish.

## VARIATION

- Ask participants beforehand to bring a small object they are prepared to give away that says something about some focus of the workshop. Do the exercise as above. At the end, have each participant identify a different object they would like to take home. This can be done either in the group, or informally.

# Process 42: Finding the higher purpose

**PURPOSE:** To find out the higher purpose of a group using a nonrational process.

**MATERIALS:** A container such as a bowl or hat.

**TIME:** 40 minutes.

## PROCESS

*Background*

Talk about the holonomic principle, which asserts that the whole is represented in the part. Just as one small part of a holographic image contains the whole hologram, or every cell contains all the DNA structure of the whole, so one person in a group can speak for the whole group.

*Step 1 (5 minutes)*

Encourage the group to explore the possibility of using non-rational processes as a valid alternative. Would they like to try one to identify the higher purpose of the group? If so, encourage people to try it out 'as if' it will really work.

Request that they acknowledge any scepticism, and be willing to suspend it. Introduce the process as a ritual to discover one person who will speak for the group. In this process the spokesperson's role will be to speak the higher purpose of the group.

*Step 2 (3–5 minutes)*

Invite everyone to relax and centre themselves. Suggest they focus on their breathing, breathe into their bellies and relax further on each breath out.

*Step 3 (5 minutes)*

When everyone is relaxed, invite each person to put a small, identifiable article such as a watch, ring or earring into a container.

*Step 4 (10 minutes)*

Without looking into the container, the facilitator takes one object from it and gives it to the owner, with the container. That person takes another object and hands it with the container to its owner, and so on. The last person to receive their object and the container is the holonomic focus and becomes the group spokesperson.

*Step 5 (5 minutes)*

In their own time and in their own way the person who is the holonomic focus—the spokesperson—centres herself or himself. The facilitator reminds the spokesperson that they have been ritually chosen by an agreed non-rational method. Everyone brings their energy and attention to the person. Then the spokesperson is asked by the facilitator:

'What is the higher purpose of this group?'

*Step 6 (5 minutes)*

In their own time, and taking as much time as they need, the spokesperson speaks. You may like to write down the spokesperson's words.

*Step 7 (3 minutes)*

After they have spoken, the person is thanked, they derole and the ritual is completed.

*Note:* Ensure that the spokesperson is deroled.

## Variations

• The spokesperson is asked questions by the group and answers them as the holonomic focus. This variation needs to be facilitated sensitively.

# Processes for facilitator training

# *Process 43: Identity check (for uncovering projections)*

**PURPOSE:** An identity check uncovers the projections we are making onto others.

This exercise is particularly useful if you are beginning a close working or personal relationship or if a relationship is becoming difficult or stuck. The exercise can be done with the person we are having difficulty with, or with another person who agrees to play that role.

**TIME:** 20 minutes (10 minutes x 2), or variable.

**PROCESS:** Sit opposite one another on the same level and maintain eye contact. Person A asks B the following questions, and encourages B to answer them as fully as possible:

'Who do I remind you of?'

'How am I like them?'

'What do you want to say to that person? Say it to me now as if I were them.'

'What do you want them to say to you?' (Person A then repeats this back to B as though they were that person.)

'How am I different from that person?' (Continue asking this question until you are both clear that you are quite distinct from that person.)

You may find that a person reminds you of more than one other, and the whole process will need to be repeated.

When Person B has completed the process, swap roles and begin again.

# Process 44: Situation check (for uncovering projections)

This process is particularly useful if you find you are reacting to a situation out of proportion to its significance, or if feelings about a situation are hanging around after the event.

**PURPOSE:** To uncover the projections we are taking from one situation on to others.

**TIME:** Variable—say, 10 minutes.

**PROCESS:** Ask yourself, or have someone else ask you, the following questions:

'What does this situation remind me/you of?'

'How is it similar?'

'What do you need to express to get complete about that situation?' (feelings, thoughts, unexpressed communications or sounds)

'What would I/you have liked to have happened differently?'

'Who do I/you need to forgive?' (including my/yourself)

'What can you let go of?'

'How is this situation different?' (Describe differences in detail until you are both clear that this situation is quite distinct from the previous situation.)

You may find that the situation reminds you of more than one other situation, in which case the whole process will need to be repeated.

**VARIATION**

- This exercise can also be reciprocal. After the exercise is completed, swap roles and repeat.

# Process 45: Working on different levels

**PURPOSE:** To explore and name the different levels in a group.

**MATERIALS:** Paper, pastels and paint.

**TIME:** 40 minutes.

**PROCESS:** Introduce the levels outlined in Part 1 Chapter 8. Ask participants to express their sense of the levels they have noticed through painting or drawing (15 minutes).

Debrief in the whole group, asking the participants to identify the levels they noticed. Invite participants to share their paintings or drawings with the whole group.

What levels did people feel comfortable or uncomfortable with?

Discuss how a facilitator can intervene to shift levels.

# Process 46: Using role-play to practise facilitator interventions

**PURPOSE:** To develop intervention skills using role-play.

**MATERIALS:** Chairs.

**TIME:** 1 hour.

## PROCESS

*Step 1* Divide the group into two groups. Invite each group to choose a type of intervention from Part 1 Chapter 7 for which they will develop a role-play.

*Step 2* Invite each group to develop a role-play using some intervention to present to the whole group. Give them 8 minutes.

Encourage them to use an example from within the group that one member has experienced. Have this person play one of the key participant roles in the group and have another group member act as facilitator. Have other group members play other participants. Ensure that each group participant knows how they respond to the situation sufficiently that they can respond to different interventions the facilitators may make spontaneously. It isn't necessary or helpful to have the whole role-play scripted; it is very helpful for the participants to have a good sense of the person they are representing, more than just 'angry person'.

*Step 3* Set the group up with an audience space and a stage space. Ask which group would like to go first.

The group facilitator's role while the role-play is being done is to assist all the participants to get the learning available from the role-play.

*Step 4* Stop the role-play at any point where you feel something interesting has happened. It is useful for the participants to display their roles, and for the facilitator within the role-play to get comfortable in their role initially. After this you may pause the role-play more quickly, perhaps after each intervention.

When you pause the role-play there are two types of intervention you can make. You can ask the audience group to give feedback to the facilitator within the role-play and unfold this into some discussion. You can also ask one of the audience group to take up the role of facilitator within the role-play and demonstrate how they might intervene in the situation. You may also use a combination of these.

Do not have members of the participant group offer feedback to the facilitator or take up other roles within the role-play; once the role-play gets going any change in the roles will significantly change the whole role-play situation. If one of the participants in the role-play really wants to make comment have them do it from within their role in the role-play.

It is useful to have the attitude that you are primarily focused on the learning of the facilitator within the role-play. Therefore the feedback from the group to them is to assist them to develop a new response. If you swap facilitators at some point it is important that the original facilitator be offered another attempt after several other people have demonstrated how they might intervene in the situation, in order that they get to experience doing something new if they want to.

The participants learn through experiencing and observing the impact different interventions have on them and others.

*Step 5* Remember to get all participants to derole before the end of the session so that all role associations are removed.

## Process 47: Working with challenges as a facilitator

See also Process 46 on using role-plays to enable facilitators to develop skills in interventions.

**PURPOSE:** To develop the ability for facilitators to respond effectively to challenges.

**TIME:** Approximately an hour.

Challenges are not challenging situations; rather a challenge is when one participant or group of participants overtly challenges the facilitator about how they are fulfilling their role, or where the facilitator overtly challenges the group about how it is working.

The group divides into two groups and each group has eight minutes to develop a role-play which demonstrates one of these two types of challenges. Follow the process in the role-play for intervention training.

## Process 48: Uncovering sabotage patterns

**PURPOSE:** To identify and share the ways in which each participant's patterned behaviour is likely to get in the way of the group achieving its purpose.

Note: This is a consciousness-raising exercise, not an excuse for self (or other) blame. The mood needs to be lightly serious.

**TIME:** 30–60 minutes (depending on the size of the group).

**PROCESS:** In pairs, choose an A and a B. A asks B:

'How do you sabotage yourself?' (3 minutes x 2)

A encourages B to be specific and invites them to think of other ways:

'Yes, and how else do you sabotage yourself?'

Swap roles.

In the whole group, ask the group to share as an unstructured round:

'How do you sabotage a group?'

Ask the group to share as an unstructured round (2–3 minutes each).

Participants may like to ask the group for suggestions.

Debrief from this exercise with a group whoop or 'Arrrrrhhhh'.

## Process 49: Blaming and scapegoating

*Note:* This is a powerful exercise that can bring up strong feelings and catharsis (crying, anger and fear) for some participants as they flip into other situations which they find triggering.

**PURPOSE:** To experience the foolishness of blaming and scapegoating.

**TIME:** 30 minutes.

**PROCESS:** Find a large cushion and put it in the middle of the group circle. Ask the group to choose a name (not the same as anyone in the group) for the cushion.

*Step 1* Have participants stand up in a circle about a metre away from the cushion (for our purposes, called 'Bruce'; if there is a person in your group called Bruce choose another name). Encourage participants to give themselves full permission to blame Bruce for everything that hasn't worked in the group since it began. It's all Bruce's fault. He caused everything to go wrong, and what's more he did it on purpose. He is not aligned with the group and is unrepentant. Encourage participants to shout and yell at Bruce, laugh at him behind his back, make snide comments to him or about him, be mean to him. He is their scapegoat and they can project all their dissatisfactions onto him, really exaggerating their anger and outrage. Keep this going for 5 minutes.

*Step 2* Ask the participants to stop, sit down in the circle and share. Allow 15 minutes to explore this important issue. Suggest participants focus on:

- The things I like about blaming and scapegoating.
- The things I dislike about blaming and scapegoating.
- What is really going on?

If people have become activated, allow them to continue the catharsis while the discussion takes place, or give them some group time.

Encourage the group to attend to them through the gift of free attention rather than intervention. Just ask the person if there is anything they want to say or do. Give them physical support only if they ask for it. When ready, get the activated person to derole the cushion by describing out loud how it is not like

'Bruce' until the association is removed and he or she can hug the cushion.

# Process 50: Centring yourself when facilitating

Breathe into your belly. Ground yourself. Imagine you are a tree with roots going far down into the ground. Draw up energy from the earth. When there is an opportunity for a break go for a little walk and breathe deeply. Let go of the upset. Talk to the trees.

# Process 51: Debriefing after a facilitation

**PURPOSE:** To get clear and get the learnings after facilitating.

**TIME:** As long as needed—say, half to one hour.

**PROCESS:** Arrange to contact your coach or supervisor after each facilitation. This could be a colleague or a paid professional.
Address questions such as:

- What am I left with after the facilitation?
- What do I need to say about these?
- Is there anything I need to do?
- What are the learnings?
- What did I do well?

# Process 52: Facilitator feedback

**PURPOSE:** To give feedback to the trainee facilitator.

**TIME:** 6 minutes (or longer, as agreed).

**PROCESS:** An opportunity for giving feedback to each facilitator can be built in to each training session by taking six minutes within the time allowed at the end of each exercise for reflection, and self-and peer-assessment. You may like to choose a timekeeper and a recorder.

The process gives two minutes for the trainee facilitator, who completes the sentences:

'One thing I could improve is...'
'One thing I did well is...'
This is followed by the participants, who complete
  the sentences:
'My constructive criticism is...' (2 minutes)
'My acknowledgement to you (the trainee
  facilitator) is...'

(2 minutes)
Encourage short, pithy comments. Discourage stories, discussion or justification. Encourage trainee facilitators to receive feedback as a gift, whether they agree with it or not. Encourage participants not to repeat feedback already given.

To complete the process, the trainee facilitator chooses one constructive criticism and one acknowledgement as their 'gems' for learning.

## Some feedback guidelines

- Speak with honesty and good intent.
- Set aside labels and judgements (avoid 'ought', 'should' and 'must').
- Separate the person from the behaviour.
- Be specific, with both constructive criticism and acknowledgement. Tell people exactly what they said or did.
- Check readiness to receive feedback, and appropriate time and space.
- Focus on what's missing that will make a difference, not what's wrong.
- Present feedback so that it is perceived as an opportunity, not a threat.

# Chapter 4

# design frameworks

Here are design frameworks for workshops, meetings, projects and evaluations.

## 1. Workshop design

The facilitator will want to have a major input into the design of any workshop they are facilitating. This is process design. Process design is what ensures that the workshop objectives are met and the participants cared for (in the process).

This section provides some process design guidelines, and a workshop model to illustrate how a workshop might look. The workshop length used in this model is one day, but the guidelines apply to a workshop of any length.

## *Workshop design guidelines*

There are four phases in the design of a workshop. In a one-day workshop these phases fit broadly into the following four sessions:

| Time | Session | Phase |
| --- | --- | --- |
| 9:00–10:15am | One | Getting full participation |
| 10:15–10:30am | Break | |
| 10:30–12:30pm | Two | Exploring the group limits |

| Time | Session | Phase |
|------|---------|-------|
| 12:30–1:00pm | Lunch break | |
| 1:00–3:00pm | Three | Taking new territory |
| 3:00–3:15pm | Break | |
| 3:15–5:00pm | Four | Completion |

# Phases

Each of the four phases has its own intention and flavour. Here is a summary of the contents of each phase. Although not every facet needs to be addressed explicitly (or in exactly this order) in every workshop, the facilitator will be aware of and taking care of them all.

**Phase 1. Getting full participation** The intent of this phase is to have each participant fully present, aligned with the group purpose and ready to work as part of the whole group.

The time needed for this first phase is particularly variable. Time allocated will depend on how well the participants know one another and the clarity of the group purpose. Care taken in this phase is critical, as this stage is the foundation on which all other stages rest.

This is the phase in which participants are freshest. The facilitator will be establishing her or his credibility and rapport with the group.

This stage includes:

- Arriving.
- Welcoming—could include a ritual.

- Handling lateness and commitments to be present for the whole session.
- Introduction by the facilitator (including background if a new facilitator).
- Introductions of participants (if one or more are new to the group).
- Alignment on group purpose (and objectives of the workshop).
- Check-in by participants, including individual intentions or desired outcomes.
- Housekeeping—including requests.
- Outline of programme—process and content.
- Negotiation of and agreement to programme.
- Clarifying group culture/ground rules, including requests for confidentiality.
- Clarifying roles.
- Creating full participation.

**Phase 2. Exploring the group limits** The intent of this phase is to explore and develop what the group knows already (or has access to through the facilitator or other resources) so that it can move on in the most powerful way.

This phase includes:

- Outlining the issues to be addressed.
- Establishing the framework for addressing the issues.
- Presencing and enlarging the vision or broad picture.
- Identifying the resources available to the group.

- Receiving specific input.
- Deepening the group relationships and clearing as needed.
- Making connections.
- Maintaining focus and concentration.
- Pressing the group boundaries.
- Identifying where the group leading edges are (areas it can develop).
- Clarifying what is missing and how it can be created.
- Summarising where the group is up to.

**Phase 3. Claiming new territory** The intent of this phase is for the group to move past the known and claim new territory.

This phase includes:
- Accessing synergy.
- Leaping across chasms.
- Breaking through barriers.
- Generating creativity.
- Maintaining focus.
- Sustaining momentum.
- Sustaining full participation.
- Exploring more possibilities.
- Developing opportunities.
- Maintaining alignment.
- Working through conflict.
- Sharing withholds.
- Keeping energy recharged and moving.
- Getting to agreements.
- Transformation.

**Phase 4. Completion** The intent of this phase is to complete the group process in a way that anchors the territory gained by the group.

This stage includes:

- Completing conversations.
- Declaring what has been achieved.
- Drawing out the learning.
- Presencing the miracles.
- Recording decisions.
- Recording individual and subgroup commitments.
- Creating a structure to support commitments.
- Feedback on process and facilitation.
- Recognition of territory taken (or lost).
- Declarations of individual's intentions and desired outcomes met (or not).
- Affirmation of selves and others.
- Being ready to leave the group.
- Completion session.
- Farewells—could include a ritual.

**Workshop model**

Here is a workshop model to assist you to translate the design guidelines into a workshop design. The Project Formulation Workshop model will also be useful.

# Team-building workshop

The purpose of this workshop is to enhance teamwork (in a well-established work group).

The promised outcomes are:
- Improved team effectiveness.
- Skills in managing conflict.
- Increased communication skills.
  Outcomes are measured by:
- Feedback from participants at the end of the workshop.
- Assessment by manager and staff after two weeks, to agreed criteria.

## Programme outline

8:30am Welcome, introductions and outline of programme for the day. Housekeeping and ground rules.

8:45am Check-in—what does each participant need to say to be fully present and ready to get to work.
*Note:* If there is a lot of baggage to be cleared this session will need to be extended—continue with the clearing and move the programme times back. Shorten the conflict management section as needed. You will find you have already covered some of these skills.

9:00am: Vision for the team (presented by the manager and enlarged by the team).

9:20am: Trust-building exercise.

9:30am: What makes an effective team? (Identifying characteristics of an effective team, reaching agreement on checklist and assessing the present team through individual assessment.)

10:15am: Tea break.

10:30am: Clarification and analysis of power relationships, leadership, roles and tasks. Sharing strengths and weaknesses through self-and peer-assessment. Identifying areas of agreement and differences in perception. Participants choose an area needing improvement to work on and design a plan for this.

12:00pm: Lunch.

12:30pm Conflict management, including assertion skills, sharing feelings and making requests and promises (using role-plays).

2:00pm: Team exercise. (Building team and velocity.)

2:15pm: Tea break.

2:30pm: Developing a team charter and/or contract.

3:45pm: Identifying the learning.

4:00pm: Feedback on the day.

4:30pm: Close.

# 2. Meeting design

Here are the elements of meeting design for a cooperative group using collective decisionmaking.

## *Preparation*

Checklist:
- Is a meeting necessary? What are the alternatives?
- What is the purpose of the meeting? Is it clear?
- Who needs to be at the meeting? (Key people.)
- Are the key people available?
- Decide date, time and venue.
- Do these arrangements complement the purpose of the meeting?
- Is a written invitation needed? Telephone?
- Does an agenda need to be circulated? Discussed? With which key people?
- Do refreshments need to be organised?
- Crèche facilities?
- Transport?
- Interpreters?
- Is equipment needed? Whiteboard, video, overhead projector, paper, pens? (Generate your own list.)
- Does resource material need to be circulated? Available before the meeting?
- Do any key people need to be reminded?
- What outcomes are needed from the meeting?

# Environment

Before the meeting, ensure all required resources are prepared and at hand ready to use when appropriate. Prepare the room so it is clean and welcoming, with chairs (and tables if necessary) set up as you want them for the meeting. Provide only the number of chairs needed.

# Arrival

Ensure that people are greeted on arrival and that coats, bags and so on are attended to. People need time to arrive, greet one another and 'get there' both physically and mentally.

The culture of the group (and the organisation of which it is a part) is most readily established at the beginning of the meeting—even before the meeting proper begins. Model the behaviours that you want to promote.

Think about these questions:

What is the atmosphere you are creating?
Who is responsible for greeting people?
Are people's needs being attended to?
Do people already know one another or are introductions needed?

Sit in a circle or round a table without any gaps or empty chairs. Ensure everyone is on the same level; for example, don't have some people on chairs and some on the floor.

Make sure everyone is comfortable, not too hot or cold, and that there is air circulating in the room, and sufficient light and sound levels.

Ensure everyone is close enough to hear others clearly and see their faces. If someone is seated behind another person ask them to come forward, rearranging chairs as required. Repeat the request if necessary.

## *Ritual*

There may be a ritual way of starting your meetings such as a welcome speech or circle.

## *Establishing roles*

Establish who is taking the following roles:
- Facilitator (responsible for the group process).
- Recorder (records decisions, agenda items, and people present).
- Timekeeper (monitors timeframes and ending time of meeting).

## *Introductions*

The facilitator checks out with the group to see if introductions are needed. Introductions are needed if this is a first meeting or if new people have joined the group.

If appropriate, introduce yourself as the facilitator and then invite group members to introduce themselves. This can take the form of a round.

The facilitator checks if everyone is now ready to participate.

*Note:* People may have personal issues (births, deaths, accomplishments) that they want to share. If a group member is upset or unwell, check with them to see if they would prefer not to attend the meeting. Give them the opportunity to leave.

# Confirm meeting details

The facilitator confirms:
- The purpose of the meeting and any required outcomes (be specific).
- The ending time of the meeting.
- Housekeeping details (food arrangements, breaks, and location of toilets).

# Confirm ground rules (if needed)

Ground rules are optional but useful. They need to be clearly understood and agreed by everyone. Examples of ground rules are:
- Speaking only for yourself and not on behalf of others.
- Not interrupting.
- Speaking succinctly (short and to the point).
- Not leaving the room until the meeting is completed.

- Not answering the phone.

## *Information sharing*

Share short items of information that are relevant to the meeting and do not require discussion (such as apologies for non-attendance). If you find people always get into instant discussion, it may be preferable to put each information item on the agenda.

## *Review previous decisions*

Review all decisions made at the previous meeting and check out action taken as a result of decisions.

Record the action taken on each decision. If action has not been taken, bring forward decisions and re-enter them in the records of this meeting. If action is no longer practical or relevant, note this alongside the decision in previous records.

## *Open agenda setting*

This model is often used by groups using collective decisionmaking.

**Agenda items** Each person puts forward the agenda items they want discussed at the meeting and these are all recorded, preferably on a large sheet of paper so everyone can see them. The name of the person who initiated the agenda item is placed alongside it.

**Time setting** The initiator is asked by the facilitator to estimate how long it will take to discuss the item and the requested time is noted alongside the item. The facilitator checks this time with the meeting and adjusts it if a longer time is requested.

**Priority setting** The times of all items are added together and the ending time of the meeting checked. If the time needed is longer than the time of the meeting, have a round where each person nominates their two most important agenda items. These can be recorded alongside the item by marking one tick for each person's preferences. This will generate a priority list and items can be addressed in this order.

Keep in mind the following:
- What items must be discussed today?
- What items are important but not urgent?
- What items can be left until another meeting or be resolved by another process, for example delegation to one or two people to decide and action?

## Discussion, decisionmaking and action planning

Each agenda item is now discussed in turn. The following process may be useful.
1. The facilitator invites the initiator to:
    - Introduce the item (issue and background).
    - Say what they want from the group (feedback, ideas, alternatives or a decision).

- Suggest the process or technique they would like the group to use—for example, rounds, brainstorm, pros and cons.

2. The facilitator seeks clarification and group agreement for the ideas outlined by the initiator to be implemented. If the initiator is unclear about techniques or processes, the facilitator will suggest one. If specific feedback or ideas are requested, the facilitator may find the technique of rounds useful. Often a round will clarify the issue, and common ground and differences will become obvious.

3. When this process is complete, the facilitator summarises and checks to see what else is needed for the initiator's request to be fulfilled.

4. If group agreement is needed, request proposals from the group. Continue this process until a proposal is suggested which meets general agreement. It may be helpful to reach minor agreements along the way. Record these. If a decision is being held up by one or two people, the facilitator can ask what they propose to solve the difficulty. If agreement is still not reached, check with dissenters to see if they are directly affected by the outcome. If not, see if they will allow the decision to be made anyway.

Those directly affected by a decision need to be directly involved in the decisionmaking.

5. The timekeeper keeps an eye on the time and lets the meeting know how it is going. It is usually better not to extend the time, as there is a group 'law' that decisionmaking expands to fill the time available. Not extending time educates the group to be intentional in decisionmaking.

6. If a decision is not made, you may need an interim decision such as:

   • Defer the item to the next or a special meeting.

   • Delegate one or more people to decide on behalf of the group within given parameters.

## Records

Records of the meeting need to include:
- People present.
- Date and time.
- Agenda items.
- Decisions made (action, person, timeframe).

Write down each decision as it is reached, including specific actions, if any, to be taken. Note who will take action on the decision and by when. Always be very specific.

## Next meeting

Decide the date and time of the next meeting.

## Completion

A closing round may be held in which people express anything that is still incomplete for them from the meeting, or any acknowledgements they would like to give to other members of the group.

## Ending

The group may have a ritual for ending the meeting.

## Follow-up

After the meeting, circulate decisions to participants. Alternatively, you may keep a decision book in a central place.

A useful tool between meetings is to set up a decision management system. This could take the form of 'buddies' who coach one another towards taking the action they said they would by the time promised. Another method is to nominate a 'decision manager' who keeps in contact with people carrying out decisions and 'coaches' them to meet their commitments.

# 3. Project design

An effective group will have a clear purpose and vision, and undertake projects towards achieving its purpose.

It is very helpful for a facilitator to understand the basics of project design so that the easiest path can be found through to achieving the project.

## Examples or projects

Projects are specific results in time. They can involve one or more people. Three examples are:

- To increase the school roll by 10% by 1 March 200X.
- To complete the construction of ... building to ... standard by ... time.
- To hold a birthday party on 24 May at ... venue with ... people present.

## Project stages

There are four stages in any project—formulation, concentration, momentum, completion. Here is a summary of each phase and the kind of issues that are likely to arise.

**Formulation** This is the first stage of a project. In this stage the nature of the project is developed and clarified from the initial good idea through to a specific and measurable objective. In this stage the project will be checked for its importance towards realising the vision, its priority in relation to other projects, its feasibility, and the commitment and resources of the project group to carrying it out.

Ask the group these questions:

Does the project move the group towards its vision?

Is this project the best use of group time, effort and resources?

Is the project attainable?

Is the project a sufficient challenge?

Can every single person 'own' the project and be committed to it? What are people's concerns about the project? (Get them all out in the open.)

Is it exciting, does it 'light up' or inspire group members?

Are all the group members aligned on the project?

The project needs to be written in terms of a SMART objective: Specific, Measurable, Attainable, Results-orientated and Time-bound. Sometimes there will be more than one objective.

The project must have specific conditions of satisfaction or performance measures. The objective will need an action plan with sufficient detail to show that the project can be fulfilled. A fully formulated project will leave no doubt as to its feasibility—and this does not mean that it won't stretch every member of the team to get it done.

*Alarm bells*

- The project is unclear or unmeasurable.
- The project is not central to fulfilling the vision.
- Some group members are not excited or have gone quiet.

Until the project is clear and measurable, on line to meet the vision and the group members are fully aligned and excited, do not proceed. Any question marks now mean danger later.

**Concentration** In the concentration phase of the project, the group will put in a lot of energy fine-tuning and implementing the action plan. This is the high-energy action phase when coordinated action is required between all team members. It is 'shoulders to the wheel' time to get the 'wheel' in motion—and it takes more energy to get the 'wheel' started than to keep it in motion. It is high energy in for small results.

Ask the group these questions:

Are the action plans clear and comprehensive?

Has a project manager been appointed to manage the action plan implementation?

Is everyone clear what actions they are accountable for?

Are the timeframes clear?

Is there feedback—early warning systems in place for problems?

Is there a clear display of the project (such as a wall chart) where everyone can see at a glance what is happening?

Are there any problems with getting access to resources?

Is anyone stuck, confused and needing help?

Does anyone need coaching to carry through with their tasks?

Has anyone 'bitten off more than they can chew'?

Are there clear communication channels or lines?

Is everyone in communication or are some people stuck and withholding their problems?

Are there clear problem-solving and conflict-resolution mechanisms?

*Alarm bells*

- People are out of communication with one another—not returning phone calls or emails, not checking in as arranged, or not using the feedback systems. This is nearly always the first indication that something is wrong.
- People look hassled and avoid eye contact.
- Timeframes are starting to slip.
- The wall display (or other displays) is not up to date.
- People are withholding their problems.

Encourage the group to take action at the first signs of problems (and there will always be some—usually lots). Get people back into communication, sharing problems, recreating the vision and clarifying commitments. Trust that the group can solve any problems that arise. Celebrate small victories. Act on the assumption that 'problems not shared always get worse'. Without rigorous management the project may never get to the next stage.

**Momentum** If the concentration stage has been effective, the project will now move into momentum.

This is the stage when the 'wheel' is turning and needs to be steered rather than pushed. There is less energy needed to drive the project and results are showing up. The project is on course (or close to it) and the wall display will reflect the good results. It is clear that the project will be successful (in whole or part) and people can take some time out to reflect on progress and acknowledge the efforts and successes of one another.

Ask the group these questions:

Is management in place—who is steering the project and watching out for danger?

Is the wall display up to date?

Is the momentum being maintained?

Who is out of communication and why?

Do the action plans need updating?

Is it time to have a clearing session?

What is missing that could make a difference to achieving the project?

*Alarm bells*

- People are losing focus and concentration.
- People seem to be satisfied with less than full, successful completion of the project. ('Near enough is good enough.')
- The project manager is not being vigilant in steering the project—it is getting off course.

Focus and concentration need to be maintained to ensure the project remains on course, and that everyone is available for extra energy to solve any further problems that arise. Vigilance and watchfulness are the keys to keeping the momentum going. Remember, accidents at speed are much more dangerous than when we are travelling slowly.

**Completion** This is the final stage of the project, when the results are collated and all the loose end are tied up. Evaluations are carried out. All the learning from this project is distilled so that further projects can benefit. Any leftover gripes and disappointments are shared. Acknowledgements to one another and others are given and successes celebrated. A completion ritual is carried out. People are free to begin the next project.

Ask the group these questions:

Have the project outcomes been achieved?

Is the display complete?

Is anything missing that can still be put in?

Have all the action plans been completed or revoked?

Has all the learning from the project been spoken and written?

Has a completion meeting been held to express any unfinished business with one another?

Have full acknowledgements occurred?

Is everyone complete and freed up to move to the next project?

Has there been full celebration?

This stage is often glossed over and the full learning is not accessed. Encourage people to say everything they need to say—to withhold nothing, whether it appears large or small. A small issue on this project may be critical on the next.

Make sure people get the opportunity to fully acknowledge themselves and one another. This is the real reward everyone wants and needs—where our 'cup gets refilled'.

*Alarm bells*

- People look hassled—they are not freed up and complete.
- The learning is superficial.
- The fullness of acknowledgement is missing.
- There is no clear ending ritual.

# Project formulation workshop

This model is of a day workshop for a project group of up to 25 people using a facilitator. The purpose of the workshop is to formulate (clarify and develop) the project and get it off to a strong start. The model is suitable for an organisation project or a community project.

The promised outcomes are:
- Clear project objectives and plans of action.
- Commitment to fulfil the project.
  Outcomes to be measured by:
- Written objectives and action plans with time limits.
- Clear accountabilities.
- Ongoing meeting structure in place for the project group.

# Programme outline

9:30am Welcome by the project sponsor (or community leader) and introduction of the facilitator.

You, as facilitator, introduce yourself and explain how you will work with the group (whole group and subgroups). Outline the programme for the day. Check for agreement to proceed. (Negotiate if there are requests for changes.) Housekeeping (food, toilets, ending and break times).

9:50am Introductions. Check-in, or exercise for participants to meet each other and establish some rapport.

10:15am The project idea is introduced to the group by the initiators. (Although all participants will already know about the project and be interested in being involved, they will not have heard it as a group.)

10:30am Morning tea break.

10:45am Building the vision of the project, as a round or brainstorm. (Involve all the participants so that they contribute to the building of the project and 'own' it.) Record key words of all comments on sheets of paper.

11:30am Develop goals and objectives. (Crystallising the vision in specifics.) (Use subgroups to work on these, with five in each group. Groups report back to whole group after 20 minutes with suggestions.)

In the whole group, refine, prioritise and negotiate agreement. Ensure that objectives are specific, measurable and time-bound.

12:30pm Break for lunch.

1:15pm Strategies, resources—brainstorm strategies and resources needed to meet each objective and list them on large sheets of paper. For resources, list also where they can come from. (Use subgroups—one for each objective, for 30 minutes. Then allow 10 minutes for participants to move to other groups to add to the lists.)

Pin sheets up around the room.

2:30pm Accountabilities—request participants to form into task teams, one team for each objective. In the task teams have each team member share what time and other resources they can contribute or access. Each team records this. Have teams then choose a team leader. Each group then develops an action plan and allocates specific tasks to each person.

3:15pm Break—tea and coffee.

3:30pm Return to the whole group. Each task team shares what they will be doing. Actions may need to be coordinated in the large group.

3:50pm Ongoing structure developed—coordinating group of task team groups or other agreed structure. Further meetings arranged.

4:30pm Feedback on the day.

4:45pm Closing and acknowledgements by the project sponsor or community leader.

5:00pm Close.

# 4. Evaluation design

## *What is the purpose of evaluation?*

The purpose of evaluation is to determine the value or worth of something.

The questions underlining evaluation are:

What did we plan to achieve?

Did we achieve it?

To what standard did we achieve it?

What have we learnt that can be applied in the future?

# The design of evaluation

The design of evaluation is part of planning. At the planning phase of a workshop, project or other process we at Zenergy design how it will be evaluated. And having implemented the workshop, project or process, we then evaluate it as agreed during the planning phase.

# 'Smart' and 'Soft' evaluation

'Smart' evaluation is evaluation against measurable outcomes—for example, the achievement of a SMART objective (**S**pecific, **M**easurable, **A**ttainable, **R**esults-oriented and **T**ime-bound).

'Soft' evaluation is evaluation that is expressive and descriptive of individuals' feelings, perceptions, learnings and insights.

SMART objectives set in the planning stage allow for clear monitoring during the project and evaluation at the end. Lack of measurable outcomes means that evaluation can only be 'soft'.

**Large quantities of soft evaluation do not compensate for lack of planning with measurable outcomes such as SMART objectives.**

Make sure that each project has identified the key measurable outcomes that will show whether the project has been accomplished (or not). These then need to be displayed, tracked and available to be seen by all participants (see Project design).

We recommend a mixture of 'smart' and 'soft' evaluation: measurable outcomes (for the overall process, workshops, meetings) plus expressive and descriptive spoken and written material (from the individual participants).

# 'Smart' evaluation

'Smart' evaluation is straightforward. Clear outcomes and measures are developed in the planning stage and these are then applied in the evaluation stage. The clearer and more specific the stated outcomes, the simpler the evaluation process. Clear evaluation requires a SMART approach. These outcomes/objectives can then be measured by numbers, percentages and yes/no responses.

**'Smart' evaluation model**

1. Were the promised outcomes met?

Outcome A: Yes/No, or percentage or fraction
Outcome B: Yes/No, or percentage or fraction
Outcome C: Yes/No, or percentage or fraction
Total number of outcomes met:...

2. Outcome A: The process was implemented as agreed (yes/no)

Outcome B: The strategic plan (content) completed (yes/no)
Outcome C: All timeframes were met (yes/no)

# 'Soft' evaluation

'Soft' evaluation is useful where the outcomes are qualitative (about quality rather than quantity) or unpredictable. 'Soft' evaluation provides expression for learning that is not directly related to the stated outcomes. It allows for lateral thinking and unexpected results. It can also provide an opening for a new and different future.

'Soft' evaluation is usually in response to open questions (questions that cannot be answered by 'yes' or 'no'):

What was useful?

What was not useful?

What did you learn?

How did you feel?

What insights did you have about yourself or others?

What are your recommendations for the future?

Responses are likely to be expressive and descriptive:

'I realised that I am an excellent team leader. I have gained a lot of confidence.'

'I got a real shock to see how my behaviour affected the team results.'

'I was amazed that ... happened. I would never have predicted it.'

**'Soft' evaluation model**

1. Feedback by participants at the end of each facilitated session. Two structured or unstructured rounds:

   a) Constructive criticism.
   b) Acknowledgements.

   Comments can be recorded on a large sheet of paper.
2. Halfway evaluation by participants for a series of facilitated sessions. Participants address the following questions either as a round or in writing:

   What I have gained from the content so far is...?
   What I still want to accomplish is...?
   What I appreciate about the process is...?
   Suggestions for improvement are...?

3. Evaluation by participants at the end of a series of facilitated sessions. Participants address the following questions either as a round or in writing:

   What I have accomplished as a result of these sessions...?
   What action I will take as a result of these sessions is...?
   What was missing from these sessions was...?
   What improvements to the contents I recommend...?

> What improvements to the process I
> recommend...?

## *Softly smart*

A mixed evaluation for individual participants at a training workshop can involve each individual setting their own specific learning objectives at the beginning of the workshop and reviewing these at the end.

# 5. Contract confirmation model

Here is a model letter confirming a facilitation contract.

Date:
Address:
Name:
Job Title:
Organisation:
Address:

Dear...

This is to confirm my facilitation of the ... (process) with ... (group).

My commitment is to facilitating in accordance with the IAF code of ethics.

The purpose of the process is to...

A planning meeting was held ... (where and when) with ... and ... [names of people present].

We agreed on the following outcomes:

[Make sure they are SMART—see above.]

1.
2.
3.

Outcomes will be measured by

1.
2.
3.

[Be specific about who will do the measuring and by when.]

The agreed/proposed process is attached.

The cost of this service is $ ... to be paid [terms—for example, within 14 days of the workshop]. Please note that there is a cancellation fee of $ ... if the workshop is cancelled with less than ... notice.

If you wish to discuss any of the above matters further please contact me (phone and/or email) by ... (date).

Yours sincerely,
[signature]
[typed name]

# 6. Meeting-record sheet model

This is a suggested meeting-record sheet for all types of meetings. Adapt it for each specific purpose.

## *Meeting Record*

| Agenda Items:<br>1.<br>2.<br>3.<br>4.<br>5. | | | | |
|---|---|---|---|---|
| Agenda Item No. | Decision | Person responsible | Completion date | Status* |
| | | | | |

\* Completed, deleted or carried forward.

Date and Time:
Meeting:
Purpose:
People attending:
Facilitator:
Venue:

436

# Chapter 5

# other resources

## International Association of Facilitators (IAF)

The IAF was established in 1994, and in 2006 had 1300 members in 50 countries. The IAF website is: www.iaf-world.org.

### *Mission*

The mission of the IAF is to promote, support and advance the art and practice of professional facilitation through methods of exchange, professional growth, practical research, collegial networking and support services. This is accomplished through peer-to-peer networking, professional development and annual conferences, which are critical means for fulfilling the mission and reflecting their core values.

### *Values*

IAF core values are:
- **Inclusiveness**—including the full spectrum of personal, professional and cultural diversity in our membership and in the field of facilitation.

- **Global scope**—connecting and serving facilitators locally, nationally and internationally.
- **Participation**—advocating participative methodologies that generate ownership of decisions and actions.
- **Celebration**—celebrating life through spirit-filled quality interchange, activities and events.
- **Innovative form**—modelling a participative and flexible organisational structure that promotes growth, change and learning.
- **Social responsibility**—supporting socially responsible change within private, public and voluntary organisations.

## Code of Ethics

For the IAF Code of Ethics see Part 2 Chapter 3.

## Foundational Facilitator Competencies

The competency framework described below was developed over several years by the IAF, with the support of IAF members and facilitators from all over the world. The competencies form the basic set of skills, knowledge and behaviours that facilitators must have in order to be successful facilitating in a wide variety of environments.

# IAF Facilitator Competencies

## A. Create collaborative client relationships

1.  Develop working partnerships:
    - Clarify mutual commitment.
    - Develop consensus on tasks, deliverables, roles and responsibilities.
    - Demonstrate collaborative values and processes, such as in co-facilitation.
2.  Design and customise applications to meet client needs:
    - Analyse the organisational environment.
    - Diagnose client need.
    - Create appropriate designs to achieve intended outcomes.
    - Predefine a quality product and outcomes with the client.
3.  Manage multi-session events effectively:
    - Contract with the client for scope and deliverables.
    - Develop an event plan.
    - Deliver the event successfully.
    - Assess/evaluate client satisfaction at all stages of the event/project.

## B. Plan appropriate group processes

1.  Select clear methods and processes that:
    - Foster open participation with respect for client culture, norms and participant diversity.
    - Engage the participation of those with varied learning/thinking styles.

- Achieve a high quality product/outcome that meets the client's needs.
2. Prepare time and space to support group process:
    - Arrange physical space to support the purpose of the meeting.
    - Plan effective use of time.
    - Provide effective atmosphere and drama for sessions.

## C. Create and sustain a participatory environment

1. Demonstrate effective participatory and inter-personal communication skills:
    - Apply a variety of participatory processes.
    - Demonstrate effective verbal communication skills.
    - Develop rapport with participants.
    - Practise active listening.
    - Demonstrate the ability to observe and provide feedback to participants.
2. Honour and recognise diversity, ensuring inclusiveness:
    - Create opportunities for participants to benefit from the diversity of the group.
    - Cultivate cultural awareness and sensitivity.
3. Manage group conflict:
    - Help individuals identify and review underlying assumptions.

- Recognise conflict and its role within group learning/maturity.
- Provide a safe environment for conflict to surface.
- Manage disruptive group behaviour.
- Support the group through resolution of conflict.

4. Evoke group creativity:
- Draw out participants of all learning/thinking styles.
- Encourage creative thinking.
- Accept all ideas.
- Use approaches that best fit the needs and abilities of the group.
- Stimulate and tap group energy.

## D. Guide the group to appropriate and useful outcomes

1. Guide the group with clear methods and processes:
- Establish a clear context for the session.
- Actively listen, question and summarise to elicit the sense of the group.
- Recognise tangents and redirect to the task.
- Manage small and large group process.

2. Facilitate group self-awareness about its task:
- Vary the pace of activities according to the needs of the group.
- Identify information the group needs, and draw out data and insight from the group.

• Help the group synthesise patterns, trends, root causes and frameworks for action.

• Assist the group in reflection on its experience.

3.  Guide the group to consensus and desired outcomes:

• Use a variety of approaches to achieve group consensus.

• Use a variety of approaches to meet group objectives.

• Adapt processes to changing situations and needs of the group.

• Assess and communicate group progress.

• Foster task completion.

## E. Build and maintain professional knowledge

1.  Maintain a base of knowledge:

• Be knowledgeable in management, organisational systems and development, group development, psychology, and conflict resolution.

• Understand the dynamics of change.

• Understand learning/thinking theory.

2.  Know a range of facilitation methods:

• Understand problem-solving and decisionmaking models.

• Understand a variety of group methods and techniques.

• Know the consequences of misuse of group methods.

• Distinguish process from task and content.

&bull; Learn new processes, methods and models in support of the client's changing/emerging needs.

3.  Maintain professional standing:

&bull; Engage in ongoing study/learning related to our field.

&bull; Continuously gain awareness of new information in our profession.

# Appendix A

# Earthsong Eco-Neighbourhood Body Corporate Rules

This legal document was created specifically for this project. It is provided here for your interest. We ask that any persons wanting to directly reuse any of this material should contact the project beforehand [cohousing@xtra.co.nz].

Earthsong Eco-Neighbourhood Cohousing Project, PO Box 70001, Ranui, Auckland NZ [www.ecohousing .pl.net], May 2002

BODY CORPORATE No. 210417 (North Auckland Registry)

That the rules contained in the Second Schedule to the Unit Titles Act 1972 are revoked and replaced by the following:

(Rules that may be amended, added to or repealed by ***unanimous*** resolution)...

# Group Decision Making Process

The method for discussion and decision making shall be by Consensus, using Colour Cards as follows:

**Discussion** Each person including any facilitator taking part in the discussion has six coloured cards which are raised at any time during the discussion to indicate a wish to speak.

- Black     I have an interpersonal difficulty that is preventing my full participation.

- Red     I have a process observation, e.g. the discussion is off the subject.

- Orange     I wish to acknowledge someone or something.

- Yellow     I have a question, or need clarification.

- Green     I can provide clarification.

- Blue     I have a comment or opinion.

Cards are accorded differing priority and are heard in the order listed above.

Black cards have first priority. The facilitator first calls on the person with the black card to state their difficulty and to say how they would like the matter dealt with. The group can then decide whether this should be processed within the group or between the individuals concerned.

The red card, the 'stop the process' card, has the next priority. It is used to point out a breach in the agreed-upon procedure, such as an item has exceeded time limits.

Next, people holding up orange cards are called upon to deliver their acknowledgment(s).

People raising yellow cards to indicate questions have the next priority.

After a question has been asked, people holding green cards are called on to provide clarification to that question.

After all questions have been answered, the facilitator calls on participants holding blue cards. At this time, comments regarding the topic of the discussion can be put forth.

**Decision making** Each person, including the facilitator, taking part in the decision making has five coloured cards. When deciding on an issue, each person must raise one of the coloured cards, which now have the following meanings.

- Green       I agree with the proposal at hand.
- Blue         I am neutral or basically for it, with some slight reservation.
- Yellow      I have a question to be answered before I can make a decision.
- Orange     I have a serious reservation, but I am not willing to block Consensus.
- Red          I am entirely against the proposal and will block Consensus.

If any orange or red cards are raised, those people with reservations should voice their concerns, if they have not already done so. At this point, an amendment to the current motion could be made which may address concerns raised.

Another show of cards can then follow. It should be noted that at this point a proposal has been passed by Consensus unless there are still red cards being shown.

If consensus is still not reached after a further meeting on the topic, the decision can be made by a three quarters majority of [proprietors'] votes.

This process requires every person in the room to participate in decision making. Dominant personalities will find it harder to push their ideas through at the expense of less vocal members, and softer-spoken members find it easier to voice their concerns.

**Process for revisiting decisions** A proprietor absent from a meeting may request to revisit a decision made at that meeting at the next meeting only. Otherwise decisions may be reopened only with the prior agreement of 50% of Proprietors in the Quorum.

**Communication agreements** We have established a set of communication agreements and these are fundamental to our way of working and living together:

- I will use 'I' statements, and speak for myself, not others.
- I will speak succinctly (short and to the point).
- I will take responsibility for owning and naming my own feelings.
- I will respect others' rights to speak without interruption.
- I undertake to respect others' privacy by not discussing outside the group other people's personal issues which may arise within the group process.
- I undertake to value and respect different contributions and perspectives of all individuals.
- I undertake to keep my relationships within the group clear by dealing with issues as they arise.

- I recognise that we work best together when we remember to have fun!

# Appendix B

# Hand Signs

## I would like to say something

Raise your hand with one finger. When you make this sign, the facilitator puts you in the speakers list.

## I agree with you

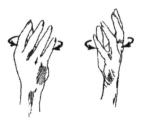

Wave two hands in the air. You agree with what the speaker is saying.

# I have a suggestion to improve the process

Raise two hands, making a 'T', when you have a suggestion to improve the discussion process. The facilitator will directly give you the word.

# I oppose/I block the decision

Raise your right fist

This sign indicates that you strongly disagree with what is said. It can be that the facilitator will ask you to express your reasons.

*In case of a decisions situation:*

Raise your right fist and yell "block!" This sign you use, when a proposal is made, with which you cannot agree. In this case the facilitator will ask you directly why you don't agree.

# It is clear what you want to say, for me you don't have to continue with this point

Turn your two arms around another. This indicates to the speaker, that it is clear what she/he said and that she/he can stop talking further. This sign is developed to help the speaker; not to criticise what she/he says. Also the facilitator can react, when a lot of people use this sign, by stopping the speaker.

\*\*\*

The Zhaba Facilitators Collective has published a range of worksheets that can help you with campaigning. These sheets can be obtained from the Internet on http://www.zhaba.cz

The Zhaba Facilitators Collective is a group of NGO facilitators. It helps non-profit organisations to improve their work. More information on http://www.zhaba.cz

© 2003 Stichting Zhaba Facilitators Collective

# Notes

## Part 1

## *Chapter 1. Preparing the ground*

[1] See V. Pierce et al., 'Facilitator Competencies', in *Group Facilitation: A Research and Applications Journal* 2(2), pp.24–31. For the International Association of Facilitators (IAF) Statement of Values and Code of Ethics for Group Facilitators. For further information on all these aspects of the IAF go to the IAF website, www.iaf-world.o rg; the Group Facilitation List serv http://www. albany.edu/cpr/gf/and see S. Schuman's *Creating a Culture of Collaboration* and *The IAF Handbook of Group Facilitation.*

[2] Gil Brenson-Lazan, personal conversation with the author.

## *Chapter 2. The role of the facilitator*

[1] See M. O'Hara, 'Person-Centered Approach as Conscientizacao: The Works of Carl Rogers and Paulo Freire'. *Journal of Humanistic Psychology* 29(1), pp.11–33 (12–13).

[2] Candace Pert, *Molecules of Emotion: The Science Behind Mind-Body Medicine.*

[3] Norman R.F. Maier, 'Assets and Liabilities in Group Problem Solving: The Need for an Integrative Function'. *Psychological Review,* 74 (4), pp.239–49.

452

[4]   Michel Avery et al., *Building United Judgment: A Handbook for Consensus Decision Making*, p.51.

[5]   Barbara Gray, *Collaborating: Finding Common Ground for Multiparty Problems*, p.163.

[6]   Thomas Kayser, *Mining Group Gold*, p.12.

[7]   Sam Kaner et al., *Facilitator's Guide to Participatory Decisionmaking*, p.32.

[8]   Tom Justice & David Jamieson, *The Facilitator's Fieldbook*, p.5.

[9]   David Straus, *How to Make Collaboration Work: Powerful Ways to Build Consensus, Solve Problems and Make Decisions*, p.118.

[10]   Roger Schwarz, *The Skilled Facilitator*, pp.4–9.

[11]   Harrison Owen, *Spirit: Transformation and Development in Organizations*, p.48.

[12]   Harrison Owen, *The Millennium Organization*.

[13]   R.K. Greenleaf, *Servant-Leadership: A Journey into the Nature of Legitimate Power and Greatness*.

## *Chapter 3. A framework for facilitation*

[1]   T. Buzan & B. Buzan, *The Mind Map Book*.

## *Chapter 9. Dialogue and storytelling*

[1]   Brian Stanfield, *The Art of Focused Conversation: 100 Ways to Access Group Wisdom in the Workplace*, p.18.

[2] See J. Cruikshank, *The Social Life of Stories: Narrative and Knowledge in the Yukon Territory.*

[3] J. Senehi, 'Constructive Storytelling: Building Community Building Peace'.

[4] New Zealand Guild of Storytellers, festival pamphlet, Glistening Waters International Festival of Storytelling, Masterton, New Zealand, 30 October– 1 November 2004.

[5] G. Copland, workshop, 'Telling Original Stories from Your Own Culture', Glistening Waters International Festival of Storytelling, Masterton, New Zealand, 30 October–1 November, 2004.

## *Chapter 10. Getting to consensus*

[1] See Tree Bressen, 'Decisionmaking in Cohousing Communities', *Communities Magazine,* Spring (106), 2000.

[2] Earthsong Eco-Neighbourhood, 'Group Decision Making Process', in *Earthsong Eco-Neighbourhood Body Corporate Rules.*

[3] Zhaba Facilitators Collective, *Shared Path Shared Goal: A Handbook on Direct Democracy and the Consensus Decision Process.*

## Part 2

## *Chapter 1. Facilitation and the client*

[1] See J. Brown & D. Isaacs, *The World Café: Shaping Our Futures Through Conversations That Matter.*

## Chapter 2. Cooperative processes in organisations

[1]  D. Hunter, *Facilitation of Sustainable Co-operative Processes in Organisations.*

[2]  D. Hunter & S. Thorpe, 'Facilitator Values and Ethics', in S. Schuman (ed.). *The IAF Handbook of Group Facilitation.*

[3]  D. Maheshananda, 'A Personal Remembrance and Conversation with Paulo Freire Educator of the Oppressed'.

[4]  C. Rogers, *Freedom to Learn.*

[5]  J. Heron, *The Complete Facilitator's Handbook.*

[6]  M. Csikszentmihalyi, *Flow: The Psychology of Optimal Experience.*

[7]  H. Owen, *The Millennium Organization.*

[8]  D. Hunter, A. Bailey & B. Taylor, *Co-operacy: A New Way of Being at Work.*

## Chapter 3. Facilitator ethics

[1]  N. Chomsky & E. Herman, *Manufacturing Consent: The Political Economy of the Mass Media.*

[2]  R. Schwarz, *The Skilled Facilitator,* p.4.

[3]  V. Pierce, D. Cheesebrow & L. Matthews Braun, 'Facilitator Competencies'. *Group Facilitation: A Research and Applications Journal* 2(2), pp.24–31 (p.24).

[4]  J. Gribbin, *In Search of Schroedinger's Cat: Quantum Physics and Reality.*

[5]   Joan Firkins, *Trust, Safety and Equity.* Unpublished essay, 2001.

[6]   R. Schwarz, *Who is the Client?* Unpublished essay, 2002, p.1.

[7]   E. Schein, *Process Consultation, Volume II: Lessons for managers and consultants,* p.125.

[8]   F. Marvin, 'Consensus is Primary to Group Facilitation'. Unpublished essay, 2002.

[9]   J. Butcher, *Consensus is Situation Dependent.* Unpublished essay, 2002.

[10]  Ibid.

[11]  International Association of Facilitators, *Statement of Values and Code of Ethics for Group Facilitators.*[www.iaf-world.org] September 2006.

# Chapter 4. A sustainable society

[1]   J. Elkington, *Cannibals with Forks: The Triple Bottom Line of 21st Century Business.*

[2]   L.W. Milbrath, 'Envisioning a Sustainable Society', in R.A. Slaughter (ed.), *New Thinking for a New Millennium.*

[3]   See Barbara Marx Hubbard, *Conscious Evolution: Awakening the Power of Our Social Potential;* Hazel Henderson, *Building a Win-Win World: Life Beyond Global Economic Warfare,* and Sohail Inayatullah, *Situating Sarkar: Tantra, Macrohistory and Alternative Futures.*

[4]   L.W. Milbrath, 'Envisioning a Sustainable Society', in R.A. Slaughter (ed.), *New Thinking for a New Millennium.*

[5]     See Stuart B. Hill's *What is Social Ecology?*[htt
        p://www.zulenet.com/see/chair.html]and'Social
        Ecology as Future Stories', in *A Social Ecology
        Journal* 1(1), pp.197–208.

## *Chapter 5. Facilitation and therapeutic groupwork*

[1]     Jacob L. Moreno, *Psychodrama Vol. 1*,
        pp.49–53.
[2]     Ibid.
[3]     G.M. Clayton, *Living Pictures of the Self: Appli-
        cations of Role Theory in Professional Practice
        and Daily Living.*
[4]     H.R. Brown, *From Coping to Creation: Develop-
        ing Generative Capacity.* Unpublished psychodra-
        ma thesis.
[5]     See Ralph D. Stacy, *Strategic Management and
        Organisational Dynamics: The Challenge of
        Complexity,* and Peter Senge, *The Fifth Disci-
        pline Fieldbook: Strategies and Tools for Build-
        ing a Learning Organization.*
[6]     Brown, *From Coping to Creation: Developing
        Generative Capacity.*
[7]     Stacy, *Strategic Management and Organisational
        Dynamics: The Challenge of Complexity.*
[8]     Senge, *The Fifth Discipline: The Art & Practice
        of the Learning Organization.*
[9]     Malcolm Pines, *Bion and Group Psychotherapy.*
[10]    G.M. Clayton, *Effective Group Leadership.*

## Chapter 6. Facilitation online

[1]    C. Halverson, et al., *World Jam: Supporting Talk Among 50,000.*

[2]    Nancy White, 'Online and Offline Facilitation: Different Yet Alike?' [www.fullcirc.com/community/onvsofflinefac.htm]

[3]    R.E. Kraut, et al., 'Informal Communication in Organizations: Form, Function, and Technology'. In R.M. Baecker (ed.), *Readings in Groupware and Computer-Supported Cooperative Work: Assisting Human-Human Collaboration.*

[4]    N. Rangarajan & J. Rohrbaugh, 'Multiple Roles of Online Facilitation: An Example of Any-Time, Any-Place Meetings'. *Group Facilitation: A Research and Applications Journal* (5) Spring 2003, pp.26–37.

[5]    S. Thorpe, 'Online Facilitation'. Paper presented at Heart Politics, 7–11 January 2004, Taupo, New Zealand. [www.zenergyglobal.com/docs/research/FacilitationOnline.pdf]

# *Chapter 7. Mapping the field of facilitation*

[1]    Royal Commission on Genetic Modification, *Report of the Royal Commission on Genetic Modification: Report and Recommendations.*

[2]    Religious Society of Friends. *Quakers: Religious Witnesses for Peace Since 1660,*[www.quaker.org], September 2006.

[3] See Fran Peavey, 'Strategic Questioning: An Approach to Creating Personal and Social Change' and *Heart Politics Revisited;* and *Heart Politics,* [www.heartpolitics.net], August 2006.

[4] AVP USA, *What Is The Alternatives To Violence Project?*

[5] K. Lewin, 'Frontiers in Group Dynamics: Channels of Group Life; Social Planning and Action Research'. *Human Relations* (1), pp.143–53.

[6] C. Rogers, *Encounter Groups.*

[7] See Will Schutz, *Elements of Encounter.*

[8] ANZPA, 'What is Psychodrama?' [http://anzpa.org/Pdis.html]

[9] D.L. Cooperrider & S. Srivastva, 'Appreciative Inquiry in Organizational Life'. In R. Woodman and W. Pasmore (eds.), *Research in Organizational Change and Development* (1), pp.129–69.

# Part 3

## *Chapter 1. Facilitator education*

[1] David Z. Albert, 'Bohm's Alternative to Quantum Mechanics', *Scientific American,* May 1994.

[2] Candace Pert, 'Healing Ourselves and Our Society'. Presentation at the Elmwood Symposium, Boston, MA, 9 December 1989. In F. Capra, *The Web of Life: A New Synthesis of Mind and Matter,* pp.276–77.

[3] R. Golten, *The Owner's Guide to the Body: How to Have a Perfectly Tuned Body and Mind.*

[4]     See L. Bendaly, *The Facilitation Skills Training Kit*; L.B. Hart, *Faultless Facilitation: An Instructor's Manual for Facilitation Training* and *Faultless Facilitation: A Resource Guide for Group and Team Leaders*; M. Havergal & J. Edmonstone, *The Facilitator's Toolkit*; L. Parry, 'Effective Facilitators: A Key Element in Successful Continuous Improvement Processes', *Training for Quality* 3(4), pp.9–14; and P.A. Sharp, 'The "Never-evers" of Workshop Facilitation', *Journal of Staff Development* 13(2), pp.38–40.

[5]     See T. Bentley, 'Facilitation: Providing Opportunities for Learning', *Journal of European Industrial Training* 18(5), pp.8–22; A. Brockbank & I. McGill, *Facilitating Reflective Learning in Higher Education*; J. Heron, *The Facilitator's Handbook, Group Facilitation: Theories and Models for Practice,* and *The Complete Facilitator's Handbook*; S. Priest et al., *The Essential Elements of Facilitation*; R. Schwarz, *The Skilled Facilitator: A Comprehensive Resource for Consultants, Facilitators, Managers, Trainers, and Coaches,* and R.G. Weaver & J. D. Farrell, *Managers as Facilitators.*

[6]     D. Hunter et al., *The Essence of Facilitation: Being in Action in Groups*; T.M. Ringer, *Group Action: The Dynamics of Groups in Therapeutic, Educational and Corporate Settings,* and C.R. Rogers, *Freedom to Learn for the 80's* and 'The Interpersonal Relationship in the Facilitation of

Learning', in H.E. Kirschenbaum (ed.), *The Carl Rogers Reader.*

[7]    p.Kirk, & M. Broussine 2000. 'The Politics of Facilitation'. *Journal of Workplace Learning: Employee Counseling Today,* 12(1) pp.13-22.

[8]    D. Hunter et al., *The Art of Facilitation,* p.201, and Glyn Thomas, 'Dimensions of Facilitator Education', in Sandy Schuman (ed.), *The IAF Handbook of Group Facilitation,* pp.525–42.

[9]    R. Schwarz, *The Skilled Facilitator.*

# *Chapter 3. Processes*

[1]    Adapted from Wayne Liebman, *Tending the Fire: The Ritual Men's Group,* pp.16–17.

# Bibliography

Albert, David Z., 1994. 'Bohm's Alternative to Quantum Mechanics'. *Scientific American,* May.

ANZPA 2005. 'What is Psychodrama?' Australian and New Zealand Psychodrama Association. [http://anzpa.org/Pdis.html] October 2005.

Argyris, C. & D. Schön, 1996. *Organisational Learning II: Theory, Method and Practice.* Reading: Addison-Wesley.

Art of Facilitation [www.artoffacilitation.com]

Atlee, T., 2003. *The Tao of Democracy: Using Co-intelligence to Create a World that Works.* Cranston: The Writers' Collective.

Avery, Michel & Brian Auvine, Barbara Streibel, Lonnie Weiss, 1981. *Building United Judgment: A Handbook for Consensus Decision Making.* The Center for Conflict Resolution.

AVP USA, 2005. *What Is The Alternatives To Violence Project?* St. Paul: AVP/USA.

Beck, D. & C. Cowan, 1995. *Spiral Dynamics: Mastering Values, Leadership, and Change.* Oxford: Blackwell.

Bendaly, L., 2000. *The Facilitation Skills Training Kit.* New York: McGraw-Hill.

Bentley, T., 1994. 'Facilitation: Providing Opportunities for Learning'. *Journal of European Industrial Training* 18(5), pp.8–22.

Bion, W.R., 1961. *Experiences in Groups.* London: Tavistock.

462

Birch, C., 1990. *A Purpose for Everything: Religion in a Postmodern Worldview.* Mystic: Twenty-Third Publications.

Booker, Christopher, 2004. *The Seven Basic Plots: Why We Tell Stories.* London: Continuum.

Brockbank, A. & I. McGill, 1998. *Facilitating Reflective Learning in Higher Education.* Buckingham: SHRE and Open University.

Brown H.R., 2005. 'From Coping to Creation: Developing Generative Capacity'. Unpublished psychodrama thesis.

Brown, J. & Isaacs D., 2005. *The World Café: Shaping Our Futures Through Conversations That Matter.* San Francisco, Berrett-Koehler.

Bressen, Tree, 2000. Decisionmaking in Cohousing Communities. *Communities Magazine,* Spring (106).

Bunker, B.B. & Billie T. Alban, 1996. *Large Group Interventions: Engaging the Whole System for Rapid Change.* San Francisco: Jossey-Bass.

Buzan, T. & Buzan, B., 2000. *The Mind Map Book.* London: BBC Books.

Campbell, J., 1988. *The Power of Myth with Bill Moyers.* New York: Doubleday.

Chomsky, N. & E. Herman, 1988. *Manufacturing Consent: The Political Economy of the Mass Media.* New York: Pantheon Books.

Clayton, G.M., 1993. *Living Pictures of the Self: Applications of Role Theory in Professional Practice and Daily Living.* Victoria, Australia: ICA Press.

Clayton, G. M., 1994. *Effective Group Leadership.* Victoria, Australia: ICA Press.

Cooperrider, D.L. & S. Srivastva, 1987. 'Appreciative Inquiry in Organizational Life', in R. Woodman & W. Pasmore (eds), *Research in Organizational Change and Development: Volume 1,* pp.129–69. San Francisco: New Lexington.

Cruikshank, J., 1998. *The Social Life of Stones: Narrative and Knowledge in the Yukon Territory.* Lincoln: University of Nebraska Press.

Csikszentmihalyi, M., 1990. *Flow: The Psychology of Optimal Experience.* New York: Harper Perennial.

Denning, Stephen, 2005. *The Leader's Guide to Storytelling: Mastering the Art and Discipline of Business Narrative.* San Francisco: Jossey-Bass.

Diamond, J., 2004. *Collapse: How Societies Choose to Fail or Survive.* London: Allen Lane.

Dick, B., 1991. *Helping Groups To Be More Effective* (2nd edn). Chapel Hill, QLD: Interchange.

Dick, B. & T. Dalmau, 1999. *Values in Action: Applying the Ideas of Argyris and Schön* (2nd edn). Chapel Hill, QLD: Interchange.

Dyer, Wayne, 2004. *The Power of Intention: Learning to Co-create Your World Your Way.* Carlsbad: Hay House.

Earthsong Eco-Neighbourhood, 2002. 'Group Decision Making Process', in *Earthsong Eco-Neighbourhood Body Corporate Rules,* Auckland: Earthsong Eco-Neighbourhood Cohousing Project. Adapted from K. McCamant & C. Durett,

464

1994, *Cohousing: A Contemporary Approach to Housing Ourselves.* Berkeley: Ten Speed Press.

Elkington, J., 1998. *Cannibals with Forks: The Triple Bottom Line of 21st Century Business.* Gabriola Island: New Society Publishers.

Emery, F.E. & Trist, E.L., 1960. 'Socio-technical systems', in C.W. Churchman & M. Verhulst (eds), *Management Sciences: Models and Techniques (2).*

Emery, Merrelyn & Ronald Purser, 1996. *The Search Conference: A Powerful Method for Planning Organizational Change and Community Action.* San Francisco: Jossey-Bass.

Freire, P., 1993. *The Pedagogy of the Oppressed.* 20th anniversary edition. New York: Continuum.

Garfield, C. & C. Spring, S. Cahill, 1998. *Wisdom Circles: A Guide to Self-Discovery and Community Building in Small Groups.* Hyperion.

Gladwell, M., 2005. *Blink: The Power of Thinking Without Thinking.* London: Allen Lane.

Golten, R., 1999. *The Owner's Guide to the Body: How to Have a Perfectly Tuned Body and Mind.* London: Thorsons.

Gray, Barbara, 1989. *Collaborating: Finding Common Ground for Multiparty Problems.* San Francisco: Jossey-Bass.

Greenleaf, R.K., 1977. *Servant Leadership: A Journey into the Nature of Legitimate Power and Greatness.* Mahwah: Paulist Press.

Gribbin, J., 1984. *In Search of Schroedinger's Cat: Quantum Physics and Reality.* New York: Bantam Books.

Halverson, C. & J. Newswanger, T. Erickson, T. Wolf, W.A. Kellogg, M. Laff, p.Malkin, 2001. *World Jam: Supporting Talk Among 50,000.* ECSCW.

Hart, L.B., 1991. *Faultless Facilitation: An Instructor's Manual for Facilitation Training.* Amherst: Human Resource Development.

Hart, L.B., 1992. *Faultless Facilitation: A Resource Guide for Group and Team Leaders.* Amherst: HRD Press.

Havergal, M. & J. Edmonstone, 1999. *The Facilitator's Toolkit.* Aldershot: Gower.

Henderson, H., 1996. *Building a Win-Win World: Life Beyond Global Economic Warfare.* San Francisco: Berrett-Koehler.

Heron, J., 1989. *The Facilitator's Handbook.* London: Kogan Page.

Heron, J., 1993. *Group Facilitation: Theories and Models for Practice.* London: Kogan Page.

Heron, J., 1999. *The Complete Facilitator's Handbook.* London: Kogan Page.

Hill, S.B., 1999. 'Social Ecology as Future Stories'. *A Social Ecology Journal* 1(1), pp.197–208.

Hill, S.B., 2000. 'Leadership and Ethics', Denis Cordner Memorial Address at a forum for Developing Tomorrow's Leaders, July 2–8, University of Sydney.

466

Hill, S.B., 2005. *What is Social Ecology?* [http://www.zulenet.com/see/chair.html] August 2005.

Hogan, C., 2003. *Practical Facilitation: A Toolkit of Techniques.* London: Kogan Page.

Houston, J., 1993. *Life Force: The Psycho-Historical Recovery of the Self.* Wheaton: The Theosophical Publishing House.

Hubbard, B.M., 1998. *Conscious Evolution: Awakening the Power of Our Social Potential.* Novato: New World Library.

Hunter, D., 2003. 'Facilitation of Sustainable Co-operative Processes in Organisations', PhD thesis, University of Western Sydney.

Hunter, D., 2006. 'Sustainable Cooperative Processes', in S. Schuman, (ed.), *Creating a Culture of Collaboration.* San Francisco: Jossey-Bass.

Hunter, D. & A. Bailey, B. Taylor, 1992. *The Zen of Groups: A Handbook for People Meeting with a Purpose.* Auckland: Tandem.

Hunter, D. & A. Bailey, B. Taylor, 1994. *The Art of Facilitation.* Auckland: Tandem.

Hunter, D. & A. Bailey, B. Taylor, 1996. *Management Zen: Facilitacion y Eficiencia de Grupos.* Translation of *The Zen of Groups.* Buenos Aires: Troquel, S.A.

Hunter, D. & A. Bailey, B. Taylor, 1997. *Co-operacy: A New Way of Being at Work.* Auckland: Tandem.

Hunter, D. & A. Bailey, B. Taylor, 1999. *The Essence of Facilitation.* Auckland: Tandem.

Hunter, D. & S. Thorpe, 2005. 'Values and Ethics', in S. Schuman, (ed.), *The IAF Handbook of Group Facilitation.* San Francisco: Jossey-Bass.

Inayatullah, S., 1999. *Situating Sarkar: Tantra, Macrohistory and Alternative Futures.* Maleny: Gurukul.

International Association of Facilitators (IAF), 2003. 'Statement of Values and Code of Ethics for Facilitators' [http://www.iaf-world.org] May 2003.

International Association of Facilitators (IAF), 2003. 'Facilitator Competencies'. [http://www.iaf-world.org] May 2003.

Jaworski, Joseph, 1996. *Synchronicity: The Inner Path of Leadership.* San Francisco: Berrett-Koehler.

Justice, Tom & David Jamieson, 1999. *The Facilitator's Fieldbook.* American Management Association.

Kaner, Sam, & Lenny Lind, Catherine Toldi, Sarak Fisk, Duane Berger, 1996. *Facilitator's Guide to Participatory Decisionmaking.* New Society Publishers.

Kayser, Thomas, 1990. *Mining Group Gold.* Serif Publishing.

Kirk, P., & M. Broussine, 2000. 'The Politics of Facilitation'. *Journal of Workplace Learning: Employee Counseling Today,* 12(1), pp.13–22.

Kraut R.E. & R.S. Fish, R.W. Root, B.L. Chalfonte, 1993. 'Informal Communication in Organizations: Form, Function, and Technology', in R.M. Baecker (ed.), *Readings in Groupware and Computer-Sup-*

468

*ported  Cooperative Work: Assisting Human-Human Collaboration,* pp.287–314. San Mateo: Morgan Kaufman.

Landsberg, M., 1996. *The Tao of Coaching.* London: HarperCollins.

Lao Tsu (translation, 1972), *Tao Te Ching (translated by Gia-Fu, F. & J. English).* New York: Vintage Books.

Leider, Richard J., 1997. *The Power of Purpose: Creating Meaning in Your Life and Work.* Berrett-Koehler Publishers.

Lewin, K., 1947. 'Frontiers in Group Dynamics: Channels of Group Life; Social Planning and Action Research'. *Human Relations* 1, pp.143–53.

Liebman, Wayne, 1991. *Tending the Fire: The Ritual Men's Group.* St Paul, MN: Ally.

McCamant, Kathryn & Charles Durrett, 1994. *Cohousing: A Contemporary Approach to Housing Ourselves.* Berkeley: Ten Speed Press.

McTaggart, Lynne, 2001. *The Field.* London: HarperCollins.

Maheshananda, D., 1997. 'A Personal Remembrance and Conversation with Paulo Freire Educator of the Oppressed'. *Global Times.* [www.proutworld.org/features/freire.html] July 2001.

Maier, Norman R.F., 1967. 'Assets and Liabilities in Group Problem Solving: The Need for an Integrative Function'. *Psychological Review* 74(4), pp.239–49.

Milbrath, L.W., 1996. 'Envisioning a Sustainable Society', in R.A. Slaughter (ed.), *New Thinking for a New Millennium.* London: Routledge.

Mittleman, D. & R. Briggs, J. Nunamaker Jr, 2000. 'Best Practices in Facilitating Virtual Meetings: Some Notes from Initial Experience'. *Group Facilitation: A Research and Applications Journal* 2(2), pp.5–14.

Moore, C., 1996. *The Mediation Process: Practical Strategies for Resolving Conflict* (2nd ed.). San Francisco: Jossey-Bass.

Moore, C., 1982. *Natural Resource Conflict Management.* Boulder: Romcoe.

Moreno, J.L., 1946. *Psychodrama, Vol. 1.* New York: Beacon House.

Moreno, J.L., 1953. *Psychodrama, Vol. 2.* New York: Beacon House.

Moreno, J. L., 1969. *Psychodrama, Vol. 3.* New York: Beacon House.

O'Hara, M., 1989. 'Person-Centered Approach as Conscientizacao: The Works of Carl Rogers and Paulo Freire'. *Journal of Humanistic Psychology* 29(1), pp.11–33.

Owen, Harrison, 1987. *Spirit: Transformation and Development in Organizations.* Potomac, MD: Abbott.

Owen, Harrison, 1994. *The Millennium Organization.* Potomac, MD: Abbott Publishing.

Parry, L., 1995. 'Effective Facilitators: A Key Element in Successful Continuous Improvement Processes'. *Training for Quality* 3(4), pp.9–14.

Peavey, F., 1985. *Heart Politics.* Philadelphia, PA: New Society.

Peavey, F., 1993. *By Life's Grace: Musings on the Essence of Social Change.* Philadelphia, PA: New Society.

Peavey, F., 1997. 'Strategic Questioning: An Approach to Creating Personal and Social Change'. In V. Hutchison. (ed.) (unpublished).

Peavey, F., 2000. *Heart Politics Revisited.* Annandale, NSW: Pluto Press.

Peck, M.S., 1987. *The Different Drum: Community-Making in Peace.* New York: Simon and Schuster.

Peck, M. Scott, 1993. *A World Waiting To Be Born: Civility Rediscovered.* New York: Bantam.

Pert, Candace, 1989. 'Healing Ourselves and Our Society', presentation at Elmwood Symposium, December 9, Boston, MA. In F. Capra, 1996, *The Web of Life: A New Synthesis of Mind and Matter.* London: HarperCollins.

Pert, Candace, 1999. *Molecules of Emotion: The Science Behind Mind-Body Medicine.* New York: Scribner.

Pierce, V. & D. Cheesebrow, L. Matthews Braun, 2000. 'Facilitator Competencies'. *Group Facilitation: A Research and Applications Journal* 2(2), pp.24–31.

Pines, Malcolm, 2000. *Bion and Group Psychotherapy.* London: Routledge & Kegan.

Priest, S., & M. Gass, L. Gillis, 2000. *The Essential Elements of Facilitation.* Dubuque: Kendall/Hunt.

Rangarajan, N. & Rohrbaugh, J., 2003. 'Multiple Roles of Online Facilitation: An Example of Any-Time, Any-Place Meetings'. *Group Facilitation: A Research and Applications Journal* (5) Spring, pp.26–37.

Religious Society of Friends. *Quakers: Religious Witnesses for Peace Since 1660.*[www.quaker.org] September 2006.

Ringer, T.M., 2002. *Group Action: The Dynamics of Groups in Therapeutic, Educational and Corporate Settings.* London: Jessica Kingsley.

Rogers, C., 1969. *Freedom to Learn.* Columbus: Charles E. Merrill.

Rogers, C., 1970. *Encounter Groups.* New York: Harper & Row.

Rogers, C., 1977. *Carl Rogers on Personal Power.* New York: Delacorte.

Rogers, C.R., 1983. *Freedom to Learn for the 80's.* London: Charles E. Merrill.

Rogers, C.R., 1989. 'The Interpersonal Relationship in the Facilitation of Learning', in H.E. Kirschenbaum (ed.), *The Carl Rogers Reader.* Boston: Houghton Mifflin.

Royal Commission on Genetic Modification, 2001. *Report of the Royal Commission on Genetic*

472

*Modification: Report and Recommendations.* Wellington: The Commission.

Schein, E., 1987. *Process Consultation: Lessons for Managers and Consultants, Vol. 2.* Reading: Addison-Wesley.

Schuman, S. (ed.), 2005. *The IAF Handbook of Group Facilitation: Best Practices from the Leading Organization in Facilitation.* San Francisco: Jossey-Bass.

Schuman, S. (ed.) 2006. *Creating a Culture of Collaboration.* San Francisco: Jossey-Bass.

Schutz, Will, 1973. *Elements of Encounter.* Big Sur: Joy Press.

Schwarz, R., 1994. *The Skilled Facilitator.* San Francisco: Jossey Bass.

Schwarz, R., 2002. *The Skilled Facilitator: A Comprehensive Resource for Consultants, Facilitators, Managers, Trainers, and Coaches* (2nd edn). San Francisco: Jossey-Bass.

Schwarz, R., 2002. *The Skilled Facilitator Fieldbook.* San Francisco: Jossey-Bass.

Senehi, J., 'Constructive Storytelling: Building Community Building Peace'. PhD thesis, Graduate School of Syracuse University, Syracuse, NY.

Senge, Peter M., 1990. *The Fifth Discipline: The Art and Practice of The Learning Organization.* New York: Currency Doubleday.

Senge, Peter M., 1994. *The Fifth Discipline Fieldbook: Strategies and Tools for Building a Learning Organization.* New York: Currency Doubleday.

Senge, p.& C.O. Scharmer, J. Jaworski, B.S. Flowers, 2004. *Presence: Human Purpose and the Field of the Future.* Cambridge, Mass.: Society for Organizational Learning.

Sharp, P.A., 1992. 'The "Never-evers" of Workshop Facilitation.' *Journal of Staff Development* 13(2), pp.38–40.

Spencer, L.J., 1989. *Winning Through Participation: Meeting the Challenge of Corporate Change with the Technology of Participation.* Iowa: Kendall/Hunt.

Stacy, Ralph D., 2003. *Strategic Management and Organisational Dynamics: The Challenge of Complexity.* Harlow: Prentice-Hall.

Stanfield, R. Brian, 2000. *The Art of Focused Conversation: 100 Ways to Access Group Wisdom in the Workplace.* Gabriola Island, BC: New Society.

Stanfield, B., 2000. *The Courage to Lead: Transform Self, Transform Society.* Gabriola Island, BC: New Society.

Starhawk, 1979. *The Spiral Dance: A Rebirth of the Ancient Religions of the Great Goddess.* San Francisco: HarperCollins.

Starhawk, 1987. *Truth or Dare: Encounters with Power, Authority and Mystery.* San Francisco: Harper & Row.

Starhawk, 1999. *The Spiral Dance.* 20th anniversary edition. New York: HarperCollins.

Straus, David, 2002. *How to Make Collaboration Work: Powerful Ways to Build Consensus, Solve Problems, and Make Decisions.* Berrett-Koehler Publishers.

474

Thomas, G., 2005. 'Facilitator Education', in S. Schuman, (ed.), *The IAF Handbook of Group Facilitation.* San Francisco: Jossey-Bass.

Thorpe, S., 2004. 'Online Facilitation'. Paper presented at Heart Politics, 7–11 January, Taupo, New Zealand. [www.zenergyglobal.com/docs/research/FacilitationOnline.pdf] January 2004.

Ting, S. & p.Scisco (eds.), 2006. *The CCL Handbook of Coaching: A Guide for the Leader Coach.* San Francisco: Jossey-Bass.

Umpleby, S. & A. Oyler, 2003. 'A Global Strategy for Human Development: The Work of the Institute of Cultural Affairs'. Proceedings of the Annual Conference of the International Society for the Systems Sciences, Crete, July 2003.

Weaver, R.G., & J.D. Farrell, 1997. *Managers as Facilitators.* San Francisco: Berrett-Koehler.

White, Nancy, 2000. *Online and Offline Facilitation: Different Yet Alike?* Seattle: Full Circle Associates. [www.fullcirc.com/community/onvsofflinefac.htm] March 2001.

Zenergy Ltd [www.zenergyglobal.com; email: zenergy@xtra.co.nz]

Zhaba Facilitators Collective, *Shared Path Shared Goal: A Handbook on Direct Democracy and the Consensus Decision Process.* Zhaba Facilitators Collective PF. 701/178 H-1399 Budapest, Hungary. Email: zhaba@ecn.cz [http://www.zhaba.cz] September 2006.

See also one-to-one facilitation;
psychotherapy,
counter-proposing solutions (conflict resolution), *352*
creativity, *91, 110, 116, 118, 135, 146, 183*
  and psychodramatic theory, *229, 231, 233, 239*
criteria setting, *333*
critical thinking, *110*
cultural differences, *83, 115*
  in online groups, *250*
culture, group, *29, 31, 33, 37-39, 71-72, 122, 147, 210*
  and challenges, *159*
  checking on, *179*
  and conflict, *147, 156*
  generating, *38-39, 338*
  interventions to set, *93*
  online groups, *244, 248, 250*
  process, *39, 338*
  and storytelling, *128, 130*
  training in establishing, *294, 296, 298*
culture, organisational, *109, 199*

**D**
decisional level of focused conversation, *125*

decisionmaking, group, *5, 84, 133*
  See also consensus;
  majority decisionmaking,
democracy,
  see majority decisionmaking,
Denning, Stephen, The Leader's Guide to Storytelling, *128*
dependence, *8*
dialogue, *110, 120, 122-123, 125-126*
  checking in, *123, 130*
  focused conversation, *125-126*
  methods of, *122-123, 327*
  strategic dialogue, *126*
  strategic questioning, *123, 125, 257*
  training in, *312, 314*
Diamond, Jared, Collapse: How Societies Choose to Fail or Survive, *223, 225*
Dick, Bob, *4*
difference, *8, 10, 55, 86*
  See also cultural differences,
  valuing, processes, *356, 358-361*
disagreement, *79, 133, 135, 140, 146*

482

47373765R00283

Made in the USA
Lexington, KY
05 December 2015